Table of Contents

Editor's Introduction

The choice of these two works – *Stratagems* and *On Military Matters* in one volume allows the reader a bookend of Roman military theory and style. *Stratagem* was written in the first century AD by noted engineer and soldier, Sextus Julius Frontius. Rather than a specific outline of tactics, it is examples of strategies employed by other generals over time that could be, presumably learned by commanders and applied as the situation arose. This is somewhat similar to the style Plutarch uses in describing the lives of the notable Greeks and Romans in his book, *Parallel Lives*. *On Military Matter*, on the other hand, was written near the end of the western Empire in the fourth century AD, as a manual of how an army should be organized and used. Little is known about its author, Publius Flavius Vegetius Renatus, beyond this work and another on veterinary medicine.

Frontius had a diverse career that includes experience as a soldier and engineer. Of his works that have survived down to us, *De aquaeductu*, consists of two books reporting on the history and description of the aqueducts of Rome to the Emperor Nerva. He served in the army in Germany under Domitian as well as in Britain. *Stratagems* consist of four books, three of which are accepted to belong to Frontius while the fourth has been in doubt. There are indications that *Stratagems* was written in conjunction with a now lost book on military theory. Frontius wrote his book while Rome was at the height of its military prowess, but wanted to remind his readers of the worthies of history and the constant need to learn from their examples in order to keep the military strong.

On Military Matters (*De Re Militari*) originally consisted of five books, only three of which are presented here while the fourth and fifth dealt with the Roman Navy and Sieges. Vegetius wrote his books when Rome was in decline as a military power, as a way to regain the might of the first century, but ignores the central problems of Rome's civil wars and lack of martial spirit.

Stratagems: The Roman Strategy at War

Stratagems by Sextus Julius Frontius
And
On Military Matters by Publius Flavius
Vegetius Renatius

Stratagems: The Roman Strategy at War

This edition is dedicated to Barbarian Bill who helped me hone my ancient tactics.

Cover by V.W.Rospond
Edited by Vincent W. Rospond
Assistant Editor Alexandra L. Rospond

Winged Hussar Publishing, LLC 2013
Point Pleasant, NJ

ISBN: 978-0-9889532-3-9
Library of Congress Control Number: 2013912352

For more information on Winged Hussar Publishing, LLC, visit us at:

http://www.WingedHussarPublishing.com

Vegetius refers to Frontius and had known about his works, possibly even another work on strategy that seems to have been lost to us. These books tease us as well with glimpses and references to books we know longer know. Vegetius ascribes Rome's problems to the quality of the recruits, not the internal warfare. By the late Empire prominent people entered civil service while military service was more or less pushed off on barbarians and the service seen as a step backwards. Based on the introduction to the second book, Vegetius indicates that the Emperor has read and favorably commented on the first book which has encouraged him to write the subsequent books.

In the middle ages, the rediscovery of these authors gave military men insight in the way of the Romans and from that time they were required reading for anyone interested in learning the art of war. Both books rely on earlier works, some now lost to us, and the knowledge of individuals in the history of Rome. The authors often qualify the names of people they cite by titles such as, "Alexander of Macedonia", "Pericles of Athens" to make sure the readers know which worthies they were talking about. While Frontius encourages the use of invoking the gods, Vegetius makes use of guile and strategy.

As with many ancient authors there is an issue with the authenticity of the transcriptions and additions of the books which have survived to the modern age. As many times as these books have been copied, errors creep in and mutate across generations. Likewise, book are sometimes added – like book 4 of Frontius or book 8 of The Gallic Wars, which might be commentaries by another author, but became part of the edition and are called into question. These two books may represent opposite ends of the spectrum when it comes to ancient knowledge on warfare, but they also complement each other in providing examples on ancient strategies and the methods one can use to implement them.

To help the reader understand the background on these books we have included appendices that explain some of the terms and people referred to in the texts. Additionally, there is an index of places referenced including their modern location where possible.

The Route of Alexander the Great

Stratagems

By Sextus Julius Frontius

Book I - Stratagems

Since I alone, of those interested in military science, have undertaken the task of shaping its rules to system, and since I seem to have fulfilled that purpose, so far as pains on my part could accomplish it, I thus still feel under obligation, in order to complete the task I have begun, to summarize in convenient sketches the adroit operations of generals, which the Greeks embrace under the one name, *Strategemata*. In this way, commanders will be furnished with specimens of wisdom and foresight, which will serve to foster their own power of conceiving and executing like deeds. This will result in the added advantage that a general will not fear on the issue of his own stratagem if he compares it with examples that have already succeeded.

I neither ignore nor deny the fact that historians have included in the compass of their works this feature as well, nor have that authors already recorded in some fashion all famous examples. However I ought, I think, out of consideration for busy men, to have regard to brevity. It is a tedious business to hunt out separate examples scattered over the vast body of history; and those who have made selections of notable deeds have overwhelmed readers by the very mass of material. My effort will be devoted to the task of setting forth, as if in response to questions, and as occasion shall demand, the illustration applicable to the case in point. Having examined the categories, I have mapped out my campaign in advance, so to speak, for the presentation of illustrative examples. In order that these may be sifted and properly classified according to the variety of subject-matter, I have divided them into three books. In the first book I have illustrations of stratagems for use before the battle begins; in the second, those that relate to the battle itself and tend to effect the complete subjugation of the enemy; the third contains stratagems connected with sieges and the raising of sieges. Under these successive classes I have grouped the illustrations appropriate to each.

It is not without justice that I shall claim indulgence for this work, and I beg that no one will charge me with negligence if he finds that I have passed over some illustration. Who could prove equal to the task of examining all the records which have come down to us in both languages; and thus I have purposely allowed myself to skip many things. I have not done this without reason, and those who read the books of others treating of the same subjects will realize this; but it will be easy for the reader to supply those examples under each category. For since this work, like my preceding ones, has been undertaken for the benefit of others, rather than for the sake of my own renown, I shall feel that I am being aided, rather than criticized, by those who will make additions to it.

If there prove to be any persons who take an interest in these books, let them remember to discriminate between "strategy" and "stratagems," which are by nature extremely similar. For everything achieved by a commander, be it characterized by foresight, advantage, enterprise, or resolution, will belong under the head of "strategy," while those things which fall under some special type of these will be "stratagems." The essential characteristic of the latter, resting, as it does, on skill and cleverness, is effective quite as much when the enemy is to be evaded as when he is to be crushed. Since in this field certain striking results have been produced by speeches, I have set down examples of these also, as well as of deeds.

Types of stratagems for the guidance of a commander in matters to be attended to before battle:

I.   On concealing one's plans.

II. On finding out the enemy's plans.

III. On determining the character of the war.

IV. On leading an army through places infested by the enemy.

V. On escaping from difficult situations.

VI. On laying and meeting ambushes while on the march.

VII.How to conceal the absence of the things we lack, or to supply substitutes for them.

VIII.   On distracting the attention of the enemy.

IX. On quelling a mutiny of soldiers.

X. How to check an unseasonable demand for battle.

XI. How to arouse an army's enthusiasm for battle.

XII.On dispelling the fears inspired in soldiers by adverse omens.

Roman Legionnaire - 1st Century BC (Antoine Gledel)

I. ON CONCEALING ONE'S PLANS

Marcus Porcius Cato believed that, when opportunity offered, the Spanish cities which he had subdued would revolt, relying upon the protection of their walls. He therefore wrote to each of the cities, ordering them to destroy their fortifications, and threatening war unless they obeyed forthwith. He ordered these letters to be delivered to all cities on the same day. Each city supposed that it alone had received the commands; had they known that the same orders had been sent to all; they could have joined forces and refused obedience.[1]

Himilco, the Carthaginian general, desiring to land in Sicily by surprise, made no public announcement as to the destination of his voyage, but gave all the captains sealed letters, in which were instructions as to which port to make, with further directions that no one should read these, unless separated from the flag-ship by a violent storm.[2]

When Gaius Laelius went as envoy to Syphax, he took with him certain tribunes and centurions as spies whom he represented to be slaves and attendants. One of these, Lucius Statorius, was frequently seen in the camp and was concerned that the enemy might recognize him so Laelius caned him like a slave, in order to conceal the man's rank.[3]

Tarquin the Proud, having decided that the leading citizens of Gabii should be put to death, and not wishing to confide this purpose to anyone, gave no response to the messenger sent to him by his son, but merely cut off the tallest poppy heads with his cane, as he happened to walk about in the garden. The messenger, returning without an answer, reported to the young Tarquin what he had seen his father doing. The son thereupon understood that the same thing was to be done to the prominent citizens of Gabii.

Gaius Caesar, distrusting the loyalty of the Egyptians, and wishing to give the appearance of indifference, indulged in riotous banqueting while devoting himself to an inspection of the city[4] and its defenses, pretending to be captivated by the charm of the place and to be succumbing to the customs and life of the Egyptians. Having made ready his reserves while he thus dissembled, he seized Egypt.[5]

---

[1] Cato's memos: 195 B.C. Cf. Appian Hisp. 41.
[2] Himilco's memos: 396 B.C. Cf. Polyaenus V.X.2.
[3] Laelius' slave: 203 B.C. Cf. Liv. XXX.4.
[4] the city: Alexandria
[5] Caesar's riotous living in Egypt: 48 B.C. Cf. Appian C. II.89.

When Ventidius was waging war against the Parthian king Pacorus, he knew that a certain Pharnaeus from the province of Cyrrhestica, was one of those that pretended to be an ally, revealed all the preparations of his own army to the Parthians. He turned the treachery of the barbarian to his own advantage by pretending to be afraid that those things would happen which he was particularly desirous should happen, and pretended to desire those things to happen which he really dreaded. And so, fearful that the Parthians would cross the Euphrates before he could be reinforced by the legions which were stationed beyond the Taurus Mountains in Cappadocia, he earnestly endeavored to make this traitor, according to his usual perfidy, advised the Parthians to lead their army across through Zeugma, where the route is shortest, and where the Euphrates flows in a deep channel. He declared that if the Parthians came by that road, he could avail himself of the protection of the hills for eluding their archers; but in reality he feared disaster if they should advance by the lower road through the open plains.[6] Influenced by this information, the barbarians led their army by a circuitous route over the lower road and spent above forty days in preparing materials and in constructing a bridge[7] across the river at a point where the banks were quite widely separated. There they built a bridge, which thus involved more work. Ventidius utilized this interval for reuniting his forces, and having assembled these three days before the Parthians arrived, he opened battle, conquered Pacorus, and killed him.[8]

When Mithridates was blockaded by Pompey and planned to retreat the next day, he wanted to conceal his purpose and made foraging expeditions over a wide territory to the valleys adjacent to the enemy. For the purpose of further averting suspicion, he also arranged conferences for a subsequent date with several of his foes, and ordered numerous fires to be lighted throughout the camp. Then, in the second watch, he led out his forces directly past the camp of the enemy.[9]

---

[6] Ventidius' tale of fears: Since Ventidius really wished the Parthians to take his longer route that his reinforcement might have time to arrive. He led Pharnaeus to believe that he hoped they would cross by the shorter route. He knew that Pharnaeus would counsel the Parthians to take the course of action not desired by him.

[7] Bridge: The text is very uncertain at this point, though the general meaning is clear.

[8] Ventidius and Pacorus: 38 B.C. Cf. Dio XLIX.19.

[9] Mithridates' foraging and fires: 66 B.C. Cf. Appian Mithr. 98.

When the Emperor Caesar Domitianus Augustus Germanicus[10] wished to crush the Germans, who were in arms, he realized they would make greater preparations for war if they foresaw the arrival of so eminent a commander as himself. He then concealed the reason for his departure from Rome under the pretext of taking a census of the Gallic provinces. Under this guise he plunged into sudden warfare, crushed the ferocity of these savage tribes, and thus acted for the good of the provinces.[11]

Even though it was essential that Hasdrubal and his troops should be destroyed before they joined Hannibal, the brother of Hasdrubal, Claudius Nero lacked confidence in the troops under his own command. He was therefore eager to unite his forces with those of his colleague, Livius Salinator, to whom the direction of the campaign had been committed. Desiring, however, that his departure should be unobserved by Hannibal, whose camp was opposite his, he chose ten thousand of his bravest soldiers, and gave orders to the lieutenants whom he left that the usual number of patrols and sentries be posted, the same number of fires lighted, and the usual appearance of the camp be maintained, in order that Hannibal might not become suspicious and venture to attack the few troops left behind. Then, when he joined his colleague in Umbria after secret marches, he forbade the enlargement of the camp, lest he give some sign of his arrival to the Carthaginian commander, who would be likely to refuse battle if he knew the forces of the consuls had been united. Accordingly, attacking the enemy unawares with his reinforced troops, he won the day and returned to Hannibal in advance of any news of his exploit. Thus by the same plan, he stole a march on one of the two shrewdest Carthaginian generals and crushed the other.[12]

---

[10] Domitian
[11] Domitian's census: 83 A.D.
[12] Claudius Nero's phantom camp: 207 B.C. Cf. Val. Max. VII.IV.4; Livy XXVII.43 ff.

Upon the urging of his fellow-citizens Themistocles speedily reconstructed the walls which, at the command of the Lacedaemonians, they had demolished, informing the envoys sent from Sparta to remonstrate about this matter, that he himself would come, to put an end to this suspicion; accordingly he came to Sparta. There, by feigning illness, he secured a considerable delay. But after he realized that his subterfuge was suspected, he declared that the rumor which had come to the Spartans was false, and asked them to send some of their leading men, whose word they would take about the building operations of the Athenians. Then he wrote secretly to the Athenians, telling them to detain those who had come to them, until, upon the restoration of the walls, he could admit to the Spartans that Athens was fortified, and could inform them that their leaders could not return until he himself had been sent back. The Spartans readily agreed to fulfill his terms that they might not atone for the death of one by that of many.[13]

Lucius Furius, having led his army into an unfavorable position, determined to conceal his anxiety, lest the others take alarm. By gradually changing his course, as though planning to attack the enemy after a wider circuit, he finally reversed his line of march, and led his army safely back, without them knowing what was going on.

When Metellus Pius was in Spain and was asked what he was going to do the next day, he replied: "If my tunic could tell, I would burn it."[14]

When Marcus Licinius Crassus was asked at what time he was going to break camp, he replied: "Are you afraid you'll not hear the trumpet?"[15]

---

[13] Themistocles plays sick: 478 B.C. Cf. Thuc. I.90 ff.

[14] Metellus Pius' talking tunic: 79- 72 B.C. Cf. Val. Max. VII.IV.5.

[15] Crassus' deaf soldier: Plut. Demetr. 28 tells the same story of Antigonus and Demetrius.

II. ON FINDING OUT THE ENEMY'S PLANS

Scipio Africanus, seizing the opportunity of sending an embassy to Syphax, commanded specially chosen tribunes and centurions to go with Laelius disguised as slaves. He entrusted this unit with the task of spying out the strength of the king. These men, in order to examine the situation of the camp more freely, purposely let loose a horse and chased it around the greatest part of the fortifications, pretending it was running away. After they had reported the results of their observations, the destruction of the camp by fire[16] brought the war to a close.[17]

During the war with Etruria, when shrewd methods of reconnoitering were still unknown to Roman leaders, Quintus Fabius Maximus commanded his brother, Fabius Caeso, who spoke the Etruscan language fluently, to put on Etruscan dress and to penetrate into the Ciminian Forest, where our soldiers had never before ventured. He showed such discretion and energy in executing these commands, that after traversing the forest and observing that the Umbrians of Camerium were not hostile to the Romans, he brought them into an alliance.[18]

When the Carthaginians saw that the power of Alexander was so great that it menaced even Africa, they ordered one of their citizens, a resolute man named Hamilcar Rhodinus, to go to the king, pretending to be an exile, and to make every effort to gain his friendship. When Rhodinus had succeeded in this, he disclosed to his fellow-citizens the king's plans.[19]

The same Carthaginian sent men to tarry a long time at Rome, in the role of ambassadors, and thus to secure information of our plans.

When Marcus Cato was in Spain, being unable otherwise to arrive at knowledge of the enemy's plans, he ordered three hundred soldiers to make a simultaneous attack on an enemy post, to seize one of their men, and to bring him unharmed to camp. The prisoner, under torture, revealed all the secrets of his side.[20]

---

[16] After they had reported the results of their observations, the destruction of the camp by fire: i.e. the information furnished by the spies enabled Scipio to set fire to the camp of Syphax.

[17] Scipio's loose horse: 203 B.C. Cf. Liv. XXX.4 ff.

[18] Fabius Caeso spies on the Etruscans: 310 B.C. Cf. Liv. IX.36.

[19] Hamilcar Rhodinus, fickle friend: 331 B.C. Cf. Justin. XXI.VI.1.

[20] Cato tortures a soldier: 195 B.C. Plut. Cat. Maj. 13 attributes this stratagem to Cato at Thermopylae four years later.

During the war with the Cimbrians and Teutons, the consul Gaius Marius, wishing to test the loyalty of the Gauls and Ligurians, sent them a letter, commanding them in the first part of the letter not to open the inner part,[21] which was specially sealed, before a certain date. Afterwards, before the appointed time had arrived, he demanded the same letter back, and finding all seals broken, he knew that acts of hostility were afoot.[22]

There is also another method of securing intelligence, by which the generals themselves, without calling in any outside help, by their own unaided efforts take precautions, as, for instance:

In the Etruscan war, the consul Aemilius Paulus was on the point of sending his army down onto the plain near the town of Vetulonia, when he saw afar off a flock of birds rise in somewhat startled flight from a forest, and realized that some treachery was lurking there; both because the birds had risen in alarm and at the same time in great numbers. He therefore sent some scouts ahead and discovered that ten thousand Boii were lying in wait at that point to meet the Roman army. He overwhelmed the enemy by sending his legions against the enemy from an area that they were not expecting.[23]

In like manner, Tisamenus, the son of Orestes, hearing that a ridge, a natural stronghold, was held by the enemy, sent men ahead to ascertain the facts; and upon their reporting that his impression was without foundation, he began his march. But when he saw a large number of birds all at once fly from the suspected ridge and not settle down at all, he came to the conclusion that the enemy's troops were hiding there; and so, leading his army by a detour, he escaped those lying in wait for him.[24]

Hasdrubal, brother of Hannibal, knew that the armies of Livius and Nero had united (although by avoiding two separate camps they strove to conceal this fact), because he observed horses rather lean from travel and men somewhat sunburned, as naturally results from marching.[25]

---

[21] the inner part: The letter was presumably in codex form, with the second and third leaves fastened together by a special seal.

[22] Marius' "don't read this": 104 B.C.

[23] Aemilius Paulus at Vetulonia: Q. Aemilius Papus, consul in 282 and 278 B.C., waged war on the Etruscans. Pliny N. H. III.138 shows a like confusion of these names. Thayer's Note: Not only it's not Aemilius Paulus, it's apparently not Vetulonia, either; or at least, there seems to be a definite bit of silent emendation in the Loeb edition, the manuscripts reading Colonia. The battle is now usually referred to as that of Telamon. George Dennis discusses several opinions: see his chapter on Rusellae.

[24] Tisamenus' birds: Cf. Polyaen. II.XXXVII.

[25] Hasdrubal's thin horses: 207 B.C. Cf. I.I.9 and Livy XXVII.47.

III. On Determining the Character of the War

Whenever Alexander of Macedon had a strong army, he chose the sort of warfare in which he could fight in open battle.

In the Civil War, Gaius Caesar having an army of veterans and knowing that the enemy had only raw recruits, always strove to fight in open battle.

When engaged in war with Hannibal, who was inflated by his success in battle, Fabius Maximus decided to avoid any dangerous hazards and to devote himself solely to the protection of Italy. By this policy he earned the name of Cunctator ("The Delayer") and the reputation of a consummate general.[26]

In their war with Philip, the Greeks avoided all risks of battle, even abandoning the defense of their territory, and retired within the walls of their city which succeeded in causing Philip to withdraw, since he could not endure the delay of a siege.

In the Second Punic War, Hasdrubal, the son of Gisco, distributed his vanquished army among the cities of Spain when Publius Scipio pressed hard upon him. As a result, Scipio, in order not to scatter his forces by laying siege to several towns, withdrew his army into winter quarters.[27]

When Xerxes was approaching, Themistocles thought the strength of the Athenians unequal to their own strength whether they found a land battle, defending their territories, or supporting a siege, advised them to remove their wives and children to Troezen and other towns, to abandon the city, and to transfer the scene of the war to the water.[28]

Pericles did the same thing in the same state, in the war with the Spartans.[29]

While Hannibal was lingering in Italy, Scipio sent an army into Africa, forcing the Carthaginians to recall Hannibal. In this way he transferred the war from his own country to that of the enemy.[30]

---

[26] Fabius Maximus' delaying: 217 B.C. Cf. Livy XXII.XII.6- 12.
[27] Impatient Philip: 339 B.C. Cf. Justin IX.1.
[28] Hasdrubal splits up his forces: 207 B.C. Cf. Livy XXVIII.2- 3.
[29] Themistocles' emergency preparations: 480 B.C. Cf. Herod. VIII.41.
[30] Pericles' emergency preparations: 431 B.C. Cf. Thuc. I.143.

When the Spartans fortified the Athenian stronghold of Decelea, and were making frequent raids there, the Athenians sent a fleet to harass the Peloponnesus, and thus secured the recall of the army of Spartans stationed at Decelea.[31]

In Accordance with their usual custom, when the Germans emerged from woodland pastures and unsuspected hiding places to attack our men, and then finding a safe refuge in the depths of the forest, the Emperor Caesar Domitianus Augustus, by advancing the frontier of the empire along a stretch of one hundred and twenty miles, not only changed the nature of the war, but brought his enemies beneath his sway by uncovering their hiding-places.[32]

---

[31] Scipio brings the war home to the Carthaginians: 204 B.C. Cf. Appian Hann. 55; Livy XXVIII.40 ff.

[32] Domitian extends the frontline: 83 A.D.

IV. On Leading an Army through Places Infested by the Enemy

When the consul Aemilius Paulus was leading his army along a narrow road near the coast in Lucania, the fleet of the Tarentines had been lying in wait for him and attacked his troops with scorpions[33], he placed prisoners as a screen to his line of march. Not wishing to harm these, the enemy ceased their attacks.[34]

Agesilaus, the Spartan, when returning from Phrygia laden with booty, was hard pressed by the enemy, who took advantage of their position to harass his line of march. He therefore placed a file of captives on each flank of his army. Since these were spared by the enemy, the Spartans found time to pass.[35]

The same Agesilaus, when the Thebans held a pass through which he had to march, changed his direction, as if he were hastening to Thebes. Then, when the Thebans withdrew in alarm to protect their walls, Agesilaus resumed his march and arrived at his goal without opposition.[36]

When Nicostratus, King of the Aetolians, was at war with the Epirotes, he could only enter their territory by narrow defiles. He appeared at one point, as if intending to break through at that place. Then, when the whole body of Epirotes rushed to that place to prevent this, he left a few of his men to produce the impression that his army was still there, while he himself, with the rest of his troops, entered at another place, where he was not expected.

Autophradates, the Persian, upon leading his army into Pisidia, and finding certain passes occupied by the Pisidians, pretended to be thwarted in his plan for crossing, and began to retreat. When the Pisidians were convinced of this, under cover of night he sent a very strong force ahead to seize the same place, and on the following day sent his whole army across.[37]

---

[33] scorpion: A military engine for throwing darts, stones, and other missiles.
[34] Aemilius Paulus' human shields: 282 B.C. Cf. Zonar. VIII.2. Since no Aemilius Paulus waged war with the Tarentines, this is probably the Papus referred to in the note to I.II.7.
[35] Agesilaus' human shields: 396 B.C. Cf. Polyaen. II.I.30.
[36] Agesilaus' feint towards Thebes: 394 or 377 B.C. Cf. Zen. Hell. V.IV.49 ff.; Polyaen. II.I.24.
[37] Autophradates' false retreat: 359- 330 B.C. Cf. Polyaen. VII.XXVII.1.

When Philip of Macedon was planning the conquest of Greece, he heard that the Pass of Thermopylae was occupied by Greek troops. Accordingly, when envoys of the Aetolians came to sue for peace, he detained them, while he himself hastened by forced marches to the pass, and since the guards had relaxed their vigilance while awaiting the return of the envoys, he surprised them by marching through the Pass.[38]

When the Athenian general Iphicrates was engaged in a campaign against the Spartan Anaxibius on the Hellespont near Abydus, he had to lead his army through places occupied by enemy patrols, hemmed in on the one side by precipitous mountains, and on the other washed by the sea. For some time he delayed, and then on an unusually cold day, when no one suspected such a move, he selected his most rugged men, rubbed them down with oil and warmed them up with wine, and then ordered them to skirt the very edge of the sea, swimming across the places that were too precipitous to pass. By this unexpected attack from the rear he overwhelmed the guards of the defile.[39]

When Gnaeus Pompey, on one occasion, was prevented from crossing a river due to the enemy's troops being stationed on the opposite bank, he adopted the device of repeatedly leading his troops out of camp and back again. Then, when the enemy was at last tricked into relaxing their watch on the roads in front of the Roman advance, he made a sudden dash and affected a crossing.[40]

When Porus, a king of the Indians, was keeping Alexander of Macedon from leading his troops across the river Hydaspes, the latter commanded his men to make a practice of running toward the water. By that maneuver he led Porus to guard the opposite bank, when he suddenly led his army across at a higher point of the stream.[41]

---

[38] Philip's dilatory peace negotiations: 210 B.C.

[39] Iphicrates' Seals: 389- 388 B.C. Cf. Polyaen. III.IX.33.

[40] Pompey's troops march around a lot: Cf. the Spartan trick at Aegospotami, Xen. Hell. II.I.21 ff.

[41] Alexander crosses the Hydaspes: 326 B.C. Cf. Polyaen. IV.III.9; Plut. Alex. 60; Curt. VIII.13.5 ff.° Frontinus, misled by different names given to the river, probably took the same story from two different sources. Cf. Introd. p. xxv.°

The same Alexander, prevented by the enemy from crossing the river Indus, began to send horsemen into the water at different points and to threaten the crossing. Then, when he had the barbarians keyed up with expectation, he seized an island a little further off, and from there sent troops to the further bank. When the entire force of the enemy rushed away to overwhelm this band, he himself crossed safely by fords left unguarded and reunited all his troops.

Xenophon once ordered his men to attempt a crossing in two places in the face of Armenians who had possession of the opposite bank. Being repulsed at the lower point, he passed to the upper; and when he was also driven back from there by the enemy's attack, he returned to the lower crossing, but only after ordering a part of his soldiers to remain behind and to cross by the upper passage, so soon as the Armenians should return to protect the lower. The Armenians, supposing that all were proceeding to the lower point, overlooked those remaining above; who, crossing the upper ford without molestation, defended their comrades as they also passed over.

When Appius Claudius was consul in the first Punic War, he was unable to transport his soldiers from the neighborhood of Regium to Messina because the Carthaginians were guarding the Straits. He spread a rumor that he could not continue the war which had been undertaken without the endorsement of the people, and turning about he pretended to set sail for Italy. Then, when the Carthaginians dispersed, believing he had gone, Appius turned back and landed in Sicily.[42]

When certain Spartan generals had planned to sail to Syracuse, but were afraid of the Carthaginian fleet anchored along the shore, they commanded that the ten Carthaginian ships which they had captured should go ahead as though victors, with their own vessels either lashed to their side or towed behind. Having deceived the Carthaginians by these appearances, the Spartans succeeded in passing by.[43]

---

[42] Appius Claudius' constitutional war powers rumour: 264 B.C. Cf. Polyb. I.XI.9. Zonar. VIII.VIII.6 gives a somewhat different account of this crossing.
[43] The Spartan navy disguises itself as Carthaginians: 397 B.C. Cf. Polyaen. II.XI.

When Philip was unable to sail through the straits called Stena[44], because the Athenian fleet kept guard at a strategic point, he wrote to Antipater that Thrace was in revolt, and that the garrisons which he had left there had been cut off, directing Antipater to leave all other matters and follow him. Philip arranged to have this letter fall into the hands of the enemy. The Athenians, imagining they had secured secret intelligence of the Macedonians, withdrew their fleet, while Philip passed through the straits with no one to hinder him.

At one time the Chersonese were controlled by the Athenians, and Philip was prevented from capturing it, owing to the fact that the strait was commanded by vessels not only of the Greeks but also of the Rhodians and Chians; but Philip won the confidence of these peoples by returning their captured ships, as pledges of the peace to be arranged between himself and the Byzantines, who were the cause of the war. While the negotiations dragged on for some time and Philip purposely kept changing the details of the terms, in the interval he got ready a fleet, and eluding the enemy while they were off their guard, he suddenly sailed into the straits.

When Chabrias, the Athenian, was unable to secure access to the harbor of the Samians on account of the enemy blockade, he sent a few of his own ships with orders to cross the mouth of the harbor, thinking that the enemy on guard would give chase. When the enemy was drawn away by this ruse, and no one was there to hinder him, he secured possession of the harbor with the remainder of his fleet.

---

[44] the straits called Stena: i.e., the Hellespont. Thayer's Note: Stena isn't really a geographical name here; the word just means "the narrows".

V. On Escaping from Difficult Situations

During the Spanish campaign, Quintus Sertorius sought to cross a river while the enemy was harassing him from the rear. He had his men construct a crescent-shaped rampart on the bank, pile it high with timber, and set fire to it. When the enemy was thus cut off, he crossed the stream without hindrance.[45]

In like manner, During the Thessalian War, Pelopidas the Theban, sought to cross a stream. Choosing a site above the bank larger than was necessary for his camp, he constructed a rampart of chevaux-de-frise and other materials, and set fire to it. Then, while the enemy was kept off by the fire, he crossed the stream.[46]

When Quintus Lutatius Catulus had been repulsed by the Cimbrians, his only hope of safety lay in passing a stream the banks of which were held by the enemy. He therefore displayed his troops on the nearest mountain, as though intending to camp there. He then commanded his men not to loosen their packs, or put down their loads, and not to quit the ranks or standards. In order to more effectively strengthen the impression made upon the enemy, he ordered a few tents to be erected in open view, and fires to be built, while some built a rampart and others went forth in plain sight to collect wood. The Cimbrians, deeming these performances genuine, and chose a place for their camp, scattering through the nearest fields to gather the supplies necessary for their stay. In this way, they afforded Catulus opportunity not merely to cross the stream, but also to attack their camp.[47]

When Croesus could not ford the Halys, and had neither boats nor the means of building a bridge, he moved upstream and constructed a ditch behind his camp, bringing the channel of the river in the rear of his army.[48]

---

[45] Quintus Sertorius' firewall: 80- 72 B.C.
[46] P Lutatius Catulus' phantom camp: 102 B.C.
[47] Lutatius Catulus' phantom camp: 102 B.C.
[48] Croesus diverts a river: 546 B.C. Cf. Herod. I.75.

When Gnaeus Pompey was at Brundisium he planned to leave Italy and to transfer the war to another field, since Caesar was heavy on his heels. Just as he was on the point of embarking, he placed obstacles in some roads; others were blocked by constructing walls across them; others he intersected with trenches, setting sharp stakes in the latter and laying hurdles covered with earth across the openings. Some of the roads leading to the harbor he guarded by throwing beams across and piling them one upon another in a huge heap. After finishing these arrangements and wishing to produce the appearance of intending to retain possession of the city, he left a few archers as a guard on the walls. He led the remainder of his troops out in good order to the ships. Then, when he was under way, the archers also withdrew by familiar roads, and overtook him in small boats.[49]

When the consul Gaius Duellius was caught by a chain stretched across the entrance to the harbor of Syracuse, which he had rashly entered, he assembled all his soldiers in the sterns of the boats, and when the boats were thus tilted up, he propelled them forward with the full force of his oarsmen. Thus lifted up over the chain, the prows moved forward. When this part of the boats had been carried over, the soldiers, returning to the prows, depressed these, and the weight thus transferred to them permitted the boats to pass over the chain.[50]

When Lysander, the Spartan, was blockaded in the harbor[51] of the Athenians with his entire fleet, by Athenian ships sunk at the point where the sea flows in through a very narrow entrance, he commanded his men to secretly disembark. Placing his ships on wheels, he transported them to the neighboring harbor of Munychia.[52]

When Hirtuleius, a lieutenant of Quintus Sertorius, was leading a few cohorts up a long narrow road in Spain between two precipitous mountains, and learned that a large detachment of the enemy was approaching, he had a ditch dug between the mountains, fenced it with a wooden rampart. He set fire to this, and made his escape, while the enemy was thus cut off from attacking him.[53]

---

[49] Pompey fortifies Brundisium: 49 B.C. Cf. Caes. B.C. I.27‑28.
[50] Chained harbor no obstacle to Duilius: 260 B.C. Zonar. VIII.16 makes Hippo, rather than Syracuse, the scene of this stratagem.
[51] harbour: Piraeus.
[52] Lysander's ships on wheels: 404 B.C.
[53] Hirtuleius' firewall: 79‑75 B.C.

When Gaius Caesar led out his forces against Afranius in the Civil War, and had no means of retreating without danger, he had the first and second lines of battle remain in arms, just as they were drawn up, while the third secretly applied itself to work in the rear and dug a ditch fifteen feet deep, within the line of which the soldiers under arms withdrew at sunset.[54]

Pericles the Athenian was driven by the Peloponnesians into a place surrounded on all sides by precipitous cliffs and provided with only two outlets. He dug a ditch of great width on one side, as if to shut out the enemy; on the other side he began to build a road, as if intending to make a sally by that direction. The besiegers, not supposing that Pericles' army would try to make its escape by the ditch which he had constructed, massed to oppose him on the side with the road. But Pericles, spanning the ditch by bridges which he had made ready, extricated his men without interference.[55]

Lysimachus, one of the heirs to Alexander's power, determined on one occasion to pitch his camp on a high hill and was conducted by the inadvertence of his men to a lower one. Fearing that the enemy would attack from above, he dug a triple line of trenches and encircled these with a rampart. Then, running a single trench around all the tents, he fortified the entire camp. Having thus shut off the advance of the enemy, he filled in the ditches with earth and leaves, and made his way across them to higher ground.[56]

When Gaius Fonteius Crassus was in Spain, he set out with three thousand men on a foraging expedition and was caught in an awkward position by Hasdrubal. At nightfall, when such a movement was least expected he burst through the enemy's patrols, communicating his plan only to the centurions of the first rank.

Lucius Furius, having led his army into an unfavorable position, determined to conceal his anxiety, lest the others take alarm. By gradually changing his course, as though planning to attack the enemy after a wider circuit, he finally reversed his line of march and led his army safely back without them knowing what was going on

.

---

[54] Caesar's stealthy retreat: 49 B.C. Cf. Caes. B.C. I.42.
[55] Pericles' backdoor escape: 430 B.C. Cf. III.IX.9. Variations of the same story. Polyaen. V.X.3 attributes this stratagem to Himilco.
[56] Lysimachus' troops dig trenches and fill them in: 323 - 281 B.C.

When the consul Cornelius Cossus was caught in a disadvantageous position by the enemy in the Samnite War, Publius Decius, tribune of the soldiers, urged him to send a small force to occupy a hill nearby and volunteered as leader of those who should be sent. The enemy, thus diverted to a different quarter, allowed the consul to escape, but surrounded Decius and besieged him. Decius, extricated himself from this predicament by making a sortie at night, escaped with his men unharmed, and rejoined the consul.[57]

Under the consul Atilius Calatinus, the same thing was done by a man whose name is variously reported. Some say he was called Laberius, and some Quintus Caedicius, but most give it as Calpurnius Flamma. This man, seeing that the army had entered a valley, the sides and all commanding parts of which the enemy had occupied, asked and received from the consul three hundred soldiers. After exhorting these to save the army by their valor, he hastened to the center of the valley. The enemy descended from all sides to crush him and his followers, but, were held in check in a long and fierce battle, affording the consul an opportunity to extricate his army.[58]

When the army of the consul Quintus Minucius marched into a defile of Liguria, the memory of the disaster of the Caudine Forks occurred to the minds of all his soldiers. Minucius ordered the Numidian auxiliaries, who were not well regarded because of their wild appearance and the ungainliness of their steeds, to ride up to the mouth of the defile which the enemy held. The enemy were alerted against attack, and threw out patrols; But when the Numidians, in order to inspire still more contempt for themselves, purposely affected to fall from their horses and to engage in ridiculous antics, the barbarians, broke ranks at the novel sight, gave themselves up to the enjoyment of the show. When the Numidians noticed this, they gradually grew nearer and putting spurs to their horses, dashed through the lightly held line of the enemy. They then set fire to the fields nearby, so that it became necessary for the Ligurians to withdraw to defend their own territory; thereby forced to release the Romans shut up at the pass.[59]

---

[57] Publius Decius' diversion: 343 B.C. Cf. Liv. VII.34 ff.
[58] Calpurnius Flamma's diversion: 258 B.C. Cf. Livy XXII.LX.11; Zonar. VIII.12. Gell. III.7 gives a different account of this incident.
[59] Minucius' clumsy Numidians: 193 B.C. Cf. Livy XXXV.11.

In the Social War, Lucius Sulla, was surprised in a defile near Aesernia by the army of the enemy under the command of Duillius. He asked for a conference, but was unsuccessful in negotiating terms of peace. Noting, however, that the enemy was careless and off their guard as a result of the truce, he marched out at night, leaving only a trumpeter, with instructions to create the impression of the army's presence by sounding the watches, and to rejoin him when the fourth watch began. In this way he conducted his troops unharmed to a place of safety, with all their baggage and engines of war.[60]

The same Sulla, when fighting in Cappadocia against Archelaus, general of Mithridates, embarrassed by the difficulties of the terrain and the large numbers of the enemy, proposed peace. Then, taking advantage of the opportunity afforded by the truce, which served to divert the watchfulness of his adversary, he slipped out of their hands.[61]

When Hasdrubal, brother of Hannibal, was unable to make his way out of a defile held by the enemy, he entered into negotiations with Claudius Nero and promised to withdraw from Spain if allowed to depart. Then, by quibbling over the terms, he dragged out negotiations for several days, during all of which time he was busy sending out his troops in detachments by way of paths so narrow that they were overlooked by the Romans. Finally he easily made his escape with the remainder, who were light-armed.[62]

When Marcus Crassus constructed a ditch around the forces of Spartacus, he filled it with the bodies of prisoners and cattle that he had slain during the night, and thus marched across it.[63]

The same Spartacus, when besieged on the slopes of Vesuvius at the point where the mountain was steepest and on that account unguarded, plaited ropes of osiers from the woods. Letting himself down by these, he not only made his escape, but then appeared in another quarter and struck such terror into Clodius that several cohorts gave way before a force of only seventy-four gladiators.[64]

---

[60] Sulla's trumpeter: 90 B.C.
[61] Sulla's truce: 92 B.C.
[62] Hasdrubal's dilatory peace negotiations: 211 B.C. Cf. Livy XXVI.17; Zonar. IX.7.
[63] Spartacus' bridge of corpses: 71 B.C.
[64] Spartacus' wicker ropes: 73 B.C. Cf. Plut. Crassus 9; Flor. III.20.

When Spartacus was enveloped by the troops of the proconsul Publius Varinius, he placed stakes at short intervals before the gate of the camp; then setting up corpses, dressed in clothes and furnished with weapons, he tied these to the stakes to give the appearance of sentries when viewed from a distance. He also lit fires throughout the camp to give the appearance that it was still populated. Having deceived the enemy by this empty show, Spartacus silently led out his troops by night.[65]

When the Spartan general Brasidas, was surprised and outnumbered near Amphipolis by a host of Athenians, he allowed himself to be enveloped in order to diminish the density of the enemy's ranks by lengthening the line of besiegers. He then broke through at the point where the line was most lightly held.[66]

When Iphicrates was campaigning in Thrace, he pitched his camp on low ground and discovered through scouts that the neighboring hill was held by the enemy. This hill came down a single road which might be utilized to overwhelm him and his men. He left a few men in camp at night and commanded them to light a number of fires. Then, leading his troops and arranging them along the sides of the road just mentioned, he allowed the barbarians to pass by. In this way the disadvantage of terrain from which he suffered had been turned against them and with part of his army he overwhelmed their rear, while with another part he captured their camp.[67]

In order to deceive the Scythians, Darius left dogs and asses when he evacuated the camp. When the enemy heard these animals barking and braying, they imagined that Darius was still there.

To produce a like misconception in the minds of our men, the Ligurians, in various places, tied bullocks to trees with halters. The animals, being thus separated, bellowed incessantly and produced the impression that the Ligurians were still there.

When Hanno, was enveloped by the enemy, he selected the point in the line best suited for a sortie, and, piling up light kindling, set fire to it. Then, when the enemy withdrew to guard the other exits, he marched his men straight through the fire, directing them to protect their faces with their shields, and their legs with their clothing.

---

[65] Spartacus' corpses stand guard: 73 B.C.

[66] Brasidas lets himself be surrounded: 424 or 422 B.C. Cf. Thuc. IV.102, 106 ff.; V.6- 11.

[67] Iphicrates' ambush: 389 B.C. This same story is told in II.XI.4. Cf. also Polyaen. III.IX.41, 46, 50.

On one occasion Hannibal was embarrassed by difficulties of terrain, by lack of supplies, and by the attacks that Fabius Maximus inflicted on his rear guard. Accordingly, he tied bundles of lighted fagots to the horns of oxen, and turned the animals loose at night. The flames spread, fanned by the motion of the panic-stricken oxen who ran wildly hither and thither over the mountains to which they had been driven, illuminating the whole scene. The Romans, who had gathered to witness the sight, at first thought a prodigy had occurred. Then when scouts reported the facts, Fabius, fearing an ambush, kept his men in camp. Meanwhile the barbarians marched away, with no one to impede them.

VI. On Laying and Meeting Ambushes While on the March

When Fulvius Nobilior was leading his army from Samnium against the Lucanians, and learned from deserters that the enemy intended to attack his rearguard. He then ordered his bravest legion to go in advance, and the baggage train to follow in the rear. The enemy regarded this circumstance as a favorable opportunity and began to plunder the baggage. Fulvius then marshaled five cohorts of the legion mentioned above on the right side of the road, and five on the left. While the enemy was consumed with plundering, Fulvius, deployed his troops on both flanks, enveloped the foe, and cut them to pieces.

On another occasion Nobilior, was hard pressed from the rear by the enemy while on the march. Across his route ran a stream, not so large as to prevent passage, but large enough to cause delay by the swiftness of the current.[68] On the nearer side of this, Nobilior placed one legion in hiding, in hopes that the enemy, despising his small numbers, might follow more boldly. When this expectation was realized, the legion which had been posted attacked the enemy from ambush and destroyed them.

When Iphicrates was leading his army in Thrace, it was formed in a long file on account of the nature of the terrain. When a report was brought to him that the enemy planned to attack his rearguard, he ordered some cohorts to withdraw to both flanks and halt, while the rest were to quicken their pace and flee. He kept the elite of his forces in a separate formation as the others made their way to the rear. Thus, when the enemy was busy with rampant pillaging, and exhausted, his men were refreshed and drawn up in order. He attacked, routing the foe and stripping them of their booty.[69]

When the Roman army passed through the Litana Forest, the Boii cut into the trees at the base leaving only a slender support by which to stand, until such time as they should be pushed over. Then the Boii hid at the further edge of the woods and by toppling over the nearest trees caused the rest to fall as soon as our men entered the forest. In that way they spread general disaster among the Romans, and destroyed a large force.[70]

---

[68] large enough to cause delay: Thus giving him time to set this ambush.
[69] Iphicrates' rested troops: 389 B.C. Cf. Polyaen. III.IX.49, 54.
[70] the Boii's falling timber: 216 B.C. Twenty-five thousand, according to Livy XXIII.24.

VII. How to Conceal the Absence of the Things We Lack, Or To Supply Substitutes for Them

When Lucius Caecilius Metellus, lacked ships to transport his elephants he fastened together large earthen jars, covered them with planking, and then, loading the elephants on these, ferried them across the Sicilian Straits.[71]

On one occasion when Hannibal, could not force his elephants to ford an especially deep stream, having neither boats nor material of which to construct them, he ordered one of his men to wound the most savage elephant under the ear, and then straightway to swim across the stream and take to his heels. The infuriated elephant, eager to pursue the author of his suffering, swam the stream, and thus set an example for the rest to make the same venture.[72]

When the Carthaginian admirals were about to equip their fleet, but lacked broom,[73] they cut off the hair of their women and employed it for making cordage.[74] The Massilians and Rhodians did the same as the Carthaginians.

When he was a refugee from Mutina, Marcus Antonius gave his soldiers bark to use as shields.[75]

Spartacus and his troops had shields made of osiers and covered with hides.[76]

This place, I think, is most appropriate for recounting that famous deed of Alexander of Macedon. Marching along the desert roads of Africa, and suffering in common with his men from most distressing thirst, when some water was brought him in a helmet by a soldier, he poured it out upon the ground in the sight of all, in this way serving his soldiers better by his example of restraint than if he had been able to share the water with the rest.[77]

---

[71] Metellus' elephant floaters: 250 B.C. Cf. Zonar. VIII.14.

[72] Hannibal's recalcitrant elephants: 218 B.C. Cf. Livy XXI.XXVIII.5- 12.

[73] broom: The Spanish broom, used for making rope.

[74] The Carthaginians make cordage: 146 B.C. Cf. Flor. II.XV.10.

[75] Mark Anthony's bark shields: 43 B.C.

[76] Spartacus' wicker shields: 73 B.C. Cf. Flor. III.XX.6.

[77] Alexander leads his men: 332- 331 B.C. Cf. Polyaen. IV.III.25. Curt. VII.V.9- 12 and Plut Alex. 42 have a slightly different version.

VIII. On Distracting the Attention of the Enemy

When Coriolanus was seeking to avenge the shame of his own condemnation by war, he prevented the ravaging of the lands of the patricians, while burning and harrying those of the plebeians, in order to arouse discord whereby to destroy the harmony of the Romans.

When Hannibal proved no match for Fabius, either in character or in generalship, in order to smirch him with dishonor, he spared his lands when he ravaged all others. To meet this assault, Fabius transferred the title to his property to the State, thus, by his loftiness of character, preventing his honor from falling under the suspicion of his fellow-citizens.

In the fifth consulship of Fabius Maximus, the Gauls, Umbrians, Etruscans, and Samnites had formed an alliance against the Roman people. Fabius' first action against these tribes was to construct a fortified camp beyond the Apennines in the region of Sentinum. Then he wrote to Fulvius and Postumius, who were guarding the City, and directed them to move on Clusium with their forces. When these commanders complied, the Etruscans and Umbrians withdrew to defend their own possessions, while Fabius and his colleague Decius attacked and defeated the remaining forces of Samnites and Gauls.

When the Sabines levied a large army to invaded Roman territory, Manius Curius by secret routes sent a force against them which ravaged their lands and villages; setting fire to them in diverse places. In order to avert this destruction of their country, the Sabines withdrew, but Curius succeeded in devastating their country while it was unguarded, in repelling their army without an engagement, and then in slaughtering it piecemeal.[78]

---

[78] Manius Curius' diversionary attacks: 290 B.C.

Titus Didius at one time lacked confidence because of the small number of his troops, but continued the war in hope of the arrival of certain legions he was anticipating. On hearing that the enemy planned to attack these legions, he called an assembly of the soldiers and ordered them to get ready for battle, and purposely exercised a careless supervision over their prisoners. As a result, a few of the latter escaped and reported to their people that battle was imminent. To avoid dividing their strength when expecting battle, the enemy abandoned their plan of attacking those they were lying in wait for, so that the legions arrived without hindrance and in perfect safety at the camp of Didius.[79]

During the Punic War, certain cities had resolved to revolt against the Romans for the Carthaginians, but, before they revolted, they wished to recover the hostages they had given, and thus they pretended that an uprising had broken out among their neighbors whom Roman commissioners ought to come and suppress. When the Romans sent these envoys, the cities detained them as counter-pledges, and refused to restore them until they themselves recovered their own hostages.

After defeat of the Carthaginians, King Antiochus sheltered Hannibal and utilized his counsel against the Romans. When Roman envoys were sent to Antiochus, they held frequent conferences with Hannibal, and causing him to become an object of suspicion to the king, to whom he was otherwise most agreeable and useful, in consequence of his cleverness and experience in war.[80]

When Quintus Metellus was waging war against Jugurtha, he bribed the envoys that were sent to betray the king into his hands. When other envoys came, he did the same; and with a third embassy he adopted the same policy. However, his efforts to take Jugurtha prisoner met with little success, for Metellus wanted the king to be delivered into his hands alive. Finally, he accomplished a great deal, for when his letters addressed to the friends of the king were intercepted, the king punished all these men, and, being thus deprived of advisers, was unable to secure any friends for the future.[81]

---

[79] Titus Didius calls for battle: 98⁻ 93 B.C. In Spain.
[80] The Romans undermine Hannibal's influence: 192 B.C. Cf. Livy XXXV.14; Nep. Hann. 2.
[81] Metellus' letters to Jugurtha's advisers: 108 B.C. Cf. Sall. Jug. 61, 62, 70, 72.

On one occasion, Gaius Caesar caught a soldier who had gone to procure water, and learned from him that Afranius and Petreius planned to break camp that night. In order to hamper the plans of the enemy, and yet not cause alarm to his own troops, in the early evening gave Caesar orders to sound the signal for breaking camp, and commanded mules to be driven past the camp of the enemy with much noise and shouting. Thinking that Caesar was breaking camp, his adversaries stayed where they were, precisely as Caesar desired.[82]

When, on one occasion, reinforcements and provisions were on the way to Hannibal, Scipio, wanted to intercept them and sent Minucius Thermus ahead, and arranged to come himself to lend his support.[83]

When the Africans were planning to send large numbers of troops over to Sicily in order to attack Dionysius, tyrant of Syracuse, the latter constructed strongholds in many places and commanded their defenders to surrender them at the coming of the enemy, and then, when they retired, to return secretly to Syracuse. The Africans were forced to occupy the captured strongholds with garrisons, whereupon Dionysius, having reduced the army of his opponents to the small numbers he desired, and now being approximately equal in number, attacked and defeated them, since he had concentrated his own forces, and separated those of his adversaries.[84]

When Agesilaus, the Spartan, was waging war against Tissaphernes, he pretended to make for Caria, as though likely to fight more advantageously in mountainous districts against an enemy strong in cavalry. When he let it be known that this was his purpose, and had thus drawn Tissaphernes off to Caria, he invaded Lydia instead, where the capital the enemy's kingdom was situated. Having crushed those in command at that place, he obtained possession of the king's treasure.[85]

---

[82] Caesar breaks camp: 49 B.C. Cf. Caes. B.C. I.66.

[83] Scipio intercepts Hannibal's reinforcements: 202 B.C. Cf. Appian Pun. 36.

[84] Dionysius ties his enemies down: 396 B.C. Cf. Polyaen. V.II.9.

[85] Agesilaus' disinformation: 395 B.C. Cf. Xen. Hell. III.IV.20; Plut. Ages. 9- 10; Nep. Ages. 3.

IX. On Quelling a Mutiny of Soldiers

When the consul, Aulus Manlius, learned that the soldiers had formed a plot in their winter-quarters in Campania to murder their hosts and seize their property, he disseminated the report that they would winter next season in the same place. Having postponed the plans of the conspirators, he rescued Campania from peril, and, so soon as occasion offered, inflicted punishment on the guilty.[86]

On one occasion, legions of Roman soldiers had broken out in a dangerous mutiny, Lucius Sulla shrewdly restored sanity to the frenzied troops; for he ordered a sudden announcement to be made that the enemy were at hand, commanding a shout to be raised by those summoning the men to arms, and the trumpets were sounded. Thus the mutiny was broken up by the union of all forces against the foe.

When the senate of Milan was massacred by Pompey's troops, Pompey, fearing that he might cause a mutiny if he should call out the guilty alone, ordered certain ones who were innocent to come interspersed among the others. In this way, the guilty came with less fear, because they had not been singled out, and so did not seem to be sent for in consequence of any wrong-doing; while those whose conscience was clear kept watch on the guilty, lest by the escape of these the innocent should be disgraced.

When certain legions of Gaius Caesar mutinied, and in such a manner that seemed to threaten the life of their commander, he concealed his fear, by advancing with grim visage to the soldiers, and readily granted discharge to those asking it. But these men were no sooner discharged than penitence forced them to apologize to their commander and to pledge themselves to greater loyalty in future enterprises.[87]

---

[86] Manlius foils a mutiny: Livy VII.38‑ 39 attributes this stratagem to C. Marcius Rutilius, consul in 342 B.C.
[87] Caesar forestalls a mutiny: 47 B.C. Cf. Suet. Caes. 70; Appian B. C. II.92.

X. How to Check an Unseasonable Demand for Battle

Quintus Sertorius had learned by experience that he was by no means a match for the whole Roman army. In order to prove this to the barbarians as well, who were rashly demanding battle, he brought into their presence two horses; one was strong, the other very feeble. Then, he brought forward two youths of corresponding physique; one robust, the other slight. The stronger youth was commanded to pull out the entire tail of the feeble horse, while the slight youth was commanded to pull out the hairs of the strong horse one by one. The slight youth succeeded in his task, while the strong one was still vainly struggling with the tail of the weak horse, Sertorius observed: "By this illustration I have exhibited to you, my men, the nature of the Roman cohorts. They are invincible to him who attacks them in a body; yet he who assails them by groups will tear and rend them."[88]

When the same Sertorius saw his men rashly demanding the signal for battle, he thought them in danger of disobeying orders unless they were allowed to engage the enemy. He permitted a squadron of cavalry to advance to harass the foe. When these troops became engaged in disadvantageous combat, he sent others to their relief, and thus rescued all, showing more safely, and without injury, what would have been the outcome of the battle they had demanded. After that, he found his men most amenable.

When Agesilaus, the Spartan, was fighting against the Thebans he encamped on the bank of a stream. He was aware that the enemy forces far outnumbered his own and wished therefore to keep his men from the desire of fighting by announcing that he had been bidden by a response of the gods to fight on high ground. Accordingly, he posted a small guard on the bank and he withdrew to the hills. The Thebans, interpreting this as a mark of fear, crossed the stream, easily dislodged the defending troops, and, following the rest too eagerly, were defeated by a smaller force, owing to the difficulties of the terrain.

---

[88] Sertorius' horsetails: 80- 72 B.C. Cf. Val. Max. VII.III.6; Plut. Sert. 16; Hor. Epist. II.I.45 ff.; Plin. Epist. III.IX.11.

Though he knew that the Romans were torn with the dissensions of the civil wars, Scorylo, a chieftain of the Dacians, did not think he ought to venture on any enterprise against them, inasmuch as a foreign war might be the means of uniting the citizens in harmony. Accordingly, he pitted two dogs in combat before the populace, and when they became engaged in a desperate encounter, exhibited a wolf to them. The dogs straightway abandoned their fury against each other and attacked the wolf. By this illustration, Scorylo kept the barbarians from a movement which could only have benefited the Romans.

XI. How to Arouse an Army's Enthusiasm for Battle

When the consuls Marcus Fabius and Gnaeus Manlius were warring against the Etruscans, and the soldiers mutinied against fighting, the consuls on their side feigned a policy of delay, until soldiers, wrought upon by the taunts of the enemy, demanded battle and swore to return from it victorious.[89]

Fulvius Nobilior, decided it was necessary to fight against a large army of the Samnites who were flushed with success with a smaller force, he pretended that one legion of the enemy had been bribed by him to turn traitor. To strengthen belief in this story, he commanded the tribunes of the "first rank,"[90] and the centurions to contribute all the ready money they had, or any gold and silver, in order that the price might be paid the traitors at once. He promised that, when victory was achieved, he would give generous presents to those who contributed for this purpose. This assurance brought such ardor and confidence to the Romans that they opened battle straightway and won a glorious victory.

When Gaius Caesar was about to fight the Germans and their king, Ariovistus, his own men had been thrown into panic, called his soldiers together and declared to the assembly that on that day he proposed to employ the services of the tenth legion alone. In this way he caused the soldiers of this legion to be stirred by his tribute to their unique heroism, while the rest were overwhelmed with mortification to think that reputation for courage should rest with others.[91]

Since Quintus Fabius Maximus knew full well that the Romans possessed a spirit of independence which was roused by insult, and since he expected nothing just or reasonable from the Carthaginians, sent envoys to Carthage to inquire about terms of peace. When the envoys brought back proposals full of injustice and arrogance, the army of the Romans was stirred to combat.[92]

---

[89] Fabius and Manlius let their troops sit on the sidelines: 480 B.C. Cf. Livy II.XLIII.11- xlv; Dionys. IX.7- 10.

[90] first rank: These were a special class of centurions.

[91] Caesar chooses the tenth legion: 58 B.C. Cf. Caes. B.C. I.XXXIX.7, XL.1, 14 ff.

[92] Fabius Maximus goes out and gets a bad treaty offer: 217- 203 B.C.

The Spartan General Agesilaus, had his camp near the allied city of Orchomenos and learned that many of his soldiers were depositing their valuables within the fortifications, he commanded the townspeople to take nothing belonging to his troops, in order that his soldiers might fight with more spirit, when they realized that they must fight for all their possessions.[93]

On one occasion Epaminondas, general of the Thebans, was about to engage in battle with the Spartans, acting as follows: so that his soldiers might not only exercise their strength, but also be stirred by their feelings, he announced in an assembly of his men that the Spartans had resolved, in case of victory, to massacre all males, to lead the wives and children of those executed into bondage, and to raze Thebes to the ground. The Thebans were so roused by this announcement that they overwhelmed the Spartans at the first onset.[94]

When Leotychides, the Spartan admiral, was on the point of fighting a naval battle on the same day his allies had been victorious, although he was ignorant of the fact, he nevertheless announced that he had received news of the victory of their side, in order that in this way he might find his men more resolute for the encounter.[95]

When two youths, mounted on horseback, appeared in the battle which Aulus Postumius fought with the Latins. Postumius roused the drooping spirits of his men by declaring that the strangers were Castor and Pollux. In this way he inspired them to fresh combat.[96]

When Archidamus, the Spartan was waging war against the Arcadians, he set up weapons in camp, and ordered horses to be led around them secretly at night. In the morning, pointing to their tracks and claiming that Castor and Pollux had ridden through the camp, he convinced his men that the same gods would also lend them aid in the battle itself.[97]

---

[93] Agesilaus prohibits safe deposits: Cf. Polyaen. II.I.18.

[94] Epaminondas terrifies his own people: 371 B.C.

[95] Leotychides' victory announcement: 479 B.C. Cf. Diodor. XI.34- 35; Polyaen. I.33. Herod. IX.100- 101 has a different version.

[96] Aulus Postumius recognizes the Dioscuri: 496 B.C. Cf. Val. Max. I.VIII.1; Cic. De Nat. Deor. II.II.6; Dionys. VI.13.

[97] Archidamus and the horses of the Dioscuri: 467 B.C. Cf. Polyaen. I.XLI.1.

On one occasion when Pericles, of the Athenians, was about to engage in battle, he noticed a grove from which both armies were visible, very dense and dark, but unoccupied and consecrated to Father Pluto. He took a man of enormous stature, made imposing by high buskins, purple robes, and flowing hair, and placed him in the grove, mounted high on a chariot drawn by gleaming white horses. This man was instructed to drive forth, when the signal for battle was given and call Pericles by name, encouraging him by declaring that the gods were lending their aid to the Athenians. As a result, the enemy turned and fled almost before a dart was hurled.

In order to make his soldiers more ready for combat, Lucius Sulla pretended that the future was foretold to him by the gods. His last act, before engaging in battle, was to pray, in the sight of his army, to a small image which he had taken from Delphi, entreating it to speed the promised victory.

Gaius Marius had a certain wise-woman from Syria, whom he pretended to learn the outcome of battles in advance.[98]

Quintus Sertorius, employed barbarian troops who were not amenable to reason. He used to take a beautiful white deer with him through Lusitania, claiming he knew from it in advance what ought to be done, and what avoided. In this way he aimed to induce the barbarians to obey all his commands as though divinely inspired.[99] [This sort of stratagem is to be not only used in cases when we deem those to whom we apply it simple-minded, but much more when the ruse invented is such as might be thought to have been suggested by the gods.]

On one occasion Alexander of Macedon about to make sacrifice using a preparation to inscribe certain letters on the hand which the priest was about to place beneath the vitals. These letters indicated that victory was vouchsafed to Alexander. When the steaming liver received the impress of these characters and was displayed by the king to the soldiers, the circumstances raised their spirits, since they thought that the god gave them assurance of victory.[100]

The soothsayer Sudines did the same thing when Eumenes was about to engage in battle with the Gauls.[101]

---

[98] Marius' Syrian wisewoman: Cf. Val. Max. I.II.3a; Plut. Mar. 17; Gell. XV.22.
[99] Sertorius' beautiful white deer: Cf. Val. Max. I.II.4; Plut. Sertor. 11; Gell. XV.22
[100] Alexander's favorable entrails: Cf. Polyaen. IV.III.14 and IV.XX. Plut. Apophth. Lacon. Ages. Magni 77 attributes this stratagem to Agesilaus.
[101] Sudines' favorable entrails: Cf. Polyaen. IV.XX.

In his contest against the Spartans, Epaminondas the Theban, thought that the confidence of his troops needed strengthening by an appeal to religious sentiment, removed the weapons which were attached to the decorations of the temples that night, and convinced his soldiers that the gods were attending his march, in order to lend their aid in the battle itself.[102]

On one occasion, Agesilaus, the Spartan, captured some Persians. The appearance of these people, dressed in uniform, inspired great terror. But Agesilaus stripped his prisoners and exhibited them to his soldiers, in order that their delicate white bodies might excite contempt.[103]

After Gelo, tyrant of Syracuse, undertook a war against the Carthaginians, he took many prisoners, stripped all the feeblest, especially from among the auxiliaries, who were very swarthy, and exhibited them nude before the eyes of his troops, in order to convince his men that their foes were contemptible.[104]

Cyrus, king of the Persians, wished to rouse the ambition of his men and employed them an entire day in the fatiguing labor of cutting down a certain forest. Then on the following day, he gave them a generous feast, and asked them which they liked better. When they had expressed their preference for the feast, he said: "And yet it is only through the former that we can arrive at the latter; for unless you conquer the Medes, you cannot be free and happy." In this way he roused them to the desire for combat.[105]

In the campaign against a general of Mithridates named Archelaus, Lucius Sulla found his troops disinclined for battle at the Piraeus. By imposing tiresome tasks upon his men, he brought them to the point where they demanded the signal for battle of their own accord.[106]

Fabius Maximus, feared that his troops would fight less resolutely in consequence of their reliance on their ships, which it was possible to retreat. He ordered the ships to be set on fire before the battle began.[107]

---

[102] Epaminondas' statues prepare for battle: 371 B.C. Cf. Polyaen. II.III.8 and 12.
[103] Agesilaus' naked prisoners: 395 B.C. Cf. Polyaen. II.I.16; Xen. Hell. III.IV.19; Plut. Ages. 9.
[104] Gelo's naked prisoners, with a racial twist: 480 B.C.
Thayer's Note: This is one of the admittedly rare places in ancient sources that suggest that the Greeks and Romans were not so free of racial prejudices as current revisionism makes them out to be.
[105] Cyrus' object lesson: 558 B.C. Cf. Herod. I.126; Polyaen. VII.VI.7; Justin. I.VI.4- 6.
[106] Sulla's work details: 86 B.C.
[107] Fabius Maximus sets his own ships on fire: 315 B.C. Cf. Livy IX.23. Thayer's Note: see also Plutarch, On the Bravery of Women, 243F.

XII. On Dispelling the Fears Inspired in Soldiers by Adverse Omens

Scipio, having transported his army from Italy to Africa, stumbled as he was disembarking. When he saw the soldiers struck aghast at this, by his steadiness and loftiness of spirit he converted their cause of concern into one of encouragement, by saying: "Congratulate me, my men! I have hit Africa hard."[108]

Gaius Caesar, slipping as he was about to embark on ship, exclaimed: "I hold thee fast, Mother Earth." By this interpretation of the incident, he made it seem that he was destined to come back to the lands from which he was setting out.[109]

When the consul Tiberius Sempronius Gracchus was engaged in battle with the Picentines, a sudden earthquake threw both sides into panic. Thereupon Gracchus put new strength and courage into his men by urging them to attack the enemy, while the latter were overwhelmed with superstitious awe. Thus he fell upon them and defeated them.[110]

When by a sudden marvel caused the outsides of the shields of his cavalrymen and the breasts of their horses to show marks of blood, Sertorius interpreted this as a mark of victory, since those were the parts which were usually spattered with the blood of the enemy.

When his soldiers were depressed because the decoration Epaminondas the Theban, had hanging from his spear like a fillet had been torn away by the wind and carried to the tomb of a certain Spartan, said: "Do not be concerned, comrades! Destruction is foretold for the Spartans. Tombs are not decorated except for funerals."[111]

The same Epaminondas, when a meteor fell from the sky at night and struck terror to the hearts of those who noticed it, exclaimed: "It is a light sent us from the powers above."

---

[108] Scipio hits Africa hard: 204 B.C.

[109] Caesar holds Earth: Cf. Suet. Caes. 59.

[110] Tiberius Gracchus makes good use of an earthquake: P. Sempronius Sophus, consul, defeated the Picentines in 268 B.C. Cf. Flor. I.19.

[111] Epaminondas on decorating tombs: 371 B.C. Cf. Diodor. XV.LII.5 ff.

When Epaminondas was about to open battle against the Spartans, the chair on which he had sat down gave way beneath him, whereat all the soldiers, greatly troubled, interpreted this as an unlucky omen. But Epaminondas exclaimed: "Not at all; we are simply forbidden to sit."[112]

Gaius Sulpicius Gallus not only announced an approaching eclipse of the moon in order to prevent the soldiers from taking it as an omen, but also gave the reasons and causes of the eclipse.[113]

When Agathocles, the Syracusan, was fighting against the Carthaginians, on the eve of battle his soldiers were thrown into panic by a similar eclipse of the moon, which they interpreted as an omen. He explained the reason why this happened, and showed them that, whatever it was, it had to do with nature, and not with their own purposes.[114]

When a thunderbolt struck his camp and terrified his soldiers, Pericles called an assembly and struck fire by knocking two stones together in the sight of all his men. He thus allayed their panic by explaining that the thunderbolt was similarly produced by the contact of the clouds.

When Timotheus, the Athenian, was about to contend against the Corcyreans in a naval battle, his pilot, heard one of the rowers sneeze, giving the signal for retreat, just as the fleet was setting out; whereupon Timotheus exclaimed: "Do you think it strange if one out of so many thousands has had a chill?"[115]

As Chabrias the Athenian, was about to fight a naval battle, a thunderbolt fell directly across the path of his ship. When the soldiers were filled with dismay at such a portent, he said: "Now is the very time to begin battle, when Jupiter, mightiest of the gods, reveals that his power is present with our fleet."[116]

---

[112] We are forbidden to sit: i.e., "we must be up and doing."
[113] Sulpicius Gallus explains an eclipse: 168 B.C. Cf. Livy XLIV.37; Cic. De Senect. xiv.49; Val. Max. VIII.XI.1. Thayer's Note: 172 B.C., actually: see my note on Plutarch, Aem. 17.7.
[114] Agathocles explains an eclipse: 310 B.C. Cf. Justin. XXII.VI.1- 5; Diodor. XX.V.5.
[115] Timotheus' sneezing rower: 375 B.C. Cf. Polyaen. III.X.2.
[116] Chabrias' thunderbolt: 391- 357 B.C

Book II - Stratagems

Having given classes of examples in Book I which, I believe, will suffice to instruct a general in those matters which are to be attended to before beginning battle, I will next present examples which bear on those things that are usually done in the battle itself, and then those that come subsequent to the engagement.

Of those which concern the battle itself, there are the following classes:

I.   On Choosing the Time for Battle.
II. On Choosing the Place for Battle.
III. On the Disposition of Troops for Battle.
IV. On Creating Panic in the Enemy's Ranks.
V.   On Ambushes.
VI. On Letting the Enemy Escape, Lest, Brought to Bay, He Renew the Battle in Desperation.
VII. On Concealing Reverses.
VIII.   On Restoring Morale By Firmness.

Of the matters which deserve attention after battle, I consider that there are the following classes:

IX. On Bringing the War to a Close After a Successful Engagement.
X.   On Repairing One's Losses After a Reverse.
XI. On Ensuring the Loyalty of Those Whom One Mistrusts.
XII. What to Do For the Defense of the Camp, in Case a Commander Lacks Confidence in His Present Forces.
XIII.   On Retreating.

1 On Choosing the Time for Battle

Roman Consuls in Camp (Bilder Atlas)

I. On Choosing the Time for Battle

When Publius Scipio was in Spain and learned that the leader of the Carthaginians, Hasdrubal, had marched out and drawn up his troops in battle array early in the morning before breakfast, he kept back his own men till one o'clock, ordering them to rest and eat. When the enemy who were exhausted with hunger, thirst, and waiting under arms, had begun to return to camp, Scipio suddenly led forth his troops, opened battle, and won the day[117].

When Metellus Pius was waging war against Hirtuleius in Spain, and the latter had drawn up his troop's immediately after daybreak to march them against Metellus' entrenchments, Metellus held his own forces in camp till noon, as the weather at that time of year was extremely hot. Then, when the enemy was overcome by the heat, he easily defeated them, since his own men were fresh and their strength unimpaired.[118]

When the same Metellus joined forces with Pompey against Sertorius in Spain and had repeatedly offered battle, the enemy declined combat, deeming himself unequal to two. Later on, however, Metellus, noticing that the soldiers of the enemy, fired with great enthusiasm, were calling for battle, baring their arms, and brandishing their spears, thought it best to retreat quickly before their ardor. Accordingly, he withdrew and caused Pompey to do the same.

When Postumius was in Sicily during his consulate, his camp was three miles apart from the Carthaginians. Every day the Punic chieftains drew up their line of battle directly in front of the fortifications of the Romans, while Postumius offered resistance by way of constant skirmishes, conducted by a small band before his entrenchments. As soon as the Carthaginian commander came to regard this as a matter of course, Postumius quietly made ready all the rest of his troops within the ramparts, meeting the assault of the force with a few, according to his former practice, but keeping them engaged longer than usual. When, after noon was past, and they were retreating, weary and suffering from hunger, Postumius, with fresh troops,

---

[117] Scipio's troops have lunch: 206 B.C. Cf.
[118] Metellus' noonday attack: 76 B.C.

put them to rout, exhausted as they were by the aforementioned embarrassments.[119]

Iphicrates, the Athenian, discovered that the enemy regularly ate at the same hour, commanded his own troops to eat at an earlier hour, and then led them out to battle. When the enemy came forth, he delayed them with no opportunity either of fighting or of withdrawing. Then, as the day drew to a close, he led his troops back, but nevertheless held them under arms. The enemy, exhausted both by standing in the line and by hunger, straightway hurried off to rest and eat, whereupon Iphicrates again led forth his troops, and finding the enemy disorganized, attacked their camp.[120]

When the same Iphicrates camped near the Lacedaemonians for several days, he determined that each side was in the habit of going forth at a regular hour for forage and wood. One day he sent out slaves and camp-followers from his service in the dress of soldiers, holding back his fighting men; and as soon as the enemy had dispersed on similar errands, he captured their camp. Then, as they came running back from all quarters to the mêlée, unarmed and carrying their bundles, he easily slew or captured them.[121]

When the consul Verginius, was involved in war with the Volscians, he saw the enemy run forward at full stretch from a distance, he commanded his own men to keep steady and hold their javelins at rest. Then, the enemy was out of breath, while his own army was still strong and fresh, he attacked and routed them.[122]

Since Fabius Maximus was well aware that the Gauls and Samnites had strong initial charges, while the tireless spirits of his own men actually grew stronger as the struggle continued, he commanded his soldiers to be content with holding the foe at the first encounter and to wear them out by delay. When this succeeded, he brought up reinforcements from the rear ranks, and attacked with his full strength; he crushed and routed the enemy.[123]

---

[119] Postumius wears the enemy down: 262 B.C.
[120] Iphicrates attacks at lunchtime: Cf. Polyaen. III.IX.53.
[121] Iphicrates uses non-combatants as a supply force: 393 392 B.C. Cf. Polyaen. III.IX.52.
[122] Verginius' breathless enemies: 494 B.C. Cf. Livy II.XXX.10 ff.
[123] Fabius Maximus wears down the Gauls and Samnites: 295 B.C. Cf. Livy X.28 ff.

At Chaeronea, Philip purposely prolonged the engagement, mindful that his own soldiers were seasoned veterans, while the Athenians were enthusiastic but untrained, and impetuous only in the charge. Then, as the Athenians began to grow weary, Philip attacked more furiously and cut them down.[124]

When the Spartans learned from scouts that the Messenians had broken out into such fury that they had come down to battle attended by their wives and children, they postponed the engagement.

In the Civil War, Gaius Caesar was besieging the army of Afranius and Petreius who were suffering from thirst, and when their troops, so frustrated with this, slayed all their beasts of burden[125] and came out for battle. Caesar held back his own soldiers, deeming the occasion ill-suited for an engagement, since his opponents were so inflamed with wrath and desperation[126].

Gnaeus Pompey, desired to check the flight of Mithridates and force him to battle, so he chose night as the time for the encounter and arranged to block his march as he withdrew. Having made his preparations accordingly, he suddenly forced his enemy to fight. In addition, he drew up his force that the moonlight falling in the faces of the Pontic soldiers blinded their eyes, while it gave his own troops a distinct and clear view of the enemy[127].

It is well known that Jugurtha, aware of the courage of the Romans, was inclined to engage in battle as the day was drawing to a close, so that, in case his men were routed, they might have the advantage of night for getting away[128].

While Lucullus was campaigning at Tigranocerta in Greater Armenia against Mithridates and Tigranes, he did not have above 15,000 armed men, while the enemy had an innumerable host, which for this very reason was unwieldy. Taking advantage of this handicap of the foe, Lucullus attacked

---

124 Philip draws out an engagement: 338 B.C. Cf. Polyaen. IV.II.7; Justin. IX.III.9.
125 their troops had slain all their beasts of burden: The motive was to be less encumbered on the march.
126 Caesar's desperate opponents: 49 B.C. Cf. Caes. B.C. I.81 ff.
127 Pompey's night-time encounter: 66 B.C. Cf. Flor. III.V.22 24; Plut. Pomp. 32 ff.
128 Jugurtha's battles late in the day: 111 106 B.C. Cf. Sall. Jug. XCVIII.2.

their line before it was in order, and quickly routed the enemy so completely that even the kings themselves discarded their trappings and fled[129].

In the campaign against the Pannonians, the barbarians were in a warlike mood and formed for battle at the very break of day. Tiberius Nero held back his own troops, and allowed the enemy to be hampered by the fog and drenched by the showers, which happened to be frequent that day. Then, when he noticed that they were weary from standing, and faint not only from exposure but also from exhaustion, he gave the signal, attacked, and defeated them[130].

When Gaius Caesar was in Gaul, he learned that it was a principle and almost a law with Ariovistus, king of the Germans, not to fight when the moon was waning. Caesar therefore chose that time above all others for engaging in battle, when the enemy were embarrassed by their superstition, and so conquered them[131].

The deified Vespasian Augustus attacked Jews on their sabbath, a day on which it is sinful for them to do any business, and so defeated them[132].

When Lysander, the Spartan, was fighting against the Athenians at Aegospotami, he began by attacking the vessels of the Athenians at a regular hour and then calling off his fleet. After this had become an established procedure, as the Athenians on one occasion, after his withdrawal, were dispersing to collect their troops, he deployed his fleet as usual and withdrew it. Then, when most of the enemy had scattered according to their wont, he attacked and slew the rest, and captured all their vessels[133].

---

[129] Lucullus attacks the Armenians before they're ready: 69 B.C. Cf. Plut. Lucul. 26 28; Appian Mithr. 84 85.
[130] Tiberius Nero delays battle: 12 10 B.C. or 6 9 A.D. The future Emperor Tiberius.
[131] Caesar takes advantage of the enemy's superstition: 58 B.C. Cf. Caes. B. G. I.50; Plut. Caes. 19.

Thayer's Note: The superstition is alive and well. Other things being equal, in horary astrology, modern Western astrologers deprecate starting an enterprise during the waning moon.
[132] Vespasian and the sabbath of the Jews: 70 A.D.
Thayer's Note: August 10th. The Torah, however, specifically permits defense on the Sabbath. For details, including the passage of Josephus, see this page.
[133] Lysander's regular attacks: 405 B.C. Cf. Xen. Hell. II.I.21 ff.; Plut. Lysand. 10 11.

II. On Choosing the Place for Battle

Manius Curius, observed that the phalanx of King Pyrrhus could not be resisted when in extended order, took pains to fight in confined quarters, where the phalanx, being massed together, would embarrass itself[134].

In Cappadocia, Gnaeus Pompey chose an elevated site for his camp. As a result, the elevation so assisted the onset of his troops that he easily overcame Mithridates by the sheer weight of his assault[135].

When Gaius Caesar was about to engage with Pharnaces, son of Mithridates, he drew up his line of battle on a hill. This move made victory easy for him, since the darts, hurled from higher ground against the barbarians charging from below, put them to flight straightway[136].

When Lucullus was planning to fight Mithridates and Tigranes at Tigranocerta in Greater Armenia, he swiftly gained the crest of the nearest hill with a part of his troops and then rushed down upon the enemy posted below, at the same time attacking their cavalry on the flank. When the cavalry broke it threw the infantry into confusion. Lucullus followed after them and gained a most notable victory[137].

When Ventidius was fighting against the Parthians, he would not lead his soldiers until the Parthians were within five hundred paces. Thus by a rapid advance, he came so near that, meeting them at close quarters, he escaped the arrows they normally shot at distance. By this scheme, showing a certain degree of confidence, he quickly subdued the barbarians[138].

When Hannibal was expecting a battle with Marcellus at Numistro, he secured a position where his flank was protected by hollows and precipitous

---

[134] Manius Curius fights in confined quarters: 281 275 B.C.
[135] Pompey bears down on the enemy from a height: 66 B.C.

[136] Caesar fires his artillery at the enemy from a height: 47 B.C. Cf. Bell. Alexandr. 73 76.
[137] Lucullus bears down on the enemy from a height: 69 B.C. Cf. Plut. Lucul. 28; Appian Mithr. 85.
[138] Ventidius — "don't fire till you see the whites of their eyes": 38 B.C. Cf. Flor. IV.IX.6.

roads. By thus making the ground serve as a defense, he won a victory over a most renowned commander[139].

Again, this time at Cannae, when Hannibal learned that the Volturnus River, at variance with the nature of other streams, sent out high winds in the morning which carried swirling sand and dust, he arranged his line of battle so that the entire fury of the elements fell on the rear of his own troops, but struck the Romans in the face and eyes. Since this difficulty was a serious obstacle to the enemy, he won that memorable victory[140].

After Marius had settled on a day for fighting the Cimbrians and Teutons, he fortified his soldiers with food and stationed them in front of his camp, in order that the army of the enemy might be exhausted by marching over the interval between the opposing armies. Then, when the enemy was exhausted, he confronted them with another embarrassment by so arranging his own line of battle so that the barbarians were caught with the sun and wind and dust in their faces[141].

In his battle against Hippias, the Athenian, Cleomenes, the Spartan, found that the latter's main strength lay in his cavalry. He thereupon felled trees and cluttered the battlefield with them, thus making it impassable for cavalry[142].

The Iberians in Africa, upon encountering a great multitude of their enemies and fearing that they would be surrounded, drew near a river which at that point flowed along between deep banks. Thus, defended by the river in the rear and enabled by their superior prowess to make frequent onsets upon those nearest them, they routed the entire host of their adversaries.

---

[139] Hannibal protects his flanks by hollows and precipitous roads: 210 B.C. According to Livy XXVII.II.4 and Plut. Marc. 24, the result of the battle was indecisive.

[140] Hannibal's enemies have sand in their eyes: 216 B.C. Cf. Val. Max. VII.IV.ext.2; Plut. Fab. 16; Livy XXII.43, 46, In none of these accounts is a river mentioned as the source of the wind. Livy speaks of theventus Volturnus.

Thayer's Note: Frontinus himself gives other examples of the effects or tactical use of dust and sand in Strat. II.2.8, 12, 4.1, and IV.7.20. The main instances of the subject in other classical writers were collected by E. Echols in Military Dust (CJ 47:285 288).

[141] Marius tires out his enemies then puts the sun and wind and dust in their eyes: 101 B.C. Cf. Plut. Mar. 26; Polyaen. VIII.X.3.

[142] Cleomenes' prepared battlefield: 510 B.C.

Xanthippus, the Spartan, by merely changing the locality of operations, completely altered the fortunes of the Punic War; when he was hired as a mercenary by the despairing Carthaginians, he noticed that the Africans, who were superior in cavalry and elephants, kept to the hills, while the Romans, whose strength was in their infantry, held to the plains, so he brought the Carthaginians down to level ground, where he broke the ranks of the Romans with the elephants. Pursuing their scattered troops with Numidians, he routed their army, which till that day had been victorious on land and sea[143].

Epaminondas, leader of the Thebans, when he was about to marshal his troops in battle array against the Spartans, ordered his cavalry to engage in maneuvers along the front. Then, when he filled the eyes of the enemy with clouds of dust and caused them to expect an encounter with cavalry, he led his infantry around to one side, where it was possible to attack the enemy's rear from higher ground, and thus, by a surprise attack, cut them to pieces[144].

Against a countless horde of Persians, three hundred Spartans seized and held the pass of Thermopylae which was capable of admitting only a like number of hand-to-hand opponents. In consequence, the Spartans became numerically equal to the barbarians, as far as opportunity for fighting was concerned, and being superior to them in valor, slew large numbers of them. They would not have been overcome, had not the enemy been led around to the rear by the traitor Ephialtes the Trachinian, and thus been enabled to overwhelm them[145].

Themistocles, leader of the Athenians, saw that the Greeks had the best advantage to fight in the Straits of Salamis against the vast numbers of Xerxes's vessels, but he was unable to persuade his fellow Athenians of this. He therefore employed a stratagem to make the barbarians force the Greeks to do what was advantageous for the latter. Under pretense of turning traitor, he sent a messenger to Xerxes to inform him that the Greeks were planning flight and that the situation would be more difficult for the King if he should besiege each city separately. This plan allowed for several things, first, he caused the host of the barbarians to be kept on the alert doing guard-duty all

---

143 Xanthippus chooses to fight in the plain: 255 B.C. Cf. Polyb. I.33 ff.; Zonar. VIII.13.
144 Epaminondas raises some dust: 362 B.C. Cf. Polyaen. II.III.14.
145 the Spartans even the odds in the pass of Thermopylae: 480 B.C. Cf. Herod. VII.201 ff.; Polyaen. VII.XV.5.

night; in the second place, he made it possible for his own followers, the next morning, with strength unimpaired, to encounter the exhausted barbarians, and (precisely as he had wished) in a confined place, where Xerxes could not utilize his superiority in numbers[146].

---

[146] Themistocles turns "traitor" and keeps the enemy awake: 480 B.C. Cf. Herod. VIII.75; Plut. Them. 12; Nep. Them. 4.

III. On the Disposition of Troops for Battle

When Gnaeus Scipio was campaigning in Spain against Hanno near the town of Indibile, he noted that the Carthaginian line of battle was drawn up with the Spaniards posted on the right wing — sturdy soldiers, to be sure, but fighting for others — while on the left was the less powerful, but more resolute, Africans. He accordingly drew back his own left wing, and keeping his battle-line at an angle with the enemy, engaging the enemy with his right wing, which he had formed from his sturdiest soldiers. After routing the Africans and putting them to flight, he easily forced the surrender of the Spaniards, who had stood apart from the battle as spectators.[147]

When Philip, king of the Macedonians, was waging war against the Hyllians, he noticed that the front of the enemy consisted entirely of picked men from the whole army, while their flanks were weaker. Accordingly, he placed the stoutest of his own men on the right wing, attacked the enemy's left, and by throwing their whole line into confusion, won a complete victory.[148]

Pammenes, the Theban, having observed the battle-line of the Persians and how the most powerful troops were posted on the right wing, drew up his own men also on the same plan, putting all his cavalry and the bravest of his infantry on the right wing, but stationing opposite the bravest of the enemy his own weakest troops, whom he directed to flee at the first onset of the foe and to retreat to rough, wooded places. In this way he negated the enemy's strength, while with the best part of his own forces, enveloped the enemy with his right wing and put them to rout[149].

On one occasion Publius Cornelius Scipio, who subsequently received the name Africanus, when waging war in Spain against Hasdrubal, leader of the Carthaginians, led out his troops day after day in such a formation that the center of his battle-line was composed of his best fighting men. When the enemy also regularly came out marshaled on the same plan, on the day was determined to fight, Scipio altered the scheme of his arrangement and stationed his strongest troops on the wings, placed his light-

---

[147] Scipio attacks the weakest forces: 218 B.C. Cn. Cornelius Scipio Calvus. Cf. Polyb. III.76.
[148] Philip attacks the weakest forces: 359 B.C. Cf. Diodor. XVI.4.
[149] Pammenes draws away his strongest opponents: 353 B.C. Cf. Polyaen. V.XVI.2.

armed troops in the center, but slightly behind the line. Thus, by attacking the enemy's weakest point in crescent formation from the flank, where he was strongest, he easily routed them[150].

In the battle in which he vanquished Hirtuleius in Spain, Metellus, discovered that Hirtuleius strongest battalions were posted in the center. Accordingly, he drew back the center of his own troops, to avoid encountering the enemy at that part of the line, until by an enveloping movement of his wings he could surround their center from all sides[151].

Having superior numbers in his campaign against the Greeks who had invaded Persia, Artaxerxes, drew up his line of battle with a wider front than the enemy, placing infantry, cavalry, and light-armed troops on the wings. He then ordered the center to advance slower than the flanks, enveloping the enemy troops and cutting them to pieces[152].

On the other hand, at Cannae, Hannibal, drew back his flanks and advanced his center, driving back the Roman troops at the first assault. Then, when the fighting began and the flanks gradually worked towards each other moving forward according to instructions, Hannibal enveloped within his own lines the impetuously attacking enemy, forcing them towards the center from both sides, and cutting them to pieces, using veteran troops to accomplish this maneuver. Nothing but a trained army, responsive to every direction, could carry out this sort of tactics[153].

In the Second Punic War, when Hasdrubal was seeking to avoid an engagement, and drew up his line on a rough hillside behind protective works, Livius Salinator and Claudius Nero diverted their own forces to the flanks, leaving their center vacant. Having in this way enveloped Hasdrubal, they attacked and defeated him[154].

After Hannibal had been defeated in frequent battles by Claudius Marcellus, he finally laid out his camp on this plan: protected by mountains, marshes, or similar advantages of terrain, he so posted his troops as to be able

---

[150] Scipio changes his formation: 206 B.C. Cf. Livy XXVIII.14 15; Polyb. XI.22 ff.
[151] Metellus nullifies his opponents' strongest forces: 76 B.C. Q. Caecilius Metellus Pius.
[152] Artaxerxes' slow centre: 401 B.C. Battle of Cunaxa. Cf. Xen. Anab. I.VIII.10.
[153] Hannibal's precision use of his army: 216 B.C. Cf. Livy XXII.47; Polyb. III.115.
[154] Xanthippus reserves his best troops: 207 B.C. Battle of the Metaurus. Cf. Livy XXVII.48.

to withdraw his army, practically without loss, within his fortifications, in case the Romans won, but also with the option to pursuit, in case they gave way.

Xanthippus, the Spartan, in the campaign conducted in Africa against Marcus Atilius Regulus, placed his light-armed troops in the front line, holding the flower of his army in reserve. Then he directed the auxiliary troops[155], after hurling their javelins, to give way before the enemy, withdrawing within the ranks of their fellow-soldiers and hurrying to the flanks from which they rushed forward to attack. Thus when the enemy met the stronger troops, they were enveloped by these light-armed forces[156].

Sertorius employed the same tactics in Spain in the campaign against Pompey[157].

When Cleandridas the Spartan, was fighting against the Lucanians, he drew up his troops in close order, to give the impression that he had a much smaller army. Then, when the enemy had thus been put off their guard, at the beginning of the engagement he opened up his ranks, enveloped the enemy on the flank, and put them to rout[158].

Gastron, the Spartan, came to assist the Egyptians against the Persians, and realizing that the Greek soldiers were more powerful and more dreaded by the Persians, interchanged the arms of the two contingents, placing the Greeks in the front line. When these merely held their own in the encounter, he sent in the Egyptians as reinforcements. Although the Persians had proved equal to the Greeks (deeming them Egyptians), they gave way, as soon as they were set upon by a multitude, of whom (as supposedly consisting of Greeks) they had stood in terror[159].

When Gnaeus Pompey was fighting in Albania, the enemy was superior in numbers and cavalry, consequently he directed his infantry to cover their helmets in order to avoid being visible in consequence of the reflection, and to take their place in a defile by a hill. He then commanded his

---

[155] auxiliary troops: These were the "light-armed troops," already mentioned.

[156] Xanthippus' use of his troops: 255 B.C.

[157] Sertorius reserves his best troops: Cf. II.V.31.

[158] Cleandridas' close-order formation: After 443 B.C. Cf. Polyaen. II.X.4.

[159] Gastron's troop switch: Cf. Polyaen. II.16.

cavalry to advance across the plain and to act as a screen to the infantry, but to withdraw at the first onset of the enemy. As soon as they reached the infantry, they were to disperse to the flanks. When these maneuvers had been executed, the infantry force suddenly rose up, revealing its position, and making a sudden attack on the enemy who they relentlessly pursued, thus cut them to pieces[160].

When Mark Antony was engaged in battle with the Parthians and they were showering his army with innumerable arrows, he ordered his men to stop and form a testudo[161]. The arrows passed over this without harm to the soldiers, and the enemy's supply was soon exhausted[162].

When Hannibal was battling against Scipio in Africa, with an army of Carthaginians and auxiliaries, part of whom were not only of different nationalities, but actually consisted of Italians, he placed eighty elephants in the forefront to throw the enemy into confusion. Behind these he stationed auxiliary Gauls, Ligurians, Balearians, and Moors, so that these might be unable to run away, since the Carthaginians were standing behind them, and in order that, being placed in front, they might at least harass the enemy, if not do him damage. In the second line he placed his own countrymen and the Macedonians, to be fresh to meet the exhausted Romans; and in the rear the Italians, whose loyalty he distrusted and whose indifference he feared, inasmuch as he had dragged most of them from Italy against their will.

Against this formation, Scipio drew up the flower of his legions in three successive front lines, arranged according to hastati, principes, and triarii[163], not making the cohorts touch, but leaving a space between the detached companies through which the elephants driven by the enemy might easily be allowed to pass without throwing the ranks into confusion. These intervals were filled with light-armed skirmishers, so that the line might show no gaps, giving them instructions to withdraw to the rear or the flanks at the first onset of the elephants. The cavalry were distributed on the flanks, placing Laelius in charge of the Roman horsemen on the right, and Masinissa

---

[160] Pompey's concealed infantry: 65 B.C. Cf. Dio XXXVII.4.
[161] testudo: In the testudo, the soldiers secured protection by holding their over-lapped shields above their heads, a formation whose appearance suggested the scales of a tortoise.
[162] Mark Antony's testudo: 36 B.C. Cf. Dio XLIX.29 30; Plut. Anton. 45.
[163] hastati, principes, and triarii: These names designate three successive lines of battle. The hastati were the first line; the two other lines were drawn up behind these.

in charge of the Numidians on the left. This shrewd scheme of arrangement was undoubtedly the cause of his victory[164].

In the battle against Lucius Sulla, Archelaus placed his scythe-bearing chariots in the front rank for the purpose of throwing the enemy into confusion. In the second line he posted the Macedonian phalanx, and in the third line auxiliaries armed in the Roman way, with a sprinkling of Italian runaway slaves, in whose doggedness he had the greatest confidence. In the last line he stationed the light-armed troops in the center, while on the two flanks, he placed his more numerous cavalry for the purpose of enveloping the enemy.

To meet these dispositions, Sulla constructed trenches of great breadth on each flank, and at their ends built strong redoubts. By this device, he avoided the danger of being enveloped by the enemy, who outnumbered him in infantry and especially in cavalry. Next, he arranged a triple line of infantry, leaving intervals through which to send, according to need, the light-armed troops and the cavalry, which he placed in the rear. He then commanded the postsignani[165], who were in the second line, to drive a large numbers stakes firmly into the ground set close together, and as the chariots drew near, he withdrew the line of antesignani[166] within these stakes. Then, he ordered the skirmishers and light-armed troops to raise a general battle-cry and discharge their spears. Using these tactics, either the chariots of the enemy were caught among the stakes, or their drivers became panic-stricken at the din and were driven by the javelins back upon their own men, throwing the formation of the Macedonians into confusion. As these gave way, Sulla pressed forward, and Archelaus met him with cavalry, whereupon the Roman horsemen suddenly darted forward, drove back the enemy, and achieved victory.[167]

In the same way, Gaius Caesar met the scythe-bearing chariots of the Gauls with stakes driven in the ground and kept them in check.

---

[164] Scipio's flexible use of the standard Roman battle formation: 202 B.C. Battle of Zama. Cf. Livy XXX.33, 35; Polyb. XV.IX.6 10, XV.XI.1 3; Appian Pun. 40 41. Livy and Polybius put Laelius on the left wing and Masinissa on the right; Appian puts Laelius on the right and Octavius on the left.

[165] postsignani: Troops posted behind the standards.

[166] antesignani: Troops posted in front of the standards and serving for their defense.

[167] Sulla against Archelaus: 86 B.C.

At Arbela, Alexander feared the numbers of the enemy, but was confident in the valor of his own troops and drew up a line of battle facing in all directions, in order that his men, if surrounded, might be able to fight from all sides[168].

When Perseus, king of the Macedonians, drew up a double phalanx of his troops and had placed them in the center of his forces, with light-armed troops on each side and cavalry on both flanks. Opposing him Paulus, drew up a triple array in wedge formation, sending out skirmishers every now and then between the wedges. Seeing nothing accomplished by these tactics, he determined to feign retreat, in order to lure the enemy after him on to rough ground, which he had selected for this purpose. While the enemy, suspected his ruse in retiring, they followed in good order, so he commanded the cavalry on the left wing to ride at full speed past the front of the phalanx, covering themselves with their shields, in order that the points of the enemy's spears might be broken by the shock of their encounter with the shields. When the Macedonians were deprived of their spears, they broke and fled[169].

When Pyrrhus was fighting in defense of the Tarentines near Asculum, he followed the Homeric verse[170], according to which the poorest troops are placed in the center, stationed Samnites and Epirotes on the right flank, Bruttians, Lucanians, and Sallentines on the left, with the Tarentines in the center, and ordered the cavalry and elephants to be held as reserves.

The consuls, on the other hand, very judiciously distributed their cavalry on the wings, posting legionary soldiers in the first line and in reserve, with auxiliary troops scattered among them. The Romans were informed that there were forty thousand men on each side. Half of Pyrrhus's army was lost; on the Roman side only five thousand[171].

---

[168] Alexander's army facing in all directions: 331 B.C. Cf. Curt. IV.XIII.30 32; Diodor. XVII.LVII.5.

[169] Paulus uses up the enemy's spears: 168 B.C. Battle of Pydna. Cf. Livy XLIV.41; Plut. Aem. 20.

Thayer's Note: The date of the battle of Pydna, although it is usually given in the English-speaking world as 168 B.C., was almost certainly in September 172.

[170] the Homeric verse: Iliad IV.299 seems to have become proverbial; cf. Ammian. Marc. XXIV.VI.9.

[171] The Romans' judicious use of different kinds of troops: 279 B.C. Cf. Plut. Pyrrh. 21.

In the battle against Caesar at Old Pharsalus[172], Gnaeus Pompey drew up three lines of battle, each one ten men deep, stationing on the wings and in the center the legions upon whose prowess he could most safely rely, and filling the spaces between these with raw recruits. On the right flank he placed six hundred horsemen, along the Enipeus River, which with its channel and banks had made the locality impassable; the rest of the cavalry he stationed on the left, together with the auxiliary troops, that from this quarter he might envelop the troops of Caesar.

Against these dispositions, Gaius Caesar also drew up a triple line, placing his legions in front and resting his left flank on marshes in order to avoid envelopment. On the right he placed his cavalry, among whom he distributed the fleetest of his foot-soldiers, men trained in cavalry fighting[173]. Then he held six cohorts for emergencies in reserve, placing them obliquely on the right, from which quarter he was expecting an attack of the enemy's cavalry. No circumstance contributed more than this to Caesar's victory on that day; for as soon as Pompey's cavalry poured forth, these cohorts routed it by an unexpected onset, and delivered it up to the rest of the troops for slaughter[174].

The Emperor Caesar Augustus Germanicus[175], when the Chatti, by fleeing into the forests, again and again interfered with the course of a cavalry engagement, commanded his men, as soon as they should reach the enemy's baggage-train, to dismount and fight on foot. By this means, he made sure that his success should not be blocked by any difficulties of terrain[176].

When Gaius Duellius saw that his heavy ships were eluded by the mobile fleet of the Carthaginians and that the valor of his soldiers was thus brought to naught, he devised a kind of grappling-hook. When this caught hold of an enemy ship, the Romans, laying gangways over the bulwarks, went

---

[172] Old Pharsalus: A town in Thessaly near Pharsalus.
[173] foot-soldiers trained in cavalry fighting: i.e. in fighting in conjunction with cavalry — doubtless after the method detailed in Caesar's Gallic War, I.48.
[174] Caesar's reserves: 48 B.C. Cf. Caes. B.C. III.89, 93, 94; Plut. Caes. 44, Pomp. 69.
[175] The Emperor Caesar Augustus Germanicus: Domitian.
[176] Domitian commands his cavalry to fight on foot: 83 A.D. Cf. Suet. Domit. 6.

on board and slew the enemy in hand-to-hand combat on their own vessels[177].

[177] Duilius' grappling-hook: 260 B.C. Cf. Flor. II.I.8 9; Polyb. I.22.

IV. On Creating Panic in the Enemy's Ranks

When Papirius Cursor, the son of the dictator, failed to win any advantage in his battle against the stubbornly resisting Samnites during his consulship, he gave no intimation on his purpose to his men, but commanded Spurius Nautius to arrange to have a few auxiliary horsemen and grooms, mounted on mules and trailing branches over the ground, race down in great commotion from a hill running at an angle with the field. As soon as these came in sight, he proclaimed that his colleague[178] was at hand, crowned with victory, and urged his men to secure for themselves the glory of the present battle before he should arrive. At this the Romans rushed forward, flush with confidence, while the enemy, disheartened at the sight of the dust, turned and fled[179].

When Fabius Rullus Maximus was in Samnium during his fourth consulship, he vainly tried in every way to break through the line of the enemy, finally withdrew the hastati[180] from the ranks and sent them round with his lieutenant Scipio, under instructions to seize a hill from which they could rush down upon the rear of the enemy. When this had been done, the courage of the Romans rose, and the Samnites, fleeing in terror, were cut to pieces.[181]

The general Minucius Rufus, hard pressed by the Scordiscans and Dacians, for whom he was no match in numbers, sent his brother and a small squadron of cavalry on ahead, along with a detachment of trumpeters, directing him, as soon as he saw the battle begin, to suddenly show himself from the opposite quarter and to order the trumpeters to blow their horns. Then, when the hill-tops echoed with the sound, the enemy had the impression of a huge multitude was at hand and fled in terror[182].

When the consul Acilius Glabrio, was confronted by the army of King Antiochus, the latter was drawn up in front of the Pass of Thermopylae in Greece. He was not only hampered by the difficulties of terrain, but would

---

178 Papirius Cursor's colleague: Spurius Carvilius.
179 Papirius Cursor's phantom reinforcements: 293 B.C. Cf. Livy X.40 41.
180 hastati: First-line troops.
181 Fabius Maximus' use of a hill: 297 B.C. Cf. Livy X.14.
182 Minucius Rufus' phantom multitude: 109 B.C.

have been repulsed with loss besides; had not Porcius Cato prevented this. Cato, although an ex-consul, was in the army as a tribune of the soldiers, elected to this office by the people. Having been sent by Glabrio to make a detour, he dislodged the Aetolians, who were guarding the crest of Mt. Callidromus, and then suddenly appeared from the rear on the summit of a hill commanding the camp of the king. The forces of Antiochus were then thrown into panic, whereupon the Romans attacked them from front and rear, repulsed and scattered the enemy, and captured their camp.[183]

When the consul Gaius Sulpicius Peticus, was about to fight against the Gauls, he ordered certain muleteers to secretly withdraw with their mules to the nearby hills. Then, after the engagement began, they exhibited themselves repeatedly to the combatants, as though mounted on horses. The Gauls, therefore, imagined that reinforcements were coming, fell back before the Romans, even though they were almost victorious.[184]

At Aquae Sextiae, Marius, purposed to fight a decisive battle with the Teutons on the morrow and sent Marcellus by night with a small detachment of horse and foot to the rear of the enemy. To complete the illusion of a large force, he ordered armed grooms and camp-followers to go along with them, as well as a large part of the pack-animals, wearing saddle-cloths, in order by this means to present the appearance of cavalry. He commanded these men to fall upon the enemy from the rear, as soon as they noticed that the engagement had begun. This scheme struck such terror into the enemy that despite their great ferocity they turned and fled.[185]

During the Slave War, Licinius Crassus, was about to lead forth his troops at Camalatrum against Castus and Cannicus, the leaders of the Gauls. Crassus sent twelve cohorts around behind the mountain led by his lieutenants Gaius Pomptinius and Quintus Marcius Rufus. When the engagement began, these troops, raising a shout, poured down the mountain

---

[183] Porcius Cato appears in the enemy's rear: 191 B.C. Cf. Livy XXXVI.14 19; Plut. Cat. Maj. 12 ff.; Appian Syr. 17 ff.
[184] Sulpicius Peticus' phantom reinforcements: 358 B.C. Peticus was dictator in this year, having been consul in 364 and 361. Cf. Livy VII.14 15. Appian Gall. 1 gives a different stratagem.
[185] Marius' phantom large cavalry unit: 102 B.C. Cf. Plut. Mar. 20; Polyaen. VIII.X.2.

in the rear, and routed the enemy so that they fled in all directions with no attempt at battle[186].

Marcus Marcellus on one occasion, fearing that a feeble battle-cry would reveal the small number of his forces, commanded that sutlers, servants, and camp-followers of every sort should join in the cry. He thus threw the enemy into panic by giving the appearance of having a larger army[187].

Valerius Laevinus, in the battle against Pyrrhus, killed a common soldier, and holding up his dripping sword, made both armies believe that Pyrrhus had been slain. The enemy, therefore, panic-stricken at the falsehood, and thinking that they had been rendered helpless by the death of their commander, retreated in terror back to camp.[188]

In his struggle against Gaius Marius in Numidia, Jugurtha, who acquired the facility to use of the Latin language as a result of his early association with Roman camps, ran forward to the front line and shouted that he had slain Gaius Marius, causing many Roman men to flee.[189]

In an indecisive battle which he was waging against the Thebans, Myronides the Athenian, suddenly darted forward to the right flank of his own troops and shouted that he had already won victory on the left. By inspiring courage in his own men and fear in the enemy, he gained the day.[190]

Against overwhelming the force of the enemy's cavalry, Croesus once opposed a troop of camels. At the strange appearance and smell of these beasts, the horses were thrown into panic, and not merely threw their riders, but also trampled the ranks of their own infantry under foot, thus delivering them into the hands of the enemy to defeat[191].

---

[186] Licinius Crassus sends a small force around the enemy's rear: 71 B.C.

[187] Marcus Marcellus' loud battle-cry: 216 B.C. Cf. Livy XXIII.XVI.13 14.
[188] Valerius Laevinus' bloody sword: 280 B.C. Cf. Plut. Pyrrh. 17.
[189] Jugurtha's disinformation: 107 B.C. Cf. Sall. Jug. ci.6 8.
[190] Myronides' victory: 457 B.C. Cf. Polyaen. I.XXXV.1.
[191] Croesus' camels: 546 B.C. Cf.Herod. I.80; Polyaen. VII.VI.6; they attribute this stratagem to Cyrus.

Pyrrhus, king of the Epirotes, fighting on behalf of the Tarentines against the Romans, employed elephants in the same way, in order to throw the Roman army into confusion[192].

The Carthaginians also often did the same thing in their battles against the Romans[193].

The Volscians pitched their camp near some brush and woods on one occasion, and Camillus set fire to everything which would carry the conflagration up to their entrenchments, thus depriving his adversaries of their camp.

In the same way, Publius Crassus in the Social War narrowly escaped being cut off with all his forces.

The Spaniards, fighting against Hamilcar, hitched steers to carts and placed them in the front line. These carts they filled with pitch, tallow, and sulfur, and when the signal for battle was given, set them afire. Then, driving the steers against the enemy, they threw the line into panic and broke through[194].

The Faliscans and Tarquinians disguised a number of men as priests, and had them hold torches and snakes in front of them, like Furies. Thus they threw the army of the Romans into panic[195].

On one occasion the men of Veii and Fidenae snatched up torches and did the same thing[196].

When Atheas, king of the Scythians, was contending against the more numerous tribe of the Triballi, he commanded that herds of asses and cattle should be brought up in the rear of the enemy's forces by women, children, and all the non-combatant population, and that spears, held aloft, should be carried in front of these. He then spread the rumor that reinforcements were

---

[192] Pyrrhus' elephants: 280 B.C. Cf. Flor. I.XVIII.8; Plut. Pyrrh. 17.
[193] the Carthaginian elephants: Cf. II.V.4.
[194] Incendiary cattle: 229 B.C. Cf. Appian Hisp. 5.
[195] The Faliscan and Tarquinian Furies: 356 B.C. Cf. Livy VII.XVII.3.
[196] The Veientine and Fidenate Furies: 426 B.C. Cf. Livy IV.33; Flor. I.XII.7.

coming to him from the more distant Scythian tribes. By this declaration, he forced the enemy to withdraw[197].

[197] Atheas' phantom reinforcements: Cf. Polyaen. VII.XLIV.1.

V. On Ambushes

As Romulus drew near to Fidenae, he distributed a portion of his troops in ambush and pretended to flee. When the enemy recklessly followed, he led them on to the point where he was holding his men in hiding, whereupon the latter attacked from all sides, and taking the enemy off their guard, cut them to pieces in their onward rush[198].

The consul Quintus Fabius Maximus was sent to aid the Sutrians against the Etruscans, and caused the full brunt of the enemy's attack to fall upon himself. Then, feigning fear, he retired to higher ground, as though in retreat; when the enemy rushed upon him pell-mell he attacked, and not merely defeated them in battle, but captured their camp[199].

Sempronius Gracchus, when waging war against the Celtiberians, feigned fear and kept his army in camp. Then, by sending out light-armed troops to harass the enemy and retreat forthwith, he caused the enemy to come out; whereupon he attacked them before they could form, and crushed them so completely that he also captured their camp[200].

When the consul Lucius Metellus was waging war in Sicily against Hasdrubal — and with all the more alertness because of Hasdrubal's immense army and his one hundred and thirty elephants — he withdrew his troops, under pretense of fear, inside Panormus[201] and constructed a huge trench in front. Then, observing Hasdrubal's army, with the elephants in the front rank, he ordered the hastati to hurl their javelins at the beasts and straightway to retire within their defenses. The drivers of the elephants, enraged at such derisive treatment, drove the elephants straight towards the trench. As soon as the beasts were brought up to this, part were dispatched by a shower of darts, part were driven back to their own side, and threw the entire host into confusion. Then Metellus, who was biding his time, burst forth with his whole force, attacked the Carthaginians on the flank, and cut them to pieces. Not to mention, he captured the elephants themselves[202].

---

[198] Romulus' ambush at Fidenae: Cf. Livy I.14; Polyaen. VIII.III.2.
[199] Fabius Maximus' ambush at Sutri: 310 B.C. Q. Fabius Maximus Rullianus. Cf. Livy IX.35.
[200] Gracchus lures the enemy out: 179 B.C. Cf. Livy XL.48.
[201] Panormus: The modern Palermo.
[202] Lucius Metellus baits the Carthaginian elephants: 251 B.C. Cf. Polyb. I.40.

When Thamyris, queen of the Scythians, and Cyrus, king of the Persians, were engaged in an indecisive combat, the queen, feigned fear and lured Cyrus into a defile that was occupied by her own troops. There, suddenly turned on him, and aided by the nature of the locality, won a complete victory[203].

The Egyptians, when about to engage in battle on a plain near a marsh, covered the marsh with seaweed, and then, when the battle began, feigning flight and drew the enemy into a trap; for the latter, while advancing too swiftly over the unfamiliar ground, were caught in the mire and surrounded.

Viriathus, who rose from being a bandit to become leader of the Celtiberians, on one occasion, while pretending to give way before the Roman cavalry, led them on to a place full of deep holes. While he made his way out by familiar paths that afforded good footing, the Romans, ignorant of the locality, sank in the mire and were slain[204].

Fulvius, commander in the Cimbrian war, having pitched his camp near the enemy and ordered his cavalry to approach the fortifications of the barbarians to attack, withdraw in pretended flight. Having done this for several days, with the Cimbrians in hot pursuit, he noticed that their camp was regularly left exposed. Accordingly, maintaining his usual practice with part of his force, he himself, with light-armed troops, secretly took a position behind the camp of the enemy, and as they poured forth according to their custom, he suddenly attacked and demolished the unguarded rampart and captured their camp[205].

A force of Faliscans far superior to the Romans had encamped on our territory, when Gnaeus Fulvius had his soldiers set fire to certain buildings at a distance from the camp, in order that the Faliscans, thinking their own men had done this, might scatter in hope of plunder.

---

[203] Thamyris' ambush: 529 B.C. Cf. Justin. I.8; Herod. I.204 ff.
[204] Viriathus lures the enemy into bad terrain: 147 139 B.C. In II.XIII.4, Viriathus is dux Lusitanorum.
[205] Fulvius deceives the enemy into betraying themselves: Livy XL.30 32 says that Q. Fulvius Flaccus used this stratagem with the Celtiberians in 181 B.C. There is no account of Fulvius's warring with the Cimbrians.

Alexander, the Epirote, when waging war against the Illyrians, placed a force in ambush, and then dressed up some of his own men in Illyrian garb, ordering them to lay waste his own, that is to say, Epirote territory. When the Illyrians saw that this was being done, they began to pillage right and left — the more confidently since they thought that those who led the way were scouts. But when they had been purposely brought by the latter into a disadvantageous position, they were routed and killed.

Leptines, the Syracusan, was waging war against the Carthaginians, ordered his own lands to be laid waste and certain farm-houses and forts to be set on fire. The Carthaginians, thinking this was done by their own men, went out themselves also to help; whereupon they were set upon by men lying in wait, and were put to rout[206].

Maharbal[207], sent by the Carthaginians against rebellious Africans, knowing that the tribe was passionately fond of wine, mixed a large quantity of wine with mandragora, which in potency is something between a poison and a soporific. Then after an insignificant skirmish, he deliberately withdrew. At dead of night, leaving in the camp some of his baggage and all the drugged wine, he feigned flight. When the barbarians captured the camp and in a frenzy of delight greedily drank the drugged wine, Maharbal returned, and either took them prisoners or slaughtered them while they lay stretched out as if dead[208].

Hannibal was aware that both his own camp and that of the Romans were in places deficient in wood, deliberately abandoned the district, leaving many herds of cattle within his camp. The Romans, secured possession of these as booty, gorged themselves with flesh, which, owing to the scarcity of firewood, was raw and indigestible. Hannibal, returned by night with his army and found them off their guard and gorged with raw meat, thus proceeded to inflict great loss upon them.

Tiberius Gracchus, was in Spain, when learning that the enemy was suffering from lack of provisions, provided his camp with an elaborate supply of all kinds of edibles of all kinds and then abandoned it. When the enemy

[206] Leptines lays waste his own land: 397 396 B.C. Cf. Polyaen. V.VIII.1.
[207] Maharbal: A Carthaginian officer under Hannibal.
[208] Maharbal poisons the water: Polyaen. V.X.1 attributes this stratagem to Himilco, 396 B.C.

had got possession of the camp and had gorged themselves to repletion with the food they found, Gracchus brought back his army and crushed them.

When the Chians, were waging war against the Erythreans, they caught an Erythrean spy on a high hill and put him to death. They then gave his clothes to one of their own soldiers, who, by giving a signal from the same location, lured the Erythreans into an ambush.

Since the Arabian's, custom of giving notice of the arrival of the enemy by means of smoke by day and by fire at night was well known, issued orders on one occasion that these practices should continue without interruption until the enemy actually approached, when they should be discontinued. The enemy, imagining from the absence of the fires that their approach was unknown, advanced too eagerly and was overwhelmed.

Alexander of Macedon, when the enemy had fortified their camp on a high wooded hill, withdrew a portion of his forces and commanded those whom he left to kindle fires as usual, to give the impression of the complete army. He then lead his forces around through untraveled regions, attacked the enemy and dislodged them from their commanding position[209].

Memnon the Rhodian, being superior in cavalry, and wishing to drawn an enemy down to the plains who staid to the hills, sent certain of his soldiers under the guise of deserters to the camp of the enemy to say that the army of Memnon was inspired with such a serious spirit of mutiny that a portion of it was constantly deserting. To lend credit to this assertion, Memnon ordered small redoubts to be fortified here and there in view of the enemy, as though the disaffected were about to retire to these. Convinced by these representations, those who had been keeping themselves on the hills came down to level ground, and, as they attacked the redoubts and were surrounded by the cavalry[210].

When Harrybas, king of the Molossians, was attacked by Bardylis the Illyrian, who commanded a considerably larger army, he dispatched the non-combatant portion of his subjects to the neighboring district of Aetolia, and spread the report that he was yielding up his towns and possessions to the

---

[209] Alexander's phantom army: 327 B.C. Polyaen. IV.III.29 and Curt. VII.XI.1 tell of the employment of a different stratagem.

Aetolians. Harrybas, along with those who could bear arms, placed ambuscades here and there on the mountains and in other inaccessible places. The Illyrians, fearful lest the possessions of the Molossians should be seized by the Aetolians, began to race along in disorder, in their eagerness for plunder. As soon as they became scattered, Harrybas, emerging from his concealment and taking them unawares, routed them and put them to flight.

Titus Labienus, lieutenant of Gaius Caesar, eager to engage in battle with the Gauls before the arrival of the Germans, who he knew were coming to their aid, pretended discouragement, and, pitching his camp across the stream, announced his departure for the following day. The Gauls, imagining that he was in flight, began to cross the intervening river. Labienus, facing about with his troops, cut the Gauls to pieces in the very midst of their difficulties of crossing[211].

Hannibal learned that the camp of Fulvius, the Roman commander, was carelessly fortified and that Fulvius himself was taking many rash chances besides. Accordingly, at daybreak, when dense mists afforded cover, he permitted a few of his horsemen to show themselves to the sentries of our fortifications; whereupon Fulvius suddenly advanced. Meanwhile, Hannibal, at a different point, entered Fulvius's camp, and overwhelming the Roman rear, slew eight thousand of the bravest soldiers along with their commander.

Once, when the Roman army had been divided between the dictator Fabius and master of the horse Minucius, Fabius was watching for a favorable opportunity. While Minucius was burning with eagerness for battle, the same Hannibal pitched his camp on the plain between the hostile armies, and having concealed a portion of his troops among rough rocks, sent others to seize a neighboring hillock, as a challenge to the foe. When Minucius led out his forces to crush these troops, the men placed here and there in ambush by Hannibal suddenly sprang up, and would have annihilated Minucius's army, had not Fabius come to help them in their distress[212].

When the same Hannibal was encamped in the depths of winter at the Trebia, the camp of the consul, Sempronius Longus, was in plain view

---

[210] Memnon's deserters: Polyaen. V.XLIV.2 has a slightly different version.
[211] Labienus' departure: 53 B.C. Cf. Caes. B. G. VI.7 8; Dio XL.31.
[212] Hannibal capitalizes on the enemy's internal divisions: 217 B.C. Cf. Livy XXII.28; Polyb. III.104 105.

with only the river flowing between. He placed Mago and picked men in ambush and commanded the Numidian cavalry to advance up to Sempronius's fortifications, in order to lure forth the simple-minded Roman. At the same time, he ordered these troops to retire by familiar fords if the Romans should sally forth. By heedlessly attacking and pursuing the Numidians, the consul gave his troops a chill, as a result of fording the stream in the bitter cold and without breakfast. Then, when the Romans were suffering from numbness and hunger, Hannibal led his own troops against them, whom he had got in condition for that purpose by warm fires, food, and rubbing down with oil. Mago also did his part, and cut the rear of his enemy to pieces at the point where he had been posted for the purpose[213].

At Trasimenus, where a narrow way[214], which ran out between the lake and the base of the hills, led out to the open plain, the same Hannibal, feigning flight, made his way through the narrow road to the open districts and pitched his camp there. Then, posting soldiers by night at various points over the rising ground of the hill and at the ends of the defile, at daybreak, under cover of a fog, he marshaled his line of battle. Flaminius, pursuing the enemy, who seemed to be retreating, entered the defile and did not see the ambush until he was surrounded in front, flank, and rear, and was annihilated with his army.

When Hannibal was contending against the dictator Junius[215], he ordered six hundred cavalrymen to break into a number of squadrons, and at dead of night to appear in successive detachments without intermission around the camp of the enemy. Thus, all night long the Romans were harassed and worn out by sentry duty on the rampart and by the rain, which happened to fall continuously, so that in the morning, when Junius gave the signal for recall, Hannibal led out his own troops, who had been well rested, and took Junius's camp by assault[216].

---

213 Hannibal's cold-water ambush: 218 B.C. Cf. Livy XXI.54 ff.; Polyb. III.71.
214 A narrow way at Trasimenus: Generally considered to be the narrow passage between the lake and Monte Gualandro, near Borghetto. Livy's description suits this locality; that of Polybius does not.
215 the dictator Junius: M. Junius Pera.
216 Hannibal wears out the enemy: 216 B.C. At Capua. Cf. Polyaen. VI.XXXVIII.6; Zonar. IX.3.

In the same way, when the Spartans had drawn entrenchments across the Isthmus and were defending the Peloponnesus, Epaminondas the Theban, with the help of a few light-armed troops, harassed the enemy all night long. Then at daybreak, after he had recalled his own men and the Spartans also retired, he suddenly moved forward the entire force which he had kept at rest, and burst directly through the ramparts, which had been left without defenders[217].

At the battle of Cannae, Hannibal, drew up his line of battle and ordered six hundred Numidian cavalry to go over to the enemy. To prove their sincerity, they surrendered their swords and shields to the Romans and were dispatched to the rear. As soon as the engagement began, they drew out small swords that they had secretly hidden, and picking up the shield of the fallen, they slaughtered the troops of the Romans[218].

Under pretense of surrender, the Iapydes handed over some of their best men to Publius Licinius, the Roman proconsul. These were received and placed in the last line, whereupon they cut to pieces the Romans who were bringing up the rear.

Scipio Africanus, when facing the two hostile camps of Syphax and the Carthaginians, decided to make a night attack on that of Syphax, where there was a large supply of inflammable material, and to set fire to it. This was done to cause terror in the Numidian army, and Scipio cut them down as they scurried in terror from their camp. By laying ambuscades, he was able to catch the Carthaginians, who he knew, would rush forward to assist their allies. When the enemy rushed forward unarmed, thinking the conflagration accidental, Scipio fell upon them and cut them to pieces[219].

After repeated defeats in battle at the hands of Lucullus, Mithridates, made an attempt against his life by treachery. He hired a certain Adathas, a man of extraordinary strength, to desert and to perpetrate the deed, as soon as he should gain the confidence of the enemy. This plan the deserter did his best to execute, but his efforts failed. For, though admitted by Lucullus to the cavalry troop, he was quietly kept under surveillance, since it was neither well

---

[217] Epaminondas wears out the enemy: 369 B.C. Cf. Polyaen. II.III.9.
[218] Hannibal's Numidian cavalry infiltrators: 216 B.C. Cf. Livy XXII.48; Val. Max. VII.IV.ext.2; Appian Hann. 20 ff. Livy and Appian give the number as five hundred.
[219] Scipio Africanus's fires: 203 B.C. Cf. Livy XXX.5 6; Polyb. XIV.4.

to put trust at once in a deserter, nor to prevent other deserters from coming. After this fellow exhibited a ready and earnest devotion on repeated raids and had won confidence, he chose a time when the dismissal of the staff-officers brought with it repose throughout the camp, and caused the general's headquarters to be less frequented. Chance favored Lucullus; for while the deserter expected to find Lucullus awake, in which case he would have been at once admitted to his presence, he actually found him at that time fast asleep, exhausted with revolving plans in his mind the night before. Then, when Adathas pleaded to be admitted, on the ground that he had an unexpected and imperative message to deliver, he was kept out by the determined efforts of the slaves, who were concerned for their master's health. Fearing consequently that he was an object of suspicion, he mounted the horse which he held in readiness outside the gate, and fled to Mithridates without accomplishing his purpose[220].

When Sertorius was encamped next to Pompey near the town of Lauron in Spain, there were only two tracts from which forage could be gathered, one nearby, the other farther off. Sertorius gave orders that the one nearby should be continually raided by light-armed troops, but that a more remote one should not be visited by any troops. Thus, he finally convinced his adversaries that the more distant tract was safer. When Pompey's troops had gone to this region, on one occasion, Sertorius ordered Octavius Graecinus, with ten cohorts armed in the Roman fashion, and ten cohorts of light-armed Spaniards along with Tarquinius Priscus and two thousand cavalry, to lay an ambush against the foragers. These men executed their instructions with energy; for after examining the ground, they hid the above-mentioned forces by night in a neighboring wood, posting the light-armed Spaniards in front, as best suited to stealthy warfare, the shield-bearing soldiers a little further back, and the cavalry in the rear, in order so that the plan might not be betrayed by the neighing of the horses. They then ordered all to repose in silence till the third hour of the following day[221]. When Pompey's men, entertaining no suspicion and loaded down with forage, thought of returning, and those who had been on guard, lured on by the situation, were slipping away to forage, suddenly the Spaniards, darting out

---

[220] Mithridates's foiled attempt at assassination: 72 B.C. Cf. Appian Mithr. 79; Plut. Lucull. 16. The name of the deserter varies in the different accounts.
[221] The third hour: About 9 A.M.

with the swiftness characteristic of their race, poured forth upon the stragglers, inflicted many wounds upon them, and put them to rout, to their great amazement.

Then, before resistance to this first assault could be organized, the shield-bearing troops, bursting forth from the forest to overthrow and routed the Romans who were returning to the ranks, while the cavalry, dispatched after those in flight, followed them all the way back to the camp, cutting them to pieces. Provision was also made that no one should escape. Two hundred and fifty reserve horsemen, sent ahead for the purpose, found it a simple matter to race forward by shortcuts, and then to turn back and meet those who had first fled before they reached Pompey's camp. On learning of this, Pompey sent out a legion under Decimus Laelius to reinforce his men, whereupon the cavalry of the enemy, withdrawing to the right flank, pretended to give way, and then, passing round the legion, assaulted it from the rear, while those who had followed up the foragers attacked it from the front also. Thus the legion with its commander was crushed between the two lines of the enemy. When Pompey led out his entire army to help the legion, Sertorius exhibited his forces drawn up on the hillside, and thus baulked Pompey's purpose. Thus, in addition to inflicting a twofold disaster, as a result of the same strategy, Sertorius forced Pompey to be the helpless witness of the destruction of his own troops. This was the first battle between Sertorius and Pompey. According to Livy, ten thousand men were lost in Pompey's army, along with the entire transport[222].

When Pompey, was warring in Spain, he posted troops in scattered locations to attack from ambush, and by feigning fear, he would draw the enemy on in pursuit, until they reached the place of the ambuscade. Then when the opportune moment arrived, wheeling about, he slaughtered the foe in front and on both flanks, and likewise captured their general, Perperna[223].

The same Pompey, in Armenia, when Mithridates was superior to him in the number and quality of his cavalry, stationed three thousand light-armed men and five hundred cavalry by night in a valley under cover of

---

[222] Battle of Lauron: 76 B.C. Cf. Plut. Sert. 18; Appian B.C. I.109. The allusion to Livy cannot be identified.
[223] Pompey's ambush in Spain: 72 B.C. Cf. Livy Per. 96; Oros. V.XXIII.13; Appian B.C. I.115.

bushes lying between the two camps. Then at daybreak, he sent forth his cavalry against the position of the enemy, planning that as soon as the full force of the enemy, cavalry and infantry, became engaged in battle, the Romans would gradually fall back, still keeping ranks, until they afford room to those who had been stationed for the purpose of attacking from the rear to arise and do so. When this design turned out successfully, those who had seemed to flee turned about, enabling Pompey to cut to pieces the enemy thus caught in panic between his two lines. The Roman infantry also, engaging in hand-to-hand encounter, stabbed the horses of the enemy. That battle destroyed the faith which the king had reposed in his cavalry[224].

In the Slave War[225], Crassus fortified two camps close beside the camp of the enemy near Mt. Cantenna. Then, one night, he moved his forces, leading them all out and posting them at the base of the mountain mentioned above, leaving his headquarters tent in the larger camp in order to deceive the enemy. Dividing the cavalry into two detachments, he directed Lucius Quintius to oppose Spartacus with one division and fool him with a mock encounter; with the other to lure to combat the Germans and Gauls, of the faction of Castus and Cannicus, and, by feigning flight, to draw them on to the spot where Crassus himself had drawn up his troops in battle array. When the barbarians followed, the cavalry fell back to the flanks, and suddenly the Roman force disclosed itself and rushed forward with a shout. In that battle, Livy tells us that thirty-five thousand armed men, with their commanders, were slain; five Roman eagles and twenty-six standards were recaptured, along with much other booty, including five sets of rods and axes[226].

Gaius Cassius fighting in Syria against the Parthians and their leader Osaces, exhibited only cavalry in front, but had posted infantry in hiding on rough ground in the rear. Then, when his cavalry fell back and retreated over familiar roads, he drew the army of the Parthians into the ambush prepared for them and cut them to pieces[227].

Ventidius, keeping his own men in camp on pretense of fear, caused the Parthians and Labienus, who were elated with victorious successes, to

---

[224] Pompey's ambush in Armenia: 66 B.C. Cf. Appian Mithr. 98; Dio XXXVI.XLVII.3 4.
[225] The Spartacus Rebellion
[226] Rods and axes forming the fasces
[227] Cassius' ambush in Syria: 51 B.C. Cf. Dio XL.29.

come out for battle. Having lured them into an unfavorable situation, he attacked them by surprise and so overwhelmed them that the Parthians refused to follow Labienus and evacuated the province[228].

The same Ventidius, having himself only a small force available for use against the Parthians under Pharnastanes, but observing that the confidence of the enemy was growing in consequence of their numbers, posted eighteen cohorts at the side of the camp in a hidden valley, with cavalry stationed behind the infantry. Then, he sent a very small detachment against the enemy. When these by feigning flight had drawn the enemy in hot pursuit beyond the place of ambush, the force at the side rose up, whereupon Ventidius drove the Parthians in precipitate flight and slaughtered them, Pharnastanes among them[229].

On one occasion when the camps of Gaius Caesar and Afranius were pitched in opposite plains, it was the special ambition of each side to secure possession of the neighboring hills — a task of extreme difficulty on account of the jagged rocks. In these circumstances, Caesar marshaled his army as though to march back again to Ilerda, a move supported by his deficiency of supplies. Then, within a short time, making a small detour, he suddenly started to seize the hills. The followers of Afranius, alarmed at sight of this, just as though their camp had been captured, started out themselves at top speed to gain the same hills. Caesar, having forecast this turn of affairs, fell upon Afranius's men, before they could form — partly with infantry, which he had sent ahead, partly with cavalry sent up in the rear[230].

Antonius, was near Forum Gallorum, having heard that the consul Pansa was approaching, met his army by means of ambuscades, set here and there in the woodland stretches along the Aemilian Way, routed his troops and inflicting a wound on Pansa himself from which he died in a few days[231].

Juba, King in Africa at the time of the Civil War, by feigning a retirement, once roused unwarranted elation in the heart of Curio. Under the influence of this mistaken hope, Curio, pursuing Sabboras, the king's general,

---

[228] Ventidius' surprise attack: 39 B.C.Cf. Dio XLVIII.39 40; Justin. XLII.IV.7 8.
[229] Ventidius ambushes the Parthians: 39 B.C. Cf. Dio XLVIII.XLI.1 4; Plut. Ant. 33.
[230] Caesar feigned attack on a hill: 49 B.C. Cf. Caes. B.C. I.65 72.
[231] Antonius ambushes Pansa: 43 B.C. Mutina. Cf. Appian B.C. III.66 ff.; Cic. ad Fam. X.30.

who, he thought was in flight, came to open plains, where, surrounded by the cavalry of the Numidians, he lost his army and perished himself[232].

Melanthus, the Athenian general, on one occasion came out for combat, in response to the challenge of the king of the enemy, Xanthus, the Boeotian. As soon as they stood face to face, Melanthus exclaimed: "Your conduct is unfair, Xanthus, and contrary to agreement. I am alone, but you have come out with a companion against me." When Xanthus wondered who was following him and looked behind, Melanthus dispatched him with a single stroke, as his head was turned away[233].

Iphicrates the Athenian, on one occasion in the Chersonesus, aware that Anaxibius, commander of the Spartans, was proceeding with his troops by land, disembarked a large force of men from his vessels and placed them in ambush, but directed his ships to sail in full view of the enemy, as though loaded with all his forces. When the Spartans were thus thrown off their guard and apprehended no danger, Iphicrates, attacking them by land from the rear as they marched along, crushed and routed them[234].

On one occasion the Liburnians, had taken a position among some shallows, by allowing only their heads to appear above the surface of the water caused the enemy to believe that water was deep. In this way a galley which followed them became stranded on the shoal, and was captured.

Alcibiades, commander of the Athenians at the Hellespont against Mindarus of the Spartans, had a large army and numerous vessels. He landed some of his soldiers by night, and hid part of his ships behind certain headlands. He advancing with a few troops, so as to lure the enemy on in scorn of his small force, fled when pursued, until he finally drew the foe into the trap which had been laid. Then attacking the enemy in the rear, as he disembarked, he cut him to pieces with the aid of the troops which he had landed for this very purpose[235].

---

[232] Juba's false retreat: 49 B.C. Cf. Caes. B.C. II.40 42; Dio XLI.41 42; Appian B.C. II.45.
[233] Melanthus, "Whozat behind you?": Cf. Polyaen. I.19.
[234] Iphicrates' nearly empty ships: 389 388 B.C. Cf. Xen. Hell. IV.VIII.32 ff.
[235] Alcibiades' amphibian ambush: 410 B.C. Cf. Xen. Hell. I.I.11 ff.; Polyaen. I.XL.9; Diodor. XIII.50.

The same Alcibiades, on one occasion, was about to engage in a naval combat, erected a number of masts on a headland, and commanded the men whom he left there to spread sails on these as soon as they noticed that the engagement had begun. By this means he caused the enemy to retreat, since they imagined another fleet was coming to his assistance.

Memnon the Rhodian, in a naval encounter, possessed a fleet of two hundred ships, and wishing to lure the vessels of the enemy out to battle, made arrangements for raising the masts of only a few of his ships, ordering these to proceed first. When the enemy saw the number of masts from a distance and from that inferred the number of vessels, they offered battle, but were fallen upon by a larger number of ships and defeated.

Timotheus, leader of the Athenians, was about to engage in a naval encounter with the Spartans. As soon as the Spartan fleet came out arrayed in line of battle, he sent ahead twenty of his swiftest vessels, to baulk the enemy in every way by various tactics. Then, as soon as he observed that the enemy was growing less active in their maneuvers, he moved forward and easily defeated them, since they were already worn out[236].

---

[236] Timotheus wears the enemy down: 375 B.C. Cf. Polyaen. III.X.6, 12, 16.

VI. On Letting the Enemy Escape, lest, Brought to Bay, He Renew the Battle in Desperation

After the battle fought against Camillus, the Gauls sought boats to cross the Tiber, the Senate voted to send them across and to supply them with provisions as well.

On a subsequent occasion, free passage was afforded to the people of the same race when retreating through the Pomptine district. This road goes by the name of the "Gallic Way."[237]

A Roman knight Titus Marcius was given supreme command of the army after the two Scipios were slain and succeeded in enveloping the Carthaginians. When the latter, in order not to die unavenged, fought with increasing fury, Marcius opened up the maniples, afforded room for escape, and as the enemy became separated, slaughtered them without danger to his own men[238].

When fighting against the Germans, Gaius Caesar penned in a group that fought fiercely out of desperation, so he ordered them to be allowed to escape, and then attacked them as they fled.

At Trasimenus, when the Romans were enveloped and fighting with great fury, Hannibal opened up his ranks and gave them an opportunity of escape, whereupon, as they fled, he overwhelmed them without loss of his own troops[239].

When the Aetolians, blockaded by Antigonus, King of the Macedonians, were suffering from famine and had resolved to make a sally in face of certain death. Antigonus afforded them an avenue of flight in order to cool their passions. He then attacked them from the rear and cut them to pieces[240].

---

[237] the Romans let the Gauls go: 349 B.C. L. Furius Camillus, son of the great Camillus
[238] Titus Marcius lets the enemy escape, sort of: 212 B.C. Livy XXV.37 gives his praenomen as Lucius.
[239] Hannibal lets the enemy escape, sort of: 217 B.C.
[240] Antigonus lets the enemy escape, sort of: 223 221 B.C. Antigonus Doson.

When Agesilaus, the Spartan, was engaged in battle with the Thebans, he noticed that the enemy, hemmed in by the nature of the terrain, was fighting with greater fury on account of their desperation. Accordingly he opened up his ranks and afforded the Thebans a way of escape. But when they tried to retreat, he enveloped them again, and cut them down from behind without loss of his own troops[241].

The consul Gnaeus Manlius, returned from battle and found the Roman camp in possession of the Etruscans. He therefore posted guards at all the gates and roused the enemy that was shut up within to such a pitch of fury that he himself was slain in the fighting. When his lieutenants realized the situation, they withdrew the guards from one gate and afforded the Etruscans an opportunity of escape. But when the latter poured forth, the Romans pursued them and cut them to pieces, with the help of the other consul, Fabius, who happened to come up[242].

When Xerxes was defeated and the Athenians wished to destroy his bridge,[243] Themistocles prevented this, showing that it was better for them that Xerxes should be expelled from Europe than be forced to fight in desperation. He also sent to the king a messenger to tell him the danger that would befall him, in case he failed to make a hasty retreat[244].

When King Pyrrhus of the Epirotes, captured a certain city he noticed that the inhabitants, shut up inside had closed the gates and were fighting valiantly from dire necessity he decided to give them an opportunity to escape.

The same Pyrrhus, among many other precepts on the art of war, recommended never pressing too relentlessly on the heels of an enemy in flight. This was not merely in order to prevent the enemy from resisting too furiously out of desperation, but also to make him more inclined to withdraw

---

[241] Agesilaus lets the enemy escape, sort of: 394 B.C. Cf. Polyaen. II.I.19; Plut. Agesil. 18. Xen. Hell. IV.3 notes the failure of Agesilaus to employ this stratagem.
[242] Gnaeus Manlius' lieutenants let the enemy escape, sort of: 480 B.C. Cf. Livy II.47
[243] Xerxes' bridge: i.e. the bridge which Xerxes had constructed across the Hellespont at the time of his invasion of Greece.
[244] Themistocles lets Xerxes flee: 480 B.C. Cf. Justin. II.XIII.5 ff.; Polyaen. I.XXX.4. Plut. Them. 16 and Herod. VIII.108 attribute the advice against destroying the bridge to Aristides and Eurybiades respectively

another time, knowing that the victor would not strive to destroy him when in flight.

VII. On Concealing Reverses

Tullus Hostilius, king of the Romans, was engaged in battle on one occasion with the Veientines, when the Albans, deserting the Roman army, made for the neighboring hills. Since this action disconcerted the Roman troops, Tullus shouted in a loud voice that the Albans had done that by his instructions, with the object of enveloping the foe. This declaration struck terror into the hearts of the Veientines and lent confidence to the Romans. By this device he turned the tide of battle[245].

When a lieutenant of Lucius Sulla had gone over to the enemy at the beginning on an engagement accompanied by a considerable force of cavalry, Sulla announced that this had been done by his own instructions. He thereby not merely saved his men from panic, but encouraged them by a certain expectation of advantage to result from this plan.

The same Sulla, when certain auxiliary troops dispatched by him had been surrounded and cut to pieces by the enemy, feared that his army would become panicked on account of this disaster and announced that he had purposely placed the auxiliaries in a place of danger, since they had plotted to desert. In this way he concealed a possible reverse under the guise of discipline, and encouraged his soldiers by convincing them that he had done this.

When the envoys of King Syphax told Scipio in the name of their king not to cross over to Africa from Sicily in expectation of an alliance, Scipio, feared the spirits of his men would receive a shock if the hope of a foreign alliance were cut off, summarily dismissed the envoys, and spread abroad the report that he was expressly sent for by Syphax[246].

Once when Quintus Sertorius was engaged in battle, he plunged a dagger into the barbarian who had reported to him that Hirtuleius had fallen, for fear the messenger might spread this news to others and in this way the spirit of his own troops should be broken[247].

---

[245] Tullus Hostilius masks a desertion: Cf. Livy I.27; Val. Max. VII.IV.1; Dionys. III.24. Nep. Ages. 6 and Datam. 6 attributes like stratagems to Agesilaus and Datames.
[246] Scipio simulates an alliance: 204 B.C. Cf. Livy XXIX.23 24; Polyaen. VIII.XVI.7.
[247] Sertorius enforces silence: 75 B.C.

When Alcibiades, the Athenian, was hard pressed in battle by the Abydenes he suddenly noticed a courier approaching at great speed and with dejected countenance. He prevented the courier from openly telling what tidings he brought. Having learned privately that his fleet was beset by Pharnabazus, the commander of the king, he concealed the fact both from the enemy and from his own soldiers, and finished the battle. He then marched quickly to rescue his fleet and brought aid to his friends[248].

When Hannibal entered Italy, three thousand Carpetani deserted him. Fearing that rest of his troops might be affected by their example, he proclaimed that they had been discharged by him, and as further proof of that, he sent home a few others whose services were of very little importance[249].

When Lucius Lucullus noticed that his auxiliary Macedonian cavalry were suddenly deserting to the enemy en mass, he ordered the trumpets to sound and sent out squadrons to pursue the deserters. The enemy, thinking that an engagement was beginning, received the deserters with javelins, whereupon the Macedonians, seeing that they were not welcomed by the enemy and were attacked by those whom they were deserting, were forced to resort to a genuine battle and assaulted the enemy[250].

Datames, commander of the Persians against Autophradates in Cappadocia, learned that part of his cavalry were deserting and ordered the rest of his troops to follow with him. Upon catching up with the deserters, he commended them for outstripping him in their eagerness, and urged them to attack the enemy courageously. Seized with shame and penitence, the deserters changed their purpose, imagining that it had not been detected[251].

When the Romans yielded ground in battle the consul Titus Quinctius Capitolinus falsely claimed that the enemy had been routed on the

---

[248] Alcibiades keeps quiet: 409 B.C.
[249] Hannibal masks a desertion: 218 B.C. Cf. Livy XXI.23.
[250] Lucullus converts a desertion into a cavalry charge: 74 66 B.C.
[251] Datames averts a desertion: 362 B.C. Nep. Datam. 6, Diodor. XV.91 and Polyaen. VII.XXI.7 give a slightly different version of this episode.

other flank. By lending courage to his men in this manner, he won a victory[252].

When Marius was fighting against the Etruscans, his colleague Marcus Fabius commanding the left flank, was wounded, and that section of the army gave way, imagining that the consul had been slain. Thereupon Manlius confronted the broken line with squadrons of horse, shouting that his colleague was alive and that he himself had been victorious on the right flank. By this dauntless spirit, he restored the courage of his men and won the victory[253].

When Marius was fighting against the Cimbrians and Teutons, his engineers had heedlessly chosen a site for the camp that allowed the barbarians to control the water supply. In response to the soldiers' demand for water, Marius pointed with his finger toward the enemy and said: "There is where you must get it." Thus inspired, the Romans straightway drove the barbarians from the place[254].

After the Battle of Pharsalia, when Titus Labienus' side was defeated and he had fled to Dyrrhachium, he combined falsehood with truth, and while not concealing the outcome of the battle, pretended that the fortunes of the two sides had been equalized in consequence of a severe wound received by Caesar. By this pretense, he created confidence in the other followers of Pompey's party[255].

Marcus Cato, inadvertently landed with a single galley in Ambracia at a time when the allied fleet was blockaded by the Aetolians. Although he had no troops with him, he nevertheless began to make signals by voice and gesture, in order to give the impression that he was summoning the approaching ships of his own forces. By this deception he alarmed the enemy, just as though the troops, whom he pretended to be summoning from near at hand, were visibly approaching. The Aetolians, accordingly, feared that they would be crushed by the arrival of the Roman fleet, abandoned the blockade.

---

[252] Capitolinus' disinformation: 468 B.C. Cf. Livy II.LXIV.5 7; Dionys. IX.57.

[253] Marius gets the news out: 480 B.C. According to Livy II.46 47 and Dionys. IX.11, Q. Fabius and Manlius were wounded, and Marcus Fabius was the author of this stratagem.

[254] Marius' source of water: 102 B.C. Cf. Flor. III.III.7 10; Plut. Mar. 18.

[255] Labienus' disinformation: 48 B.C.

VIII. On Restoring Morale by Firmness

In the battle in which King Tarquinius was pitted the Sabines, Servius Tullius, then a young man, noticing that the standard-bearers fought halfheartedly, seized a standard, and hurled it into the ranks of the enemy. To recover it, the Romans fought so furiously that they not only regained the standard, but also won the day[256].

The consul Furius Agrippa was in battle when his flank gave way. Snatching a military standard from a standard-bearer, he hurled it into the hostile ranks of the Hernici and Aequi. Through this action the day was saved, because the Romans pressed forward with the greatest eagerness to recapture the standard[257].

The consul Titus Quinctius Capitolinus hurled a standard into the midst of the hostile ranks of the Faliscans and commanded his troops to regain it[258].

When his troops held back, Marcus Furius Camillus, a military tribune with consular power, seized a standard-bearer by the hand and dragged him into the hostile ranks of the Volscians and Latins, whereupon the rest were shamed into following[259]. Salvius, the Pelignian, did the same in the Persian War[260].

Marcus Furius, meeting his army in retreat, declared he would not receive anyone in camp who was not victorious. Thereupon he led them back to battle and won the day[261].

Scipio, at Numantia, seeing his forces in retreat, proclaimed that he would treat whoever should return to camp as an enemy[262].

---

[256] This type of stratagem was very frequently resorted to. Cf. Florus I.11; Val. Max. III.II.20; Caes. B. G. 4.25; Livy IV.XXIX.3 and passim.
[257] Furius Agrippa throws a standard into the ranks of the enemy: 446 B.C. Cf. Livy III.LXX.2 11.
[258] There is no other record of Titus Quinctius Capitolinus's warring with the Faliscans. Livy IV.29 attributes this stratagem to Titus Quinctius Cincinnatus in the war with the Volscians, 431 B.C.
[259] Camillus throws a standard-bearer into the ranks of the enemy: 386 B.C. Cf. Livy VI.7 8.

The dictator Servilius Priscus, commanded that the standards of the legions were to be carried forward against the hostile Faliscans and then executed the standard-bearer for hesitating to obey. The rest, cowed by this example, advanced against the foe[263]. Cornelius Cossus, master of the horse, did the same in an engagement with the people of Fidenae[264].

When his cavalry showed hesitation in the battle against the Sabines Tarquinius, , he ordered them to fling away their bridles, put spurs to their horses, and break through the enemy's line.

In the Samnite War, the consul Marcus Atilius, saw his troops quit battle and take refuge in camp, metting them with his own command and declared that they would have to fight against him and all loyal citizens, unless they preferred to fight against the enemy. In this way he marched them back in a body to the battle[265].

When Sulla's legions broke before the hosts of Mithridates led by Archelaus, Sulla advanced with drawn sword into the first line and, addressing his troops, told them, in case anybody asked where they had left their general, to answer: "Fighting in Boeotia." Shamed by these words, they followed him to a man[266].

The deified Julius, when his troops gave way at Munda, ordered his horse to be removed from sight, and strode forward as a foot-soldier to the front line. His men, ashamed to desert their commander, thereupon renewed the fight[267].

On one occasion, Philip, fearing that his troops would not withstand the onset of the Scythians, stationed the trustiest of his cavalry in the rear, and

---

[260] Salvius throws a standard-bearer into the ranks of the enemy: Plut. Aem. 20 attributes to Salvius a stratagem similar to the first three of this chapter. 168 B.C.

[261] Marcus Furius meets his army in retreat: 381 B.C. Camillus. Cf. Livy VI.24.

[262] Scipio sees his forces retreating: 133 B.C.

[263] Servilius Priscus executes a standard-bearer: 418 B.C. According to Livy IV.46 47, the battle was with the Aequi, not the Faliscans.

[264] Cornelius Cossus executes a standard-bearer: 426 B.C. Cf. Livy IV.XXXIII.7; Flor. I.XI.2 3. This stratagem is similar to number 10, rather than number 8.

[265] Marcus Atilius, "You're going to have to fight me": 294 B.C. Cf. Livy X.36. A slightly different version of this story is told in IV.I.29.

[266] Whether his army comes along or not, Sulla fights in Boeotia: 85 B.C. Cf. Plut. Sulla 21; Polyaen. VIII.IX.2; Appian Mithr. 49.

[267] 45 B.C. Cf. Plut. Caes. 56; Polyaen. VIII.XXIII.16; Vell. II.55

commanded them to permit no one of their comrades to quit the battle, with orders to kill them if they persisted in retreating. This proclamation induced even the most timid to prefer to be killed by the enemy rather than by their own comrades, and enabled Philip to win the day.

IX. On Bringing the War to a Close after a Successful Engagement

After Gaius Marius defeated the Teutons in battle, and night had put an end to the conflict, he camped amidst the remnants of his opponents. By causing a small group of his own men to raise loud cries from time to time, he kept the enemy in a state of alarm and prevented them from securing rest. In this manner he succeeded in easily crushing them on the following day, since they had had no sleep.

Claudius Nero, met the Carthaginians on their way from Spain to Italy under the command of Hasdrubal, defeated them and threw Hasdrubal's head into Hannibal's camp. As a result, Hannibal was overwhelmed with grief and the army gave up hope of receiving reinforcements[268].

When Lucius Sulla was besieging Praeneste, he fastened the heads of Praenestine generals who had been slain in battle on spears, and exhibited them to the besieged inhabitants, thus breaking their stubborn resistance[269]. Arminius, leader of the Germans, likewise fastened on spears the heads of those he had slain, and ordered them to be brought up to the fortifications of the enemy.

When Domitius Corbulo was besieging Tigranocerta and the Armenians seemed likely to make an obstinate defense, Corbulo executed Vadandus, one of the nobles he had captured, shot his head out of a ballista, and sent it flying within the fortifications of the enemy. It happened to fall in the midst of a council which the barbarians were holding at that very moment, and the sight of it (as though it were some portent) so filled them with concern that they quickly surrendered.

When Hermocrates, the Syracusan, had defeated the Carthaginians in battle, and was afraid that the enormous number of prisoners he had taken would be carelessly guarded, since the victory in battle might prompt the victors to revelry and neglect, he pretended that the cavalry of the enemy were planning an attack on the following night. By instilling this fear, he

---

[268] 207 B.C. Cf. Livy XXVII.51; Zonar. IX.9.
[269] 82 B.C. Cf. Appian B.C. I.93 94.

succeeded in having the guard over the prisoners maintained even more carefully than usual.

The same Hermocrates achieved certain success in battle, and for that reason his men, through a spirit of over-confidence, had abandoned all restraint leading them to sink into a drunken stupor. He sent a deserter into the camp of the enemy to prevent their flight by declaring that ambuscades of Syracusans had been posted everywhere. Out of fear from this, the enemy remained in camp. Having thus detained them, on the following day when his own men were more fit, Hermocrates, defeated the enemy and ended the war[270].

When Miltiades defeated a huge host of Persians at Marathon, and the Athenians were rejoicing over the victory, he forced them to hurry aid to the city, where the Persian fleet was headed. Arriving before the enemy, he filled the walls with warriors, so that the Persians, thinking that there was vast numbers of Athenians and that they had met one army at Marathon while another was now confronting them on the walls, straightway turned their vessels about and laid their course for Asia[271].

The Megarian fleet approached Eleusis at night with the object of kidnapping the Athenian matrons who had made sacrifice to Ceres. Pisistratus, the Athenian, engaged it in battle and, by ruthlessly slaughtering the enemy, avenged his own countrymen. He then filled the captured ships with Athenian soldiers, placing certain matrons dressed as captives in full view. The Megarians were deceived by these appearances, thinking their own people were sailing back, and that they were crowned with victory, rushed out to meet them, in disorder and without weapons, whereupon they were overwhelmed a second time[272].

Cimon, the Athenian general, having defeated the Persian fleet near the island of Cyprus, fitted out his men with the weapons of the prisoners and in the barbarians' own ships set sail to meet the enemy in Pamphylia, near the Eurymedon River. The Persians, recognizing the vessels and the garb of

---

[270] 413 B.C. Cf. Polyaen. I.XLIII.2; Thuc. VII.73; Plut. Nic. 26.
[271]: 490 B.C. Cf. Herod. VI.115 ff.
[272] 604 B.C. Cf. Justin. II.8; Polyaen. I.XX.2; Plut. Solon 8.

those standing on deck, were off their guard. Thus on the same day, they were suddenly crushed in two battles, one on sea and one on land[273].

[273] 466 B.C. Cf. Thuc. I.100; Polyaen. I.XXXIV.1; Diodor. XI.61.

X. On Repairing One's Losses after a Reverse

When Titus Didius was fighting in Spain, he fought an extremely bitter engagement that only ended due to darkness, leaving a large number of slain on both sides. He provided for the burial that night of his own men and on the following day, the Spaniards, coming out to perform a like duty, found more of their men slain than of the Romans, and arguing according to this calculation that they had been beaten, came to terms with the Roman commander[274].

Titus Marcius, a Roman knight, had charge of the remnants of the army [of the Scipios] in Spain. He found two camps of the Carthaginians nearby, a few miles distant from each other, urged on his men and attacked the nearer camp in the dead of night. Since the enemy, was flushed with victory, and disorganized, Marcius' attack did not leave as much as a single man to report the disaster. Granting his troops a brief rest, and outstripping the news of his exploit, he attacked the second camp the same night. Thus, by a double success, he destroyed the Carthaginians in both places and restored to the Roman people the lost provinces of Spain[275].

[274] 98 93 B.C.
[275] 212 B.C. Livy XXV.37 gives his praenomen as Lucius.

XI. On Ensuring the Loyalty of Those Whom One Mistrusts

Publius Valerius had an insufficient garrison at Epidaurus and feared perfidy on the part of the townspeople, he prepared to celebrate athletic contests at some distance from the city. When nearly all the population had gone there to see the show, he closed the gates and refused to admit the Epidaurians until he had taken hostages from their leading families.

Gnaeus Pompey, suspecting the Chaucensians and fearing that they would not admit a garrison, asked that they would meanwhile permit his invalid soldiers to recover among them. Then, sending his strongest men in the guise of invalids, he seized the city and held it.

When Alexander had conquered and subdued Thrace and was setting out for Asia, he feared that after his departure the Thracians would take up arms. He therefore took with him, under the pretext of conferring honor, their kings and officials — all in fact who seemed to take to heart the loss of freedom. He placed common and ordinary persons left behind in charge, thus preventing the officials from wishing to make any change, being bound to him by favors, and the common people from even being able to do so, since they had been deprived of their leaders[276].

When Antipater beheld the army of the Peloponnesians, who had assembled to overthrow his rule upon hearing of the death of Alexander, he pretended not to understand with what purpose they had come, and thanked them for having gathered to aid Alexander against the Spartans adding that he would write to the king about this[277]. Inasmuch as he did not need their assistance at present, he urged them to go home, and by this statement dispelled the danger which threatened him from the unruly crowd.

When Scipio Africanus was warring in Spain, among the captive women brought before him was a noble maiden of surpassing beauty who attracted the gaze of everyone. Scipio guarded her with the greatest pains and restored her to her betrothed, Alicius by name, presenting to him likewise, as

---

[276] 334 B.C. Cf. Justin. XI.V.1 3.
[277] He intentionally acted on the assumption that they had not heard of the death of Alexander, though he knew this assumption to be false.

a marriage gift, the gold which her parents had brought to Scipio as a ransom. Overcome by this manifold generosity, the whole tribe leagued itself with the government of Rome[278].

The story goes that Alexander of Macedon likewise, having taken captive a maiden of exceeding beauty betrothed to the chief of a neighboring tribe, treated her with such extreme consideration that he refrained even from gazing at her. When the maiden was later returned to her lover, Alexander, as a result of this kindness, secured the attachment of the entire tribe[279].

When the Emperor Caesar Augustus Germanicus[280], was fighting the war in which he earned his title by conquering the Germans, he built forts in the territory of the Cubii, he ordered compensation to be made for the crops which he had included within his fortifications. Thus the renown of his justice won the allegiance of all.

---

278 210 B.C. Cf. Livy XXVI.50; Val. Max. IV.III.1; Gell. VII.8; Polyb. X.19.
279 Cf. Gell. VII.8; Ammian. Marc. XXIV.IV.27.
280 the Emperor Caesar Augustus Germanicus: Domitian.

XII. What to do for the Defense of the Camp, in case a Commander lacks Confidence in his Present Forces

As the Volscians were about to attack the camp of the consul, Titus Quinctius, he kept only one cohort on duty, and dismissed the remainder of the army to take their rest. Quinctius directed the trumpeters to mount their horses and make the round of the camp sounding their trumpets. By exhibiting this semblance of strength, he kept the enemy off balance and held them throughout the night. Then at daybreak, he attacked them by a sudden sortie when they were exhausted with watching, he easily defeated them[281].

When he was in Spain, Quintus Sertorius was completely outmatched by the cavalry of the enemy, who in their excessive confidence advanced up to his very fortifications. Accordingly during the night, he constructed trenches and drew up his line of battle in front of them. Then when the cavalry approached, as was their wont, he drew back his line. The enemy following close on his heels, fell into the trenches and thus were defeated[282].

Chares, the Athenian commander, was expecting reinforcements, but feared that meanwhile the enemy, knowing he had a small force, would attack his camp. He therefore ordered that a number of the soldiers under his command should pass out at night by the rear of the camp, and should return by a route where they would be clearly observed by the enemy, thus creating the impression that fresh forces were arriving. In this way, he defended himself by pretended reinforcements, until he was equipped with those he was expecting[283].

Iphicrates, the Athenian, was camped on a plain when he learned that the Thracians were intending to come down from the hills, over which there was but a single line of descent, with the purpose of plundering his camp by night. He therefore secretly led out his troops and posted them on both sides of the road over which the Thracians were expected to pass. Then when the enemy descended upon the camp, in which a large number of watch-fires,

---

[281] 468 B.C. Cf. Livy II.64 65.
[282] Sertorius' surprise for an overconfident cavalry: 80 72 B.C.

built by the hands of a few men, he produced the impression that a mighty host was still there, Iphicrates was enabled to attack them on the flank and crush them[284].

[283] Chares' phantom reinforcements: 366/ 338 B.C.
[284] 389 B.C. This same story is told in I.V.24. Cf. also Polyaen. III.IX.41, 46, 50.

XIII. On Retreating

When the Gauls were about to fight with Attalus, they handed over all their gold and silver to trusty guards, with instructions to scatter, in case their forces should be routed in battle, in order that the enemy would be preoccupied in picking up the spoils and they might more easily escape[285].

When Tryphon, king of Syria, was defeated he scattered money along the whole line of his retreat. While the cavalry of Antiochus delayed to pick this up, he effectively escaped.

When Quintus Sertorius was defeated in battle by Quintus Metellus Pius, he was convinced that not even an organized retreat was safe, so he commanded his soldiers to disband and retire, informing them at what point he desired them to reassemble[286].

Viriathus, leader of the Lusitanians, extricated himself from an awkward position, and from the menace of Roman troops, by the same method as Sertorius, disbanded his forces and then reassembled[287].

When Porsenna's army was pressing hard upon him, Horatius Cocles, commanded his supporters to return over the bridge to the City, and then to destroy the bridge in order that the foe might not follow them. While this was being done, he held up the oncoming enemy as defender of the bridgehead. Then, when the crash told him that the bridge had been destroyed, he threw himself into the stream, and swam across it in his armor, exhausted though he was by wounds[288].

When Afranius was fleeing from Caesar near Ilerda in Spain, he pitched a camp while Caesar was pressing close upon him. When Caesar did the same and sent his men off to gather forage, Afranius suddenly gave the signal to continue the retreat[289].

As Anthony was retreating, hard pressed by the Parthians, often broke camp at daybreak, his retiring troops were assailed by volleys of arrows

---

[285] Cic. Pro Lege Manil. ix.22 and Flor. III.V.18 attribute a similar stratagem to Mithridates.
[286] 75 B.C. Cf. Plut. Pomp. 19
[287] 147 139 B.C. Cf. Appian Hisp. 62. Cf. note to II.V.7.
[288] 507 B.C. Cf. Livy II.10; Dionys. V.23 25; Plut. Publ. 16.

from the barbarians. Accordingly, one day he kept his men back till nearly noon, thus producing the impression that he had made a permanent camp. As soon as the Parthians had become persuaded of this and had withdrawn, he accomplished his regular march for the remainder of the day without interference[290].

When Philip suffered defeat in Epirus, in order so that the Romans might not overwhelm him in flight, he secured the grant of a truce to bury the dead. In consequence of this, the guards relaxed their vigilance and Philip slipped away[291].

Publius Claudius was defeated by the Carthaginians in a naval engagement and thinking it necessary to break through the forces of the enemy, ordered his twenty remaining vessels to be dressed out as though victorious. The Carthaginians, therefore, thought our men had proved themselves superior in the encounter. Claudius became an object of fear to the enemy and thus made his escape[292].

On one occasion when the Carthaginians were defeated in a naval battle, they desired to shake off the Romans who were close upon them, pretending that their vessels were caught on shoals and imitated the movement of stranded galleys. In this way they caused the victors, in fear of meeting a like disaster, to afford them an opportunity of escape.

Commius, the Atrebatian, was defeated by the deified Julius and fled from Gaul to Britain, reaching the Channel at a time when the wind was fair, but the tide was out. Although the vessels were stranded on the flats, he nevertheless ordered the sails to be spread. Caesar, who was following them from a distance, seeing the sails swelling with the full breeze, and imagining Commius to be escaping from his hands and to be proceeding on a prosperous voyage, abandoned the pursuit.

---

[289]: 49 B.C. Cf. Caes. B.C. I.80.
[290] Anthony sets up camp: 36 B.C.
[291] Philip's truce to bury the dead: 198 B.C.
[292] 249 B.C. Battle of Drepanum. Eutrop. II.26, Polyb. I.LI.11 12, and Oros. IV.X.3, give the number of ships as thirty.

Book III - Stratagems

If the preceding books have corresponded to their titles, and I have held the attention of the reader up to this point, I will now treat of ruses that deal with the siege and defense of towns. Waiving any preface, I will first submit those things which are useful in the siege of cities, then those which offer suggestions to the besieged. Laying aside all consideration of works and engines of war, the invention of which has long since reached its limit[293], and for the improvement of which I see no further hope in the applied arts, I shall recognize the following types of stratagems connected with siege operations:

I. On surprise attacks
II. On deceiving the besieged.
III. On inducing treachery.
IV. By what means the enemy may be reduced to want.
V. How to persuade the enemy that the siege will be maintained.
VI. On distracting the attention of a hostile garrison.
VII. On diverting streams and contaminated waters.
VIII. On terrorizing the besieged.
IX. On attacks from an unexpected quarter.
X. On setting traps to draw out the besieged.
XI. On pretended retirements.

On the other hand, stratagems connected with the protection of the besieged:

XII. On the stimulating the vigilance of one's own troops.
XIII. On sending and receiving messages.
XIV. On introducing reinforcement and supplying provisions.
XV. How to produce the impression of abundance of what is lacking.
XVI. How to meet the menace of treason and desertion.
XVII. On Sorties
XVIII. Concerning steadfastness on the part of the besieged.

---

[293] A curious illustration of the rashness of prophecy.

Roman Maniples in Battle formation (1851 Winkles)

I. On Surprise Attacks

Having conquered the Aequians and Volscians in an engagement, the consul Titus Quinctius decided to storm the walled town of Antium. Accordingly, he called an assembly of the soldiers and explained how necessary this project was and how easy, if only it were not postponed. Then, having roused enthusiasm by his address, he assaulted the town[294].

When Marcus Cato was in Spain, he saw that he could only gain possession of a certain town if he could assault the enemy by surprise. Accordingly, in only two days, he marched what was normally four days' march through rough and barren districts and crushed his foes, who thought they were safe. Then, when his men asked the reason of so easy a success, he told them that they had won the victory as soon as they had accomplished the four days' march in two[295].

---

[294] Titus Quinctius' rational pep talk: 468 B.C.
[295] Cato's forced march: 195 B.C.

II. On Deceiving the Besieged

When Domitius Calvinus was besieging Lueria, a town of the Ligurians, that was not only protected by its location and siege-works, but also by the superiority of its defenders, he instituted the practice of marching around the walls frequently with all his forces and then marching back to camp. The townspeople became used to this routine believing that the Roman commander did this for the purpose of drill, and consequently took no precautions against his efforts when he transformed the practice of parading into a sudden attack, and gaining possession of the walls, forcing the inhabitants to surrender.

The consul Gaius Duellius, frequently exercised his soldiers and sailors, succeeding in preventing the Carthaginians from taking notice of a practice which was innocent enough, until suddenly he brought up his fleet and seized their fortifications[296].

Hannibal captured many cities in Italy by sending ahead certain of his own men dressed in the garb of Romans and speaking Latin, which they had acquired as a result of long experience in the war[297].

While the Arcadians, were besieging a stronghold of the Messenians, they fabricated certain weapons to resemble those of the enemy. Then, when they learned that another force was to relieve the first, they dressed themselves in the uniform of those who were expected, and being admitted as comrades in consequence of this confusion, they secured possession of the place and wrought havoc among the foe.

Cimon, the Athenian general, had designs on a certain city in Caria. While under cover of night he set fire to a temple of Diana that was held in high reverence by the inhabitants, and also to a grove outside the walls. When the townspeople poured out to fight the conflagration, Cimon captured the city since it was left without defenders[298].

---

[296] Duilius' naval exercises: 260 B.C.
[297] 216 203 B.C.
[298] About 470 B.C.

Alcibiades, the Athenian commander, was besieging the strongly fortified city of the Agrigentines and requested a conference with its citizens. He addressed them at length, as though discussing matters of common concern, as was done in the theatre, as was the custom of the Greeks to afford a place for consultation. Then, while he held the crowd on the pretense of deliberation, the Athenians, whom he had previously prepared for this move, captured the city, which was left unguarded[299].

When Epaminondas, the Theban, was campaigning in Arcadia, on a certain holiday when the women of the enemy strolled in large numbers outside the walls, he sent a number of his own troops dressed in women's attire among them. In consequence of this disguise, the men were admitted to the town towards nightfall, whereupon they seized it and threw it open to their companions[300].

When the whole population had gone out of the city to celebrate the rites of Minerva on a holiday of the Tegeans, Aristippus, the Spartan, sent a number of mules laden with grain-bags filled with chaff to Tegea. The mules were driven by soldiers disguised as traders, who, escaping notice, threw open the gates of the town to their comrades.

When Antiochus was besieging the fortified town of Suenda in Cappadocia, he intercepted some beasts of burden which had gone out to procure grain. Then, killing their attendants, he dressed his own soldiers in their clothes and sent them in as though bringing back the grain. The sentinels fell into the trap and, mistaking the soldiers for teamsters, let the troops of Antiochus enter the fortifications.

When the Thebans were unable to gain possession of the harbor of the Sicyonians despite their utmost efforts, they filled a large vessel with armed men, exhibiting a cargo in full view on deck under the guise of traders, in order to deceive their enemies. At a point where the fortifications were remote from the sea, they stationed a few men with whom certain unarmed members of the crew upon disembarking were to engage in a fracas on the pretense of a quarrel. When the Sicyonians were summoned to stop the

---

[299] 415 B.C. Thuc. VI.51, Polyaen. I.XL.4 and Diodor. XIII.IV.4, make Catana, and not Agrigentum, the scene of this stratagem.
[300] 379 B.C. Polyaen. II.III.1 has a different version of this story, but in II.IV.3 attributes a somewhat similar stratagem to Pelopidas.

altercation, the Theban crews seized both the unguarded harbor and the town[301].

Timarchus, the Aetolian, having killed Charmades, general of King Ptolemy[302], arrayed himself in Macedonian fashion in the cloak and helmet of the slain commander. Through this disguise, he was admitted as Charmades into the harbor of the Sanii and secured possession of it.

301 V.XVI.3 makes Pammenes the author of this stratagem, 369 B.C.
302 Ptolemy Ceraunus, king of Macedonia, 280 B.C.

III. On Inducing Treachery

When the consul Papirius Cursor was besieging Tarentum, and Milo was holding the town with a force of Epirotes, Papirius promised safety to Milo and the townspeople if he should secure possession of the town through Milo's agency. Bribed by these inducements, Milo persuaded the Tarentines to send him as ambassador to the consul, from whom, in conformity with their understanding, he brought back liberal promises by means of which he caused the citizens to relapse into a feeling of security, and was thus enabled to hand the city over to Cursor since it was left unguarded[303].

Marcus Marcellus, having tempted a certain Sosistratus of Syracuse to turn traitor, learned from him that the guards would be less strict on a holiday when a certain citizen named Epicydes made a generous distribution of wine and food. Taking advantage of the gaiety and the consequent laxness of discipline, he scaled the walls, slew the sentinels, and threw open to the Roman army a city already made famous as the scene of noted victories[304].

When Tarquinius Superbus was unable to induce Gabii to surrender, he scourged his son Sextus with rods and sent him among the enemy, where he arraigned the cruelty of his father and persuaded the Gabians to utilize his hatred against the king. Accordingly, he was chosen leader in the war, and delivered Gabii over to his father[305].

Cyrus, king of the Persians, having proved the loyalty of his attendant Zopyrus, deliberately mutilated his face and sent him among the enemy. In consequence of their belief in his wrongs, he was regarded as implacably hostile to Cyrus, and promoted this belief by running up and discharging his weapons against Cyrus, whenever an engagement took place, till finally the city of the Babylonians was entrusted to him and by him delivered into the hands of Cyrus[306].

When Philip, was prevented from gaining possession of the town of the Sanians, he bribed one of their generals, Apollonides, to turn traitor,

---

[303] 272 B.C. Cf. Zonar. VIII.6.
[304] 212 B.C. Livy XXV.23 ff., Plut. Marc. 18, and Polyaen. VIII.11 name Damippus a Spartan, rather than Sosistratus, as the source of the information.
[305] Cf. Livy I.53; Val. Max. VII.IV.2; Polyaen. VIII.6.
[306] 518 B.C. Herod. III.153, Justin. I.X.15, and Polyaen. VII.13.

induced him to plant a cart laden with dressed stone at the very entrance to the gate. Then straightway giving the signal, he followed after the townspeople, who were huddled in panic around the blocked entrance of the gate, and succeeded in overwhelming them[307].

When Hannibal was attacking Tarentum, the town was held by a Roman garrison under the command of Livius. He induced a certain Cononeus of Tarentum to turn traitor, and arraigned a stratagem with him where he would go out at night for the purpose of hunting, on the ground that enemy rendered this impossible by day. When he went out, Hannibal supplied him with boars to present to Livius as trophies of the chase. When this had repeatedly been done, and for that reason was less noticed, Hannibal dressed one night a number of Carthaginians in the garb of hunters and introduced them among Cononeus's attendants. When these men were admitted by the guards loaded with the game, they immediately attacked and slew the latter. Then breaking down the gate, they admitted Hannibal with his troops, who slew all the Romans, save those who had fled for refuge to the citadel[308].

When Lysimachus, king of the Macedonians, was besieging the Ephesians, they were assisted by the pirate chief Mandro, who was in the habit of bringing galleys into Ephesus laden with booty. Accordingly, Lysimachus bribed Mandro to turn traitor, and attached a number of dauntless Macedonians to him to be taken into the city as captives, with their hands pinioned behind their backs. These men subsequently snatched weapons from the citadel and delivered the town into the hands of Lysimachus[309].

---

[307] 359 336 B.C

[308] 212 B.C. Cf. Appian Hann. 32; Livy XXV.8 9; Polyb. VIII.26.

[309] 287 B.C. Cf. Polyaen. V.19.

IV. By What Means the Enemy May be Reduced to Want.

Fabius Maximus was laying waste to the lands of the Campanians, in order that they might have nothing left to warrant the confidence that a siege could be sustained, withdrew at the time of the sowing, so that inhabitants might plant what seed they had remaining. Then, returning, he destroyed the new crop and thus made himself master of the Campanians, whom he had reduced to famine[310].

Antigonus employed the same device against the Athenians[311].

Dionysius captured many cities and wished to attack the Rhegians, who were well provided with supplies. He pretended to desire peace and begged them to furnish provisions for his army. When he had secured his request and consumed the grain of the inhabitants, he attacked their town, now stripped of food, and conquered it[312]. He is said to have employed the same device also against the people of Himera[313].

When Alexander was about to besiege Leucadia, a town well-supplied with provisions, he first captured the fortresses on the border and allowed all the people from there to flee for refuge to Leucadia, in order that the food-supplies were consumed with greater rapidity of being shared by many.

Phalaris of Agrigentum, was besieging certain places in Sicily protected by fortifications, pretended to make a treaty and deposited all the wheat which he said he had remaining with the Sicilians, taking pains, however, that the chambers of the buildings in which the grain was stored should have leaky roofs. Then when the Sicilians, relying on the wheat which Phalaris had deposited with them, had used up their own supplies, Phalaris attacked them at the beginning of summer and as a result of their lack of provisions forced them to surrender[314].

---

[310] Cf. Livy XXIII.XLVIII.1 2 and XXV.XIII. 215 or 211 B.C.
[311] Antigonus lets the enemy sow their crops: 263 B.C. Cf. Polyaen. IV.VI.20.
[312] 391 B.C. The version of Diodor. XIV.108 is slightly different.
[313] 387 B.C. Cf. Polyaen. V.II.10.
[314] 570/ 554 B.C. Cf. Polyaen. V.I.3. According to Polyaenus, the Sicilians were to return to Phalaris not the grain he had left with them but the crops from their later harvests.

V. How to Persuade the Enemy that the Siege will be Maintained.

When the Spartan Clearchus, learned that the Thracians had conveyed all things necessary for their subsistence to the mountains and they were buoyed by the sole hope that he would withdraw owing to the lack of supplies. At this time he had surmised their envoys would come and thus ordered one of the prisoners to be put to death in full view. His body was then distributed in pieces among the tents, as though for the mess. The Thracians, believing that Clearchus would stop at nothing in order to hold out, since he brought himself to try such loathsome food, delivered themselves up[315].

When the Lusitanians told Tiberius Gracchus that they had supplies for ten years and for that reason stood in no fear of a siege, he answered: "Then I'll capture you in the eleventh year." Terror-stricken by this language, the Lusitanians, though well supplied with provisions, at once surrendered[316].

When Aulus Torquatus was besieging a Greek city and was told that the young men of the city were engaged in earnest practice with the javelin and bow, he replied: "Then the price at which I shall presently sell them shall be higher."

---

[315] 402/ 401 B.C. Cf. Polyaen. II.II.8.
[316] 179/ 178 B.C.

VI. On Distracting the Attention of a Hostile Garrison

When Hannibal returned to Africa, many towns were still held by strong forces of the Carthaginians. Scipio's policy demanded that these towns should be reduced. Accordingly, he often sent troops to assault them and finally he would appear before the towns as though bent on sacking them, and would then retire, feigning fear. Hannibal, thinking his alarm real, withdrew the garrison from all points, and began to follow, as though determined to fight a decisive battle. Scipio, having thus accomplished what he intended, with the assistance of Masinissa and the Numidians, captured the towns, which had thus been stripped of their defenders[317].

Publius Cornelius Scipio, appreciating the difficulty of capturing Delminus, because it was defended by the concerted efforts of the population of the district, began to assault other towns. Then, when the inhabitants of the various towns had been called back to defend their homes, Scipio took Delminus, which had been left without support[318].

Pyrrhus, king of Epirus, in his war against the Illyrians, aimed to reduce their capital, but despairing of this, began to attack the other towns. He then succeeded in making the enemy disperse to protect their other cities, since they had confidence in the apparently adequate fortification of the capital. When he had accomplished this, he recalled his own forces and captured the town, now left without defenders[319].

The consul Cornelius Rufinus for some time besieged the city of Crotona without success, since it had been made impregnable by the arrival of a band of Lucanian reinforcements. He therefore pretended to desist from his undertaking, and by offers of great rewards, induced a certain prisoner to go to Crotona. This emissary, by feigning to have escaped from custody, persuaded the inhabitants to believe his report that the Romans had withdrawn. The people of Crotona, thinking this to be true, dismissed their

---

[317] 202 B.C.
[318] 155 B.C.
[319] 296 280 B.C.

allies. Then, weakened by being stripped of their defenders, they were surprised and captured[320].

Mago, general of the Carthaginians, having defeated Gnaeus Piso and having blockaded the tower wherein he had taken refuge, suspected that reinforcements would come to his relief and sent a deserter to persuade the approaching troops that Piso was already captured. Having thus scared them off, Mago made his victory complete[321].

Alcibiades, wishing to capture the city of Syracuse in Sicily, chooses from among the people of Catana, where he was encamped, a certain man of tested shrewdness and sent him to the Syracusans. This man, when brought before the public assembly of the Syracusans, persuaded them that the people of Catana were very hostile to the Athenians, and that if assisted by the Syracusans, they would crush the Athenians and Alcibiades along with them. Induced by these representations, the Syracusans left their own city and set out in full force to join the people of Catana, whereupon Alcibiades attacked Syracuse from the rear, and finding it unprotected, as he had hoped, brought it under subjection[322].

When the people of Troezen were held in subjection by troops under the command of Craterus, the Athenian, Cleonymus assaulted the town and hurled missiles inscribed with messages within its walls, stating that Cleonymus had come to liberate their state. At the same time, certain prisoners whom he had won over to his side were sent back to disparage Craterus. By this plan, he stirred up internal strife among the besieged and, bringing up his troops, gained possession of the city[323].

---

[320] 277 B.C. Cf. Zonar. VIII.6.

[321] 216 203 B.C.

[322] 415 B.C. This account agrees with that of Polyaen. I.XL.5. Thuc. VI.64 ff., and Diodor. XIII.VI.2 ff., attribute the stratagem to Nicias and Lamachus, and give a different version of its result.

[323] 277/ 276 B.C. Polyaen. II.XXIX.1 calls Cleonymus a king of Sparta.

VII. On Diverting Streams and Contaminating Waters

Publius Servilius diverted the stream from which the inhabitants of Isaura drew their water, and thus forced them to surrender in consequence of thirst.

Gaius Caesar, in one of his Gallic campaigns, deprived the city of the Cadurcia of water, although it was surrounded by a river and abounded in springs; he diverted the springs by subterranean channels, while his archers shut off all access to the river[324].

Lucius Metellus, fighting in Hither Spain, diverted the course of a river and directed it from a higher level against the camp of the enemy, which was located on low ground. Then, when the enemy was in a panic from the sudden flood, he had them slain by men whom he had stationed in ambush for this very purpose[325].

At Babylon, which is divided into two parts by the river Euphrates, Alexander constructed both a ditch and an embankment. The enemy supposed that the earth was merely being taken out to form the embankment. Alexander, diverted the stream, entered the town along the former dried up river bed, and thus afforded an entrance to the town[326]. Semiramis is said to have done the same thing in the war against the Babylonians by diverting the same Euphrates.

Clisthenes of Sicyon cut the water-pipes leading into the town of the Crisaeans. Then when the townspeople were suffering from thirst, he turned on the water again, now poisoned with hellebore. When the inhabitants used this, they were so weakened by diarrhea that Clisthenes overcame them[327].

---

[324] 51 B.C. Cf. Hirt. B. G. VIII.40 ff.

[325] 143 142 B.C. Quintus Caecilius Metellus Macedonicus, although the better manuscript readings give L. as the praenomen.

[326]: Herod. I.191, Xen. Cyrop. vii.5, and Polyaen. VII.VI.5, attribute this stratagem to Cyrus rather than Alexander.

[327]: 595/ 585 B.C. Polyaen. VI.13 attributes this stratagem to Eurylochus; Pausan. X.XXXVII.7, to Solon.

VIII. On Terrorizing the Besieged

When Philip was unable to capture the fortress of Prinassus through his utmost exertions, he excavated earth directly in front of the walls and pretended to be constructing a tunnel. The men within the fortress, imagining that they were being undermined, surrendered[328].

Pelopidas, the Theban, planned to make a simultaneous attack on two towns of the Magnetes, not very far from each other. As he advanced against one of these towns, he gave orders that, in accordance with previously agreed signals, four horsemen came from the other camp with garlands on their heads and with the marked eagerness of those who announce a victory. To complete the illusion, he arranged to have a forest between the two cities set on fire, to give the appearance of a burning town. Besides this, he ordered prisoners to be led along, dressed in the costume of the townspeople. When the besieged had been terrified by these demonstrations, deeming themselves already defeated in one quarter, they ceased to offer resistance[329].

Cyrus, king of the Persians, at one time forced Croesus to take refuge in Sardis. On one side, was a steep hill preventing access to the town. Near the walls, Cyrus erected masts of equal height of the ridge of the hill, and on them placed dummies of armed men dressed in Persian uniforms. At night, he brought these to the hill. Then at dawn, he attacked the walls from the other side. As soon as the sun rose and the dummies, flashing in the sunlight, revealed the garb of warriors, the townspeople, imagining that their city had been captured from the rear, scattered in flight and left the field to the enemy[330].

---

[328] 201 B.C. Cf. Polyb. XVI.11; Polyaen. IV.XVIII.1.
[329] Pelopidas' early victory: 369 364 B.C. Cf. Polyaen. II.IV.1.
[330] 546 B.C. Cf. Polyaen. VII.VI.10; Ctes. ed. Müller, pp46 60. Herod. I.84 makes no mention of this stratagem.

IX. On Attacks from an Unexpected Quarter

When Scipio was fighting at Carthage, he approached the walls of the city, just before the turn of the tide, guided, as he said, by some god. Then, when the tide went out in the shallow lagoon, he burst in at that point, the enemy not expecting him there[331].

Fabius Maximus, son of Fabius Cunctator, found Arpi occupied by Hannibal's forces, first inspected the site of the town, and then sent six hundred soldiers on a dark night to mount the walls with scaling-ladders at a part of the town which was fortified and therefore less guarded in order to tear down the gates. These men were aided in the execution of their orders by the noise of the falling rain, which deadened the sound of their operations. In another quarter, Fabius lead an attack at a given signal and captured Arpi[332].

In the Jugurthine War, Gaius Marius was besieging a fortress situated near the Mulucha River. It stood on a rocky eminence, accessible on one side by a single narrow path, while the other side, as though by special design, was precipitous. It happened that a certain Ligurian, a common soldier from among the auxiliaries, had gone out to procure water, and while gathering snails among the rocks of the mountain, had reached the summit. This man reported to Marius that it was possible to clamber up to the stronghold. Marius accordingly sent a few centurions in company with his fleetest soldiers, including also the most skilled trumpeters. These men went bare-headed and bare-footed, so that they might see better and make their way more easily over the rocks; their shields and swords were fastened to their backs. Guided by the Ligurian and aided by straps and staffs, in order to support themselves, they made their way up to the rear of the fortress, which, owing to its position, was without defenders, and then began to sound their trumpets and make a great uproar, as they had previously been directed. At this signal, Marius, steadfastly urging on his men, began to advance with renewed fury against the defenders of the fortress. The latter were recalled from the defense by the populace, who had lost heart under the impression

---

[331] 210 B.C. Cf. Livy XXVI.45 46; Polyb. X.10 ff.; Appian Hisp. 21 ff.
[332] 213 B.C. Cf. Livy XXIV.46 47.

that the town had been captured from the rear, so that Marius was enabled to press on and capture the fort[333].

The consul Lucius Cornelius Rufinus captured numerous towns in Sardinia by landing powerful detachments of troops at night, with instructions to remain in hiding and to wait till he himself drew near to land with his ships. Then as the enemy came to meet him at his approach, he led them a long chase by pretending to flee, while his other troops attacked the cities thus abandoned by their inhabitants[334].

Pericles, the Athenian general, was once besieging a city which was protected by very determined defenders. At night he ordered the trumpet sounded and a loud outcry to be raised at a quarter of the walls adjacent to the sea. The enemy, thinking that the town had been entered at that point, abandoned the gates, whereupon, as soon as these were left without defense, Pericles burst into the town.

Alcibiades, the Athenian general, planning to assault Cyzicus, approached the town unexpectedly at night, and commanded his trumpeters to sound their instruments at a different part of the fortifications. The defenders of the walls were ample, but since they all flocked to the side where alone they imagined themselves to be attacked, Alcibiades succeeded in scaling the walls at the point where there was no resistance[335].

Thrasybulus, general of the Milesians, in his efforts to seize the harbor of the Sicyonians, made repeated attacks on the inhabitants from the land side. Then, when the enemy directed their attention to the point where they were attacked, he suddenly seized the harbor with his fleet[336].

Philip, was besieging a coast town, when he secretly lashed ships together in pairs, with a common deck over all, and erected towers on them. He launched an attack with other towers from the land, distracting the attention of the defenders of the city, until he brought up the ships with the

---

[333] 107 B.C. Cf. Sall. Jug. 92 94; Flor. III.I.14.

[334] Probably a confusion of names: Lucius Cornelius Scipio invaded Sardinia in 259 B.C. (cf. III.X.2). Publius Cornelius Rufinus was consul in 277, but waged war only in Italy.

[335] According to Thuc. VIII.107 and Diodor. XIII.XL.6, Cyzicus was not fortified by walls. This stratagem belongs rather to the taking of Byzantium, 409 B.C. Cf. III.XI.3;Diodor. XIII.66 67; Plut. Alcib. 31.

[336] About 600 B.C.

attached towers, and advanced against the walls at the point where no resistance was offered.

Pericles, was about to lay siege to a fortress of the Peloponnesians to which there were only two avenues of approach, one of these was cut off by a trench and he began to fortify the other. The defenders of the fortress, thrown off their guard at one point, began to watch only the other where they saw the building going on. Pericles prepared bridges, laid them across the trench and entered the fortress at the point where no guard was kept[337].

Antiochus, when fighting against the Ephesians, directed the Rhodians, whom he had as allies, to make an attack on the harbor at night with a great uproar. When the entire population rushed headlong to this quarter, leaving the rest of the fortress without defenders, Antiochus attacked at a different quarter and captured the town.

---

[337] 430 B.C. Cf. I.V.10 and note.

X. On Setting Traps to Draw out the Besieged

When Cato was besieging the Lacetani, he sent away all his other troops in full view of the enemy, while ordering certain Suessetani, who were the least martial of his allies, to attack the walls of the town. When the Lacetani, made a sortie, they were easily repulsed and pursued them eagerly as they fled. The soldiers whom Cato had placed in hiding rose up and by their help he captured the town[338].

When campaigning in Sardinia, Lucius Scipio, in order to draw out the defenders of a certain city, abandoned the siege which he had begun and pretended to flee with a detachment of his troops. Then, when the inhabitants followed him pell-mell, he attacked the town with the help of those whom he had placed in hiding near at hand[339].

When Hannibal was besieging the city of Himera, he purposely allowed his camp to be captured, ordering the Carthaginians to retire, on the ground that the enemy was superior. The inhabitants were so deceived by this turn of affairs that in their joy they came out of the city and advanced against the Carthaginian breast-works, whereupon Hannibal, finding the town vacant, captured it by means of the troops whom he had placed in ambush for this very contingency[340].

In order to draw out the Saguntines, Hannibal advanced against their walls with a thin line of troops. Then, at the first sally of the inhabitants, they feigned flight. He withdrew, and interposed troops between the pursuing foe and the city, he slaughtered the enemy thus cut off from their fellows between the two forces[341].

When campaigning near Agrigentum, Himilco, the Carthaginian, placed part of his forces in ambush near the town, and directed them to set fire to some damp wood as soon as the soldiers from the town came forth. Then, advancing at daybreak with the rest of his army for the purpose of

---

[338] 195 B.C. Cf. Livy XXXIV.20.
[339] 259 B.C. Cf. III.IX.4 and note.
[340] 409 B.C. The Hannibal here mentioned is the son of Gisgo. Diodor. XIII.59 62 represents the Carthaginians as withdrawing in flight rather than executing a stratagem.
[341] 219 B.C. Son of Hamilcar Barca. The identity of names led to the confusion between these two generals.

luring out the enemy, he feigned flight and drew the inhabitants after him for a considerable distance by his retirement. The men in ambush near the walls applied the torch to the wood-piles as directed. The Agrigentines, beholding the smoke ascend, thought their city on fire and ran back in alarm to protect it. Encountering those lying in wait for them near the walls and beset in the rear by those whom they had just been pursuing, they were caught between two forces and so cut to pieces[342].

Viriathus, on one occasion, placed men in ambush and sent a few others to drive off the flocks of the Segobrigenses. When the latter rushed out in great numbers to defend their flocks and followed up the marauders who pretended to flee, they were drawn into an ambush and cut to pieces[343].

When Lucullus was put in charge of a garrison of two cohorts at Heraclea, the cavalry of the Scordisci, pretended to drive off the flocks of the inhabitants, provoked a sortie. Then, when Lucullus followed, they drew him into an ambush, feigning flight, and killed him together with eight hundred of his followers.

The Athenian general, Chares, was about to attack a city on the coast, hidding his fleet behind certain promontories and then ordered his swiftest ship to sail past the forces of the enemy. At sight of this ship, all the forces guarding the harbor darted out in pursuit, while Chares sailed in with the rest of his fleet and took possession of the undefended harbor and likewise of the city itself[344].

On one occasion, when Roman troops were blockading Lilybaeum by land and sea, the general of the Carthaginians in Sicily, Barca, ordered a part of his fleet to appear in the offing ready for action. When the Romans darted out at the sight of this, Barca seized the harbor of Lilybaeum with the ships which he had held in hiding[345].

---

[342] 406 B.C. Cf. Polyaen. V.X.4. In the Old Testament (Josh. viii.), a similar stratagem is employed by Joshua.
[343] 147/ 139 B.C.
[344] 366/ 336 B.C.
[345] 249 B.C. Cf. Polyb. I.44, where Hannibal, rather than Barca, is the general.

XI. On Pretended Retirements

The Athenian general Phormio was ravaging the lands of the Chalcidians, and their envoys complained of this action. He answered them graciously, and at evening, when he was about to dismiss them, pretended that a letter had come from his fellow-citizens requiring his return. Accordingly, he retired a short distance and dismissed the envoys. When these reported that all was safe and that Phormio had withdrawn, the Chalcidians in view of the promised consideration and of the withdrawal of the troops, relaxed the guard of their town. Phormio then suddenly returned and the Chalcidians were unable to withstand his unexpected attack[346].

When the Spartan commander, Agesilaus, was blockading the Phocaeans and when he learned that those who were then lending them support were weary with the burdens of war, he retired a short distance as though for other objects, thus leaving the allies free opportunity to withdraw. Not long after, bringing back his troops, he defeated the Phocaeans thus left without assistance[347].

When fighting against the Greeks, who kept within their walls, Alcibiades laid an ambush and, feigning a retirement, took them off their guard and crushed them[348].

After retreating for three days, Viriathus, suddenly turned around and traversed the same distance in one day. He thus crushed the Segobrigenses, taking them off their guard at a moment when they were intently engaged in sacrifice[349].

In the operations around Mantinea, Epaminondas, noticed that the Spartans had come to help his enemies, so he conceived the idea that Sparta might be captured if he secretly set out against it. He accordingly ordered numerous watch-fires to be built at night, so that, by appearing to remain in camp, he might conceal his departure. However, he was betrayed by a deserter and pursued by the Lacedaemonian troops, and abandoning his

---

[346] 432 B.C. Cf. Polyaen. III.IV.1.
[347] 396/ 394 B.C. Cf. Polyaen. II.I.16.
[348] 409 B.C. Cf. Diodor. XIII.66 67; Plut. Alcib. 31.
[349]: 147/ 139 B.C.

march to Sparta, and employed the same scheme against the Mantineans. By building watch-fires as before, he deceived the Spartans into thinking that he would remain. Meanwhile, returning to Mantinea by a march of forty miles, he found it without defenses and captured it[350].

[350] 362 B.C. Cf. Polyb. IX.8; Diodor. XV.82 84; Plut. Ages. 34.

XII. On Stimulating the Vigilance of One's Own Troops

The Athenian commander, Alcibiades, when his own city was blockaded by the Spartans, feared negligence on the part of the guards, ordered the men on picket-duty to watch for the light which he should exhibit from the citadel at night, and to raise their own lights at sight of it, threatening that whoever failed in this duty should suffer a penalty. While anxiously awaiting the signal of their general, all maintained constant watch, and so escaped the dangers of the perilous night[351].

When Iphicrates, the Athenian general, was holding Corinth with a garrison and on one occasion personally made the rounds of the sentries as the enemy were approaching, he found one of the guards asleep at his post and stabbed him with his spear. When certain ones rebuked this procedure as cruel, he answered: "I left him as I found him."[352] Epaminondas the Theban is said, on one occasion, to have done the same thing.

---

[351] Cf. Polyaen. I.XL.3.
[352] 393/ 391 B.C. Cf. Nep. Iphic. ii.1 2.

XIII. On Sending and Receiving Messages

When the Romans were besieged in the Capitol, they sent Pontius Cominius to implore Camillus to come to their aid. To elude the pickets of the Gauls, Pontius, let himself down over the Tarpeian Rock, swam the Tiber, and reached Veii. Having accomplished his errand, he returned by the same route to his friends.[353]

When the Romans were maintaining a careful guard against the inhabitants of Capua, whom they were besieging, the latter sent a certain fellow in the guise of a deserter, and finding an opportunity to escape, conveyed to the Carthaginians a letter which he had secreted in his belt.[354]

Some have written messages on skins and then sewed these to the carcasses of game or sheep.

Some have stuffed the message under the tail of a mule while passing the picket-posts.

Some have written on the linings of scabbards.

When the Cyzicenes were besieged by Mithridates, Lucius Lucullus wished to inform them of his approach. There was a single narrow entrance to the city, connecting the island with the mainland by a small bridge. Since this was held by forces of the enemy, he sewed some letters up inside two inflated skins and then ordered one of his soldiers, an adept in swimming and boating, to mount the skins, which he had fastened together at the bottom by two strips some distance apart, and to make the trip of seven miles across. So skillfully did the soldier do this, that by spreading his legs, he steered his course as though by rudder, and deceived those watching from a distance by appearing to be some marine creature.[355]

The consul Hirtius often sent letters inscribed on lead plates to Decimus Brutus, who was besieged by Antonius at Mutina. The letters were

---

[353] 390 B.C. Cf. Livy V.46; Diodor. XIV.116; Plut. Camill. 25.
[354] 211 B.C. Livy XXVI.7 represents Hannibal as sending the letter to the Capuans.
[355] 74 B.C. Cf. Flor. III.V.15 16; Oros. VI.II.14.

fastened to the arms of soldiers, who then swam across the Scultenna River.[356]

Hirtius also shut up pigeons in the dark, starved them, fastened letters to their necks by a hair, and then released them as near to the city walls as he could. The birds, eager for light and food, sought the highest buildings and were received by Brutus, who in that way was informed of everything, especially after he set food in certain spots and taught the pigeons to alight there.[357]

[356] Hirtius' special forces messengers: 43 B.C. Cf. Dio XLVI.36.
[357] Hirtius' carrier pigeons: 43 B.C. Cf. Plin. N. H. X.37.

XIV. On Introducing Reinforcements and Supplying Provisions

In the Civil War, the Spanish city of Ategua, belonging to Pompey's party, was under blockade, when one night a Moor, pretending to be a tribune's adjutant belonging to the Caesarian party, roused certain sentries and got the password from them. He then roused others, and by continuing his deception, succeeded in conducting reinforcements for Pompey through the midst of Caesar's troops.[358]

When Hannibal was besieging Casilinum, the Romans sent big jars of wheat down the current of the Volturnus to be picked up by the besieged. After Hannibal stopped these by throwing a chain across the river, the Romans scattered nuts on the water. These floated down stream to the city and thus sustained the necessities of the allies.[359]

When the inhabitants of Mutina were blockaded by Antonius, and were greatly in need of salt, Hirtius packed some in jars and sent it in to them by way of the Scultenna River.[360]

Hirtius also sent down the river carcasses of sheep, which were received and thus furnished the necessities of life.

---

[358] 45 B.C. Cf. Dio XLIII.33 34. According to Dio, this man, Munatius Flaccus, whose real mission is to aid the Ateguans in withstanding the blockade of Caesar's troops, represents to the sentries that he has been sent by Caesar to betray the city. Thus having once learned the password, he secures an easy entrance into the city.
[359] 216 B.C. Cf. Livy XXIII.19.
[360] 43 B.C.

XV. How to Produce the Impression of Abundance of What is Lacking

When the Capitol was besieged by the Gauls, the Romans, in the extremity of famine, threw bread among the enemy. They thus produced the impression that they were well supplied with food, and so withstood the siege till Camillus came.[361] The Athenians are said to have employed the same ruse against the Spartans.

When the inhabitants of Casilinum, were blockaded by Hannibal, it was thought that they had reached the starvation point, since Hannibal cut off their food supply, even their use of the growing herbs by plowing the ground between his camp and the city walls. Since the ground was made ready, the besieged flung seed into it, giving the impression that they had enough wherewith to sustain life even till harvest time.[362]

When the survivors of the Varian disaster[363] were under siege and seemed to be running short of food, they spent an entire night in leading prisoners round their store-houses; then, having cut off their hands, they turned them loose. These men persuaded the besieging force to cherish no hope of an early reduction of the Romans by starvation, since they had an abundance of food supplies.

When the Thracians were besieged on a steep mountain inaccessible to the enemy, they got together a small amount of wheat through individual contributions. They fed this to a few sheep which they then drove among the forces of the enemy. When the sheep had been caught and slaughtered, and traces of wheat had been found in their intestines, the enemy raised the siege, imagining that the Thracians had a surplus of wheat, inasmuch as they fed it even to their sheep.

The Milesians were at one time suffering a long siege at the hands of Alyattes, who hoped they could be starved into surrender. The Milesian commander, Thrasybulus, in anticipation of the arrival of envoys from Alyattes, ordered all the grain to be brought together into the market-place,

---

361 390 B.C. Cf. Livy V.48; Val. Max. VII.IV.3; Ovid. Fast. VI.350 ff.
362 216 B.C. Cf. Livy XXIII.19.
363 The Varian disaster: i.e. the defeat of Varus by Arminius in the Teutoburg Forest in 9 A.D.

arranged for banquets to be held on that occasion, and provided sumptuous feasts throughout the city. Thus, he convinced the enemy that the Milesians had abundance of provisions with which to sustain a long siege.[364]

[364] Thrasybulus' feasts: About 611 B.C. Cf. Herod. I.21 22; Polyaen. VI.47.

XVI. How to Meet the Menace of Treason and Desertion

A certain Lucius Bantius of Nola on one occasion cherished the plan of rousing his fellow-citizens to revolt, as a favor to Hannibal, by whose kindness he had been tended when wounded among those engaged at Cannae, and by whom he had been sent back from captivity to his own people. Claudius Marcellus, learning of his purpose and not daring to put him to death, for fear that by his punishment he would stir up the rest of the people of Nola, summoned Bantius and talked with him, pronouncing him a very valiant soldier (a fact which Marcellus admitted he had not previously known), and urged him to remain with him. Besides these compliments, he presented him also with a horse. By such kindness he secured the loyalty, not only of Bantius, but also of his townspeople, since their allegiance hinged on his.[365]

When the Gallic auxiliaries of Hamilcar, the Carthaginian general, were in the habit of crossing over to the Romans and were regularly received by them as allies, Hamilcar engaged his most loyal men to pretend desertion, while actually they slew the Romans who came out to welcome them. This device was not merely of present aid to Hamilcar, but caused real deserters to be regarded in future as objects of suspicion in the eyes of the Romans.[366]

Hanno, commander of the Carthaginians in Sicily, learned on one occasion that about four thousand Gallic mercenaries had conspired to desert to the Romans, because they had received no pay for several months. Not daring to punish them, for fear of mutiny, he promised to make good the deferred payment by increasing their wages. When the Gauls rendered thanks for this, Hanno, promising that they should be permitted to go out foraging at a suitable time, sent to the consul Otacilius an extremely trustworthy steward, who pretended to have deserted on account of embezzlement, and who reported that on the coming night four thousand Gauls, sent out on a foraging expedition, could be captured. Otacilius, not immediately crediting the deserter, nor yet thinking the matter ought to be treated with disdain,

---

[365] 216 B.C. Cf. Livy XXIII.15 16; Plut. Marcel. 10 11. Variations of this stratagem and its author are found in IV.VII.36, Plut. Fab. 20 and Val. Max.VII.III.7.
[366] 260/ 241 B.C.

placed the pick of his men in ambush. These met the Gauls, who fulfilled Hanno's purpose in a twofold manner, since they not only slew a number of the Romans, but were themselves slaughtered to the last man.[367]

By a similar plan, Hannibal took vengeance on certain deserters; for, being aware that some of his soldiers had deserted on the previous night, and knowing that spies of the enemy were in his camp, he publicly proclaimed that the name of "deserter" ought not to be applied to his cleverest soldiers, who at his order had gone out to learn the designs of the enemy. The spies, as soon as they heard this pronouncement, reported it to their own side. Thereupon the deserters were arrested by the Romans and sent back with their hands cut off.

When Diodotus was holding Amphipolis with a garrison, and entertained suspicions of two thousand Thracians who seemed likely to pillage the city, he invented the story that a few hostile ships had put in at the shore nearby and could be plundered. When he had incited the Thracians at that prospect, he let them out. Then, closing the gates, he refused to admit them again.[368]

---

367 261 B.C. Cf. Diodor. XXIII.VIII.3. Zonar. VIII.10 attributes this stratagem to Hamilcar.
368 168 B.C. In Livy XLIV.44, the author of the stratagem is called Diodorus.

XVII. On Sorties

When Hasdrubal came to besiege Panormus, the Romans, who were in possession of the town, purposely placed a scanty number of defenders on the walls. In contempt of their small numbers, Hasdrubal incautiously approached the walls, whereupon they made a sortie and slew him.[369]

When the Ligurians with their entire force made a surprise attack on the camp of Aemilius Paulus, the latter feigned fear and for a long time kept his troops in camp. Then, when the enemy was exhausted, making a sortie by the four gates, he defeated the Ligurians and made them prisoners.[370]

Livius, commander of the Romans, when holding the citadel of the Tarentines, sent envoys to Hasdrubal, requesting the privilege of withdrawing undisturbed. When by this feint he had thrown the enemy off their guard, he made a sortie and cut them to pieces.[371]

Gnaeus Pompey, when besieged near Dyrrhachium, not only released his own men from blockade, but also made a sally at an opportune time and place; for just as Caesar was making a fierce assault on a fortified position surrounded by a double line of works, Pompey, by this sortie, so enveloped him with a cordon of troops that Caesar incurred no slight peril and loss, caught as he was between those whom he was besieging and those who had surrounded him from the outside.[372]

Flavius Fimbria, when fighting in Asia near the river Rhyndacus against the son of Mithridates, constructed two lines of works on his flanks and a ditch in front, and kept his soldiers quietly within their entrenchments, until the cavalry of the enemy passed within the confined portions of his fortifications. Then, making a sortie, he slew six thousand of them.[373]

When the forces of Titurius Sabinus and Cotta, Caesar's lieutenants in Gaul, had been wiped out by Ambiorix, Caesar was urged by Quintus Cicero, who was himself also under siege, to come with two legions to his

---

369 251 B.C. Cf. Polyb. I.40.
370 181 B.C. Cf. Livy XL.25, 27 28.
371 212 /209 B.C.
372 48 B.C. Cf. Caes. B.C. iii.65 70.
373: 85 B.C.

relief. The enemy then turned upon Caesar, who feigned fear and kept his troops within his camp, which he had purposely constructed on a smaller scale than usual. The Gauls, already counting on victory, and beginning to press forward as though to plunder the camp, began to fill up the ditches and to tear down the ramparts. Caesar, therefore, as the Gauls were not equipped for battle, suddenly sent forth his own troops from all quarters and cut the enemy to pieces.[374]

When Titurius Sabinus was fighting against a large force of Gauls, he kept his troops within their fortifications, and thus produced upon the Gauls the impression that he was afraid. To further this impression, he sent a deserter to state that the Roman army was in despair and was planning to flee. Spurred on by the hope of victory thus offered, the Gauls loaded themselves with wood and brush with which to fill the trenches, and at top speed started for the Roman camp, which was pitched on the top of an elevation. From there, Titurius launched all his forces against them, killing many of the Gauls and receiving large numbers in surrender.[375]

As Pompey was about to assault the town of Asculum, the inhabitants exhibited on the ramparts a few aged and feeble men. Having thus thrown the Romans off their guard, they made a sortie and put them to flight.[376]

When the Numantines were blockaded, they did not even draw up a line of battle in front of the entrenchments, but kept so closely within the town that Popilius Laenas was emboldened to attack it with scaling-ladders. Suspecting a ruse, since not even then was resistance offered, he recalled his men; whereupon the Numantines made a sortie and attacked the Romans in the rear as they were climbing down.[377]

---

[374] 54 B.C. Cf. Caes. B. G. V.37 52; Dio XL.10; Polyaen. VIII.XXIII.7.
[375] 56 B.C. Cf. Caes. B. G. III.17 19.
[376] none here but the aged and infirm: 90 B.C.
[377] : 138 B.C.

XVIII. Concerning Steadfastness on the Part of the Besieged

When Hannibal was encamped near the walls of the Romans, in order to exhibit their confidence, they sent troops out by a different gate to reinforce the armies which they had in Spain.[378]

The land on which Hannibal had his camp was vacant owing to the death of the owner, the Romans bid the price up to the figure at which the property had sold before the war.

When the Romans were besieged by Hannibal and were themselves besieging Capua, they passed a decree not to recall their army from the latter place until it was captured.[379]

---

[378] 211 B.C. Cf. Livy XXVI.11; Val. Max. III.VII.10.

[379] The Romans mandate by law the taking of Capua: 211 B.C. Cf. Livy XXVI.I.7 8.

Book IV - Stratagems[380]

Having collected examples of stratagems from extensive readings, while arranging these at no small pains, in order to fulfill the promise of my three books (if only I have fulfilled it), in the current book I shall set forth those instances which seemed to fall less naturally under the former classification (which was limited to special types), and which are illustrations of military science in general rather than of stratagems. Inasmuch as these incidents, though famous, belong to a different subject,[381] I have given them separate treatment, for fear that if any persons should happen in reading to run across some of them, they might be led by the resemblance to imagine that these examples had been overlooked by me. As supplementary material, of course, these topics called for treatment. In presenting them, I shall endeavor to observe the following categories:

I.   On Discipline
II. On the effect of Discipline
III. On Restraint and Disinterestedness
IV. On Justice
V.   On Determination ("the will to victory")
VI. On Good Will and Moderation
VII. On Sundry Maxims and Devices

---

[380] There is some question about the authenticity of this document to Frontius, but it has been associated with these books for some time. We have included it with that caveat.
[381] A different subject: That is, different from the class of stratagems proper.

Roman Legionnaires 1st Century AD (Bilder Atlas)

I. On Discipline

When the Roman army was camped outside of Numantia it became demoralized by the lack of discipline of previous commanders. Publius Scipio reformed it by dismissing an enormous number of camp-followers and by giving the soldiers to a sense of responsibility through regular daily routine. One of these changes involved the frequent marches which he enforced as part of their regime. He commanded them to carry several days' rations, so that they could became accustomed to enduring cold and rain, and to the fording of streams. The general often berated them for their timidity and indolence; often he broke utensils which only served the purpose of self-indulgence and were quite unnecessary for campaigning. A notable instance of this severity occurred in the case of the tribune Gaius Memmius, to whom Scipio is said to have exclaimed: "To me you will be worthless merely for a certain period; to yourself and the state forever!"[382]

When discipline had similarly lapsed during the Jugurthine War,[383] Quintus Metellus, restored it by like severity, while he additionally forbidden the soldiers to use meat, except when baked or boiled.[384]

Pyrrhus is said to have remarked to his recruiting officer: "You pick out the big men! I'll make them brave."

In the consulship of Lucius Paulus and Gaius Varro, soldiers were for the first time compelled to take the iusiurandum. Up to that time, the sacramentum was the oath of allegiance administered to them by the tribunes, but they used to pledge each other not to quit the force by flight, or in consequence of fear, and not to leave the ranks except to seek a weapon, strike a foe, or save a comrade.[385]

---

[382] 134 B.C. Cf. Val. Max. II.VII.1; Livy Per. 57; Polyaen. VIII.XVI.2.and Plut. Apophth. Rom., Scip. Min. 17.

[383] 109 B.C. Cf. Val. Max. II.VII.2; Sall. Jug. 45. Polyaen. VIII.XVI.2 and Plut. Apophth. Scip. Min. 16 attribute this to Scipio.

[384] No meat except baked or boiled: The point of the prohibition is not obvious to the modern sense. As unlikely as it seems today, Frontinus tells of one instance in which troops ran amok and stuffed themselves on raw meat, or at least very under-done, with unhappy results.

[385] soldiers required to take the ius iurandum: 216 B.C. Cf. Livy XXII.38. Up to the time of the Battle of Cannae, there were two military oaths, the sacramentum, which was compulsory and was administered by the consul when the soldier first enlisted, and the ius iurandum, a voluntary oath taken before a tribune when the soldiers were assigned to separate divisions. In 216 the two were united, and thereafter the ius iurandum, administered by the military tribune, was compulsory. The facts here stated are slightly at variance with the general understanding.

Scipio Africanus, noticed the shield of a certain soldier rather elaborately decorated, said he did not wonder that the man had adopted it with such care, seeing that he put more trust in it than in his sword.[386]

When Philip was organizing his first army, he forbade anyone to use a carriage. He permitted the cavalrymen to have but one attendant apiece and allowed one servant for every ten infantrymen, who was detailed to carry the mills and ropes.[387] When the troops marched out to summer quarters, he commanded each man to carry flour on his shoulders for thirty days.

Gaius Marius had his soldiers fasten their utensils and food up in bundles and hang these on forked poles, in order to make the burden easier and limit the number of pack animals, this also kept the march of the army from being hampered. This created the expression, "Marius's mules".[388]

When Theagenes, the Athenian, was leading his troops towards Megara and his men inquired as to their place in the ranks, he told them he would assign them their places when they arrived at their destination. Then he secretly sent the cavalry ahead and commanded them, in the guise of enemies, to turn back and attack their comrades. When this plan was carried out and the men whom he had with him made preparations for an encounter with the foe, he permitted the battle-line to be drawn up in such a way that a man took his place where he wished, the most cowardly retiring to the rear, the bravest rushing to the front. He thereupon assigned to each man, for the campaign, the same position in which he had found him.[389]

Lysander, the Spartan, once flogged a soldier who had left the ranks while on the march. When the man said that he had not left the line for the purpose of pillage, Lysander retorted, "I won't have you look as if you were going to pillage."

Antigonus, hearing that his son had taken lodgings at the house of a woman who had three handsome daughters, said: "I hear, son, that your lodgings are cramped, owing to the number of mistresses in charge of your house. Get roomier quarters." Having commanded his son to move, he issued an edict that no one under fifty years of age should take lodgings with the mother of a family.[390]

---

[386] 134 B.C. Cf. Livy Per. 57; Plut. Apophth. Scip. Min. 18; Polyaen. VIII.XVI.3,4.
[387] The mills were for grinding corn.° The allusion to the ropes is not clear.
[388] Cf. Fest. Paul. 24, 2; 148, 6.
[389] Polyaen. V.XXVIII.1 attributes this to Theognis; in III.IX.10, he attributes it to Iphicrates.
[390] 323/ 321 B.C. Cf. Plut. Demetr. 23, Apophth. Antig. 5

The consul Quintus Metellus, although not prevented by law from having his son with him as a regular tent-mate, yet preferred to have him serve in the ranks.[391]

The consul Publius Rutilius, though he might by law have kept his son in his own tent, made him a soldier in the legion.[392]

Marcus Scaurus forbade his son to come into his presence, since he had retreated before the enemy in the Tridentine Pass. Overwhelmed by the shame of this disgrace, the young man committed suicide.[393]

In ancient times, the Romans and other peoples used to make their camps like groups of Punic huts, distributing the troops here and there by cohorts, since the men of that time were not acquainted with the construction of walls, except in the case of cities. Pyrrhus, king of the Epirotes, was the first to inaugurate the custom of concentrating an entire army within the precincts of the same entrenchments. Later, after the Romans, defeated Pyrrhus on the Arusian Plains near the city of Maleventum,[394] they captured his camp, and, noting its plan, gradually came to the arrangement which is in vogue today.[395]

One time, when Publius Nasica was in winter-quarters, he was determined that his troops might not become demoralized by idleness, or inflict harm on their allies in consequence of the license resulting from leisure, ordered them to construct ships, although he had no need of them.[396]

Marcus Cato handed down the story that, when soldiers were caught in theft, their right hands used to be cut off in the presence of their comrades; or if the authorities wished to impose a lighter sentence, the offender was bled at headquarters.[397]

---

[391] 143 (?) 109 (?) B.C. Sall. Jug. lxiv.4 says that Metellus Numidicus kept his son with him as tent-mate.

[392] 105 B.C.

[393] 102 B.C. Cf. Val. Max. V.VIII.4.

[394] The modern Benevento. Pyrrhus was defeated here in 275 B.C.

[395] Cf. Livy XXXV.14. Plut. Pyrrh. 16 represents Pyrrhus, on the other hand, marveling at the arrangement of the Roman camp.

[396] 194/ 193 B.C.

[397] Gell. X.VIII.1 gives an interesting conjecture as to the origin of this second punishment.

The Spartan general, Clearchus, used to tell his troops that their commander ought to be feared more than the enemy, meaning that the death they feared in battle was doubtful, but that execution for desertion was certain.[398]

Appius Claudius, requested the Senate degrade those knights to the status of foot-soldiers who had been captured and afterwards sent back by Pyrrhus, king of the Epirotes, while the foot-soldiers were degraded to the status of light-armed troops, all being commanded to tent outside the fortifications of the camp until each man should bring in the spoils of two foes.[399]

The consul Otacilius Crassus ordered those who had been sent under the yoke by Hannibal and had then returned, to camp outside the entrenchments, in order that they might become used to dangers while without defenses, and so grow more daring against the enemy.[400]

In the consulship of Publius Cornelius Nasica and Decimus Junius, those who had deserted from the army were condemned to be scourged publicly with rods and then to be sold into slavery.[401]

When Domitius Corbulo, was in Armenia, he ordered two squadrons and three cohorts, which had retreated from the enemy near the fortress of Initia, to camp outside the entrenchments, until by steady work and successful raids they should atone for their disgrace.[402]

Out of extreme necessity the consul Aurelius Cotta, ordered the knights to participate in a certain work and a part of them renounced his authority. He made a complaint before the censors and had the mutineers degraded. He then convinced the senators to make sure that arrears of their wages should not be paid. The tribunes of the plebs also carried through a bill with the people on the same matter, so that discipline was maintained by the joint action of all.[403]

---

[398] 431 401 B.C. Cf. Val. Max. II.VII.extr.2; Xen. Anab. II.VI.10.

[399] 279 B.C. Cf. Val. Max. II.VII.15; Eutrop. II.13.

[400] Manius Otacilius Crassus was consul in 263 and 246 B.C. Titus Otacilius Crassus was consul in 261 B.C.

[401] 138 B.C. Cf. Livy Per. 55.

[402] 58 59 A.D. Cf. Tac. Ann. XIII.36.

[403] 252 B.C. Val. Max. II.IX.7 cites a somewhat similar case of discipline.

When Quintus Metellus Macedonicus was campaigning in Spain on one occasion when five cohorts gave way before the enemy, so he commanded the soldiers to make their wills, and then sent them back to recover the lost ground, threatening that they should not be received in camp except after victory.[404]

The Senate ordered the consul Publius Valerius to lead the army, which had been defeated near the river Siris, to Saepinum, to construct a camp there, and to spend the winter under canvas.[405]

The legions which refused to serve in the Punic War[406] were sent into a kind of banishment in Sicily, and by vote of the Senate, they were put on barley rations for seven years.[407]

Because Gaius Titius, commander of a cohort, had retreated before some runaway slaves, Lucius Piso ordered him to stand in the headquarters of the camp daily, barefooted, with the belt of his toga cut and his tunic undone, and wait till the night-watchmen came. He also commanded that the culprit should forgo banquets and baths[408].

Sulla ordered a cohort and its centurions, whose defenses the enemy had broken, to stand continuously at headquarters, wearing helmets and without uniforms.

When Domitius Corbulo was campaigning in Armenia, a certain Aemilius Rufus, a praefect of cavalry, gave way before the enemy. On discovering that Rufus had kept his squadron inadequately equipped with weapons, Corbulo directed the lictors to strip the clothes from his back, and ordered the culprit to stand at headquarters in this unseemly plight until he should be released.[409]

When Atilius Regulus was crossing from Samnium to Luceria and his troops turned away from the enemy whom they had encountered, Regulus blocked their retreat with a cohort as they fled, and ordered them to be cut to pieces as deserters.[410]

---

[404] 143 B.C. Cf. Val. Max. II.VII.10; Vell. II.5.
[405] 280 B.C. Publius Valerius Laevinus.

[406] legions refusing to serve in the Punic War: In the Second Punic War, after Cannae.
[407] Cf. Liv XXIV.18. The substitution of barley for wheat rations was a common form of punishment
[408] 133 B.C. Cf. Val. Max. II.VII.9.
[409] 58 /59 A.D.
[410] 294 B.C. Cf. II.VIII.11 and note.

When the consul Cotta was in Sicily, he flogged a certain Valerius, a noble military tribune belonging to the Valerian gens.[411]

When the same Cotta, was about to cross over to Messana to take part in the auspices afresh ceremony, he placed Publius Aurelius who was connected with him by ties of blood, in charge of the blockade of the Liparian Islands. When Aurelius's line of works was burned and his camp captured, Cotta had him scourged with rods and ordered him to be reduced to the ranks and to perform the tasks of a common soldier.[412]

The censor Fulvius Flaccus, removed his own brother Fulvius from the Senate, because the latter had disbanded the legion in which he was tribune of the soldiers without the command of the consul.[413]

On one occasion Marcus Cato, lingered on a hostile shore for several days, finally giving the signal for departure three times before setting sail, when a certain soldier, who had been left behind, cried and gestured from the land, begging to be picked up. Cato turned his whole fleet back to the shore, arrested the man, and commanded him to be put to death, preferring to make an example of the fellow than to have him ignominiously put to death by the enemy.[414]

If men quit their places in the line, Appius Claudius picked out every tenth man by lot and had him clubbed to death.

In the case of two legions which had retreated in the face of the enemy, the consul Fabius Rullus, chose men by lot and beheaded them in the sight of their comrades.

Aquilius beheaded three men from each of the centuries whose position had been broken through by the enemy.

When fire had been set to his line of works by the enemy, Marcus Antonius decimated the soldiers of two cohorts who were on the works at the time, and punished the centurions of each cohort. Besides this, he dismissed the commanding officer in disgrace, and ordered the rest of the legion to be put on barley rations.[415]

---

[411] 252 B.C.
[412] Cf. Val. Max. II.VII.4.
[413] 174 B.C. Cf. Val. Max. II.VII.5; Livy XL.41, XLI.27; Vell. I.X.6.
[414] 471 B.C. Cf. Livy II.59; Dionys. IX.50; Zonar. VII.17.
[415] 36 B.C. Cf. Plut. Ant. 39.

When a legion plundered the city of Rhegium without the orders its commander was punished as follows: four thousand men were put under guard and executed. Moreover, by decree the Senate made it a crime to bury any one of these or indulge in mourning for them.[416]

The dictator Lucius Papirius Cursor demanded that Fabius Rullus, his master of the horse, be scourged, and was on the point of beheading him, because he had engaged in battle against orders — even though he was successfully in his actions. Even in the face of the efforts and pleas of his soldiers, Papirius refused to renounce his purpose of punishment, actually following Rullus when he fled for refuge to Rome, and even there not abandoning his threats of execution until Fabius and his father fell at the knees of Papirius, and the Senate and people alike joined in their petition.[417]

Manlius, to whom the name "The Masterful" was afterwards given, had his own son scourged and beheaded in the sight of the army, because, even though he came out victorious, he had engaged in battle with the enemy contrary to the orders of his father.[418]

When the army was preparing to mutiny in his behalf against his father, the younger Manlius said that no one was of such importance that discipline will be destroyed on his account, and so induced his comrades to suffer him to be punished.

Quintus Fabius Maximus cut off the right hands of deserters.[419]

---

[416] the plundering legion: When Pyrrhus was in southern Italy, the people of Rhegium applied to Rome for assistance, and the Romans sent them a garrison of four thousand soldiers, levied among the Latin colonies in Campania. In 279 these troops seized the town, killed or expelled the male inhabitants, and took possession of the women and children. Cf. Livy XXVIII.28; Val. Max. II.VII.15; Polyb. I.VII.6 13; Oros.IV.III.3 5.

[417] 325 B.C. Cf. Livy VIII.29 ff.; Val. Max. II.VII.8, III.II.9; Eutr. II.8

[418] 340 B.C. Cf. Livy VIII.7; Val. Max. II.VII.6; Sall. Cat. 52; Cic. de Fin. I.VII.23, de Off. III.XXXI.112. The father, Titus Manlius Torquatus, was the son of Lucius Manlius, dictator in 363, who had also received the cognomen Imperiosus on account of his severity.

[419] 142 140 B.C. Quintus Fabius Maximus Servilianus. Cf. Val. Max. II.VII.11; Oros. V.IV.12.

When the consul Gaius Curio was campaigning near Dyrrhachium in the war against the Dardani,[420] one of the five legions mutinied, refusing to serve and declared it would not follow his rash leadership on a difficult and dangerous enterprise. He led out four legions in arms and ordered them to take their stand in the ranks with weapons drawn, as if in battle. Then he commanded the mutinous legion to advance without arms, and forced its members to strip for work and cut straw under the eyes of armed guards. The following day, in like manner, he compelled them to strip and dig ditches, and by no entreaties of the legion could he be induced to renounce his purpose of withdrawing its standards, abolishing its name, and distributing its members to fill out other legions.

In the consulship of Quintus Fulvius and Appius Claudius, the soldiers, who after the battle of Cannae had been banished to Sicily by the Senate, petitioned the consul Marcellus to be led to battle. Marcellus consulted the Senate, who declared it was not their pleasure that the public welfare should be trusted to those who had proved disloyal. Yet they empowered Marcellus to do what seemed best to him, provided none of the soldiers should be relieved of duty, honored with a gift or reward, or conveyed back to Italy, so long as there were any Carthaginians in the country.[421]

When Marcus Salinator, was ex-consul he was condemned by the people because he had not divided the booty equally among his soldiers.[422]

When the consul Quintus Petilius had been killed in battle by the Ligurians, the Senate decreed that that legion in whose ranks the consul had been slain should, as a whole, be reported "deficient";[423] that its year's pay should be withheld, and its wages reduced.[424]

---

[420] According to Livy Per. 92, 95 and Eutrop. VI.2, Curio was proconsul when he carried on this campaign in 75 B.C.

[421] 212 B.C. Cf. Livy XXV.5 7; Val. Max. II.VII.15; Plut. Marc. 13. Marcellus was proconsul, not consul. Cf. Livy XXVI.1.

[422] 218 B.C. Cf. Livy XXVII.34, XXIX.37.

[423] "Deficient": The term infrequens was technically applied to soldiers who were absent from or irregular in attendance on their duties.

[424] 176 B.C. Cf. Livy XLI.18; Val. Max. II.VII.15.

II. On the Effect of Discipline

During the Civil War, the armies of Brutus and Cassius were marching together through Macedonia; the story goes that the army of Brutus arrived first at a stream which had to be bridged, but that the troops of Cassius were the first in constructing the bridge and in effecting a passage. This rigorous discipline made Cassius's men superior to those of Brutus not only in constructing military works, but also in the general conduct of the war.[425]

When Gaius Marius had the option of choosing a force from two armies, one of which had served under Rutilius, the other under Metellus and later under himself, he preferred the troops of Rutilius, though fewer in number, because he deemed them of trustier discipline.[426]

By improving discipline, Domitius Corbulo withstood the Parthians with a force of only two legions and a very few auxiliaries.[427]

Alexander of Macedon conquered the world, in the face of innumerable forces of enemies, by means of forty thousand men long accustomed to discipline under his father Philip.[428]

In his war against the Persians, Cyrus overcame incalculable difficulties with a force of only fourteen thousand armed men.[429]

With four thousand men, of whom only four hundred were cavalry, Epaminondas, the Theban leader, conquered a Spartan army of twenty-four thousand infantry and sixteen hundred cavalry.[430]

A hundred thousand barbarians under Artaxerxes were defeated in battle by fourteen thousand Greeks assisting Cyrus.[431]

---

[425] 42 B.C.

[426] 104 B.C.

[427] 55 59 A.D. Cf. Tac. Ann. XIII.8, 35.

[428] 334 B.C. Cf. Livy XXXV.14; Justin. XI.6; Plut. Alex. 15. The numbers vary in the different authors.

[429] 401 B.C. Cf. IV.II.7; Xen. Anab. I.II.9; Plut. Artax. 6; Diodor. XIV.XIX.6

[430] 371 B.C. Battle of Leuctra. Diodor. XV.52 ff. and Plut. Pelop. 20 give different numbers.

[431] A few thousand disciplined Greeks better than hordes of Persians: Battle of Cunaxa. Cf. IV.II.5.

The same fourteen thousand Greeks, having lost their generals in battle, returned unharmed through difficult and unknown places; the management of their retreat was committed to by one person, Xenophon, the Athenian.[432]

When Xerxes was stymied by the three hundred Spartans at Thermopylae and difficulty in destroying them, he declared that he had been deceived, because, while he had numbers enough, yet he had none that adhered to discipline.[433]

---

[432] Discipline pulls a Greek army thru a long trek across Asia Minor: Cf. Xen. Anab. III.1 ff.
[433] 480 B.C. In Herod. VII.210, the historian himself, not the king, makes this observation.

III. On Restraint and Disinterestedness

A story goes that Marcus Cato was content with the same wine as the men of his crews.[434]

When Cineas, ambassador of the Epirotes, offered Fabricius a large amount of gold, the latter rejected it, declaring that he preferred to rule those who had gold rather than to have it himself.[435]

Atilius Regulus, though he had been in charge of the greatest enterprises, was so poor that he supported himself, his wife, and children on a small farm which was tilled by a single steward. Hearing of the death of this steward, Regulus wrote to the Senate requesting them to appoint someone to succeed him in the command, since his property was left in jeopardy by the death of his slave, and his own presence at home was necessary.[436]

After Gnaeus Scipio's successful exploits in Spain, he died in the most extreme poverty, not even leaving money enough for a dowry for his daughters. The Senate, therefore, in consequence of their poverty, furnished them dowries at public expense.[437]

The Athenians did the same thing for the daughters of Aristides, who died in the greatest poverty after directing the most important enterprises.[438]

Epaminondas, the Theban general, was a man of such simple habits that among his belongings nothing was found beyond a mat and a single spit.[439]

Hannibal was accustomed to rise while it was still dark, but never took any rest before night. At dusk, and not before, he called his friends to dinner; and not more than two couches[440] were ever filled with dinner guests at his headquarters.[441]

---

[434] Cf. Val. Max. IV.III.11; Plin. H. N. XIV.3,14.°

[435] 280 B.C. Gell. I.14 tells this story of Fabricius; usually it is related of Curius. Cf. Val. Max. IV.III.5; Cic. de Sen. xvi.55; Plut. Apophth. M'. Curii.

[436] 255 B.C. Cf. Val. Max. IV.IV.6; Livy Per. 18; Senec. ad Helv. 12; Apul. Apol. 18.

[437] Other writers, excepting Seneca, speak of but one daughter, and represent the dowry as given when Scipio was warring in Spain, in 218 211 B.C. Cf. Val. Max.IV.IV.10; Sen. Qu. Nat. I.XVII.9; Apul. Apol. 18; Ammian. Marc. XIV.VI.11.

[438] 468 B.C. Cf. Nep. Aristid. 3; Plut. Aristid. 25.

[439] 362 B.C. Cf. Plut. Fab. Max. 27; Nep. Epam. 3.

[440] Not more than two couches: Frontinus has in mind a Roman lectus, or dining-couch, which accommodated three persons.

[441] Cf. Livy XXI.4; Sil. Ital. XII.559 560.

The same general, when serving under Hasdrubal as commander, usually slept on the bare ground, wrapped only in a common military cloak.

The story goes that Scipio Aemilianus used to eat bread offered him as he walked along on the march in the company of his friends. The same story is related of Alexander of Macedon.

In his ninetieth year, Masinissa, used to eat at noon, standing or walking about in front of his tent.[442]

In honor of his defeat of the Sabines, the Senate offered Manius Curius a larger amount of acreage than the discharged troops received, he was content with the allotment of ordinary soldiers, declaring that that man was a bad citizen who was not satisfied with what the rest received.[443]

The restraint of an entire army was also often noteworthy. For example, the troops which served under Marcus Scaurus left a tree laden with fruit, at the far end of the fortified enclosure of the camp, undisturbed .throughout their whole occupation and withdrawal[444].

In the war waged under the auspices of the Emperor Caesar Domitianus Augustus Germanicus, and begun by Julius Civilis in Gaul, the very wealthy city of the Lingones,[445] which had revolted to Civilis, feared that it would be plundered by the approaching army of Caesar. But when, contrary to expectation, the inhabitants remained unharmed and lost none of their property, they returned to their loyalty and handed over to me[446] seventy thousand armed men.[447]

After the capture of Corinth, Lucius Mummius adorned not merely Italy, but also the provinces, with statues and paintings. Yet he refrained so scrupulously from appropriating anything from such vast spoils to his own use that his daughter was in actual need and the Senate furnished her dowry at the public expense.[448]

---

[442] 148 B.C. Cf. Polyb. XXXVI.16; Cic. de Sen. x.34.
[443] Cf. Val. Max. IV.III.5; Plin. H. N. XVIII.4; Plut. Apophth. M'. Curii. Nep. Thras. 4 attributes a somewhat similar reply to Pittacus.
[444] Scaurus' record: For the Memoirs of Scaurus, consul 115 B.C., cf. Val. Max. IV.IV.11; Tac. Agric. 1
[445] city of the Lingones: Civitas Lingonum, today's Langres.
[446] If this is really Frontius, this passage represents personal experiance
[447] 70 A.D. Cf. Introduction, p. xx.
[448] 146 B.C. Cf. Cic. de Off. II.XXII.76; in Verr. I.XXI.55; Plin. H. N. XXXIV.VII.17.

IV. On Justice

When Camillus was besieging the Faliscans, a school teacher took the sons of the Faliscans outside the walls, as though for a walk, and then delivered them up, saying that if they should be retained as hostages, the city would be forced to execute the orders of Camillus. Camillus not only spurned the teacher's perfidy, but tying his hands behind his back, turned him over to the boys to be driven back to their parents with switches. He thus gained by kindness a victory which he had scorned to secure by fraud; for the Faliscans, in consequence of this act of justice, voluntarily surrendered to him.[449]

The physician of Pyrrhus, king of the Epirotes, came to Fabricius, general of the Romans, and promised to give Pyrrhus poison if an adequate reward should be guaranteed him for the service. Fabricius, not considering that victory called for any such crime, exposed the physician to the king, and by this honorable act succeeded in inducing Pyrrhus to seek the friendship of the Romans.[450]

---

[449] 394 B.C. Cf. Val. Max. VI.V.1; Livy V.27; Plut. Camil. 10; Polyaen. VIII.7.
[450] 279 B.C. Cf. Livy Per. 13; Cic. de Off. III.XXII.86; Plut. Pyrrh. 21. Val. Max. VI.V.1 and Gell. III.8 represent Fabricius as disclosing the plot, but not the name of the traitor.

V. On Determination ("The Will to Victory")

When the soldiers of Gnaeus Pompey threatened to plunder the money which was being carried for the triumph, Servilius and Glaucia urged him to distribute it among the troops, in order to avoid the outbreak of a mutiny. Thereupon Pompey declared he would forgo a triumph, and would die rather than yield to the insubordination of his soldiers; and after upbraiding them in vehement language, he threw in their faces the fasces wreathed with laurel, that they might start their plundering by seizing these. Through the odium thus aroused, he reduced his men to obedience.[451]

When a mutiny broke out that ran rampant from the tumult of the Civil War, Gaius Caesar dismissed an entire legion from service, and beheaded the leaders of the mutiny. Later, when the very men he had dismissed entreated him to remove their disgrace, he restored them and had in them the very best soldiers.[452]

When Postumius was ex-consul, he appealed to the courage of his troops, and having been asked by them what commands he gave, told them to imitate him. Thereupon he seized a standard and led the attack on the enemy. His soldiers followed and won the victory.

Having unexpectedly come upon some Gallic troops, Claudius Marcellus turned his horse about in a circle, looking around for a way of escape. Seeing danger on every hand, with a prayer to the gods, he broke into the midst of the enemy. By his amazing audacity, he threw them into consternation, slew their leader,[453] and actually carried away the spolia opima[454] in a situation where there had scarcely remained a hope of saving his life.[455]

After the loss of his army at Cannae, Lucius Paulus, was offered a horse by Lentulus with which to affect his escape, refused to survive the disaster, although it had not been occasioned by him, and remained seated on the rock against which he had leaned when wounded, until he was overpowered and stabbed by the enemy.[456]

---

451 79 B.C. Cf. Plut. Pomp. 14, Apophth. Pomp. 5; Zonar. X.2. There is no mention of Glaucia in this connection elsewhere.

452 49 B.C. Cf. Suet. Caes. 69; Appian B.C. II.47; Dio XLI.26 ff.

453 Their leader: Viridomarius, the Insubrian Gaul.

454 spolia opima: Spoils taken from a victorious commander from the leader of the enemy.

455 222 B.C. Cf. Val. Max. III.II.5; Livy Per. 20; Plut. Marc. 6 ff.; Flor. II.4.

456 216 B.C. Cf. Livy XXII.49.

Paulus's colleague, Varro, showed even greater resolution in continuing alive after the same disaster, and both the Senate and the people alike thanked him "because," they said, "he did not despair of the commonwealth." Throughout the rest of his life he gave proof that he had remained alive not from desire of life, but because of his love of country. He suffered his beard and hair to remain untrimmed and never afterwards reclined when he took food at table. Even when honors were offered him by the people, he declined them, saying that State needed more fortunate magistrates than himself.[457]

After the complete rout of the Romans at Cannae, when Sempronius Tuditanus and Gnaeus Octavius, tribunes of the soldiers, were besieged in the smaller camp,[458] where they urged their comrades to draw their swords and accompany them in a dash through the forces of the enemy. They declared that they themselves were resolved on this course, even if no one else possessed the courage to break through. Although only twelve knights and fifty foot-soldiers were found who had the courage to accompany them, among the wavering crowd to reached Canusium unscathed.[459]

When Gaius Fonteius Crassus was in Spain, he set out with three thousand men on a foraging expedition and was enveloped in an awkward position by Hasdrubal. In the early part of the night, at a time when such a thing was least expected, having communicated his purpose only to the centurions of the first rank, he broke through the pickets of the enemy.

When the consul Cornelius had been caught in an awkward position by the enemy in the Samnite War, Publius Decius, tribune of the soldiers, urged him to send a small force to occupy a neighboring hill, and volunteered to act as leader of those who should be sent. With the enemy's attention in a different direction, the consul was allowed to escape, while Decius was surrounded and besieged. Decius, however, extricated himself from this predicament also by making a sortie at night, and escaped unharmed along with his men and rejoined the consul.[460]

---

[457] Cf. Livy XXII.LXI.14 15; Val. Max. III.IV.4, IV.V.2.

[458] When the Romans reached Cannae, they pitched two camps, the larger one on the N.W. bank of the Aufidus, the smaller on the S.E. bank, about a mile and a quarter apart, according toPolyb. III.CX.10. Before the battle, Hannibal transferred his camp from the east side of the river to the west.

[459] 216 B.C. Cf. Livy XXII.50; Appian Hann. 16. Livy gives the number of those escaping from the smaller camp as six hundred. Appian says ten thousand from the larger camp escaped. One leader only is mentioned by both.

[460] Cf. I.V.14 and note.

Under the consul Atilius Calatinus, the same thing was done by a man whose name is variously reported. Some say he was called Laberius, and some Quintus Caedicius, but most give it as Calpurnius Flamma. This man, seeing that the army had entered a valley which was commanded on all sides by the enemy, He asked and received three hundred soldiers from the consul. After exhorting these to save the army by their valor, he hastened to the center of the valley. To crush him and his followers, the enemy descended on all sides, but, being held in check in a long and fierce battle, they afforded the consul an opportunity of extricating his army.[461]

When Gaius Caesar was about to fight the Germans and their king Ariovistus at a time when his own men had been thrown into panic, he called his soldiers together and declared to the assembly that on that day he proposed to employ the services of the tenth legion alone. In this way, he caused the soldiers of this legion to be stirred by his tribute to their unique heroism, while the rest were overwhelmed with mortification to think that reputation for courage should be confined to others.[462]

When Philip declared he would cut them off from many things, unless the state surrendered to him, a certain Spartan noble asked: "He won't cut us off from dying in defense of our country, will he?"[463]

Leonidas, the Spartan, in reply to the statement that the Persians would create clouds by the multitude of their arrows, was reported to have said: "We shall fight all the better in the shade."[464]

On one occasion when Gaius Aelius, a city praetor, was holding court a woodpecker lighted upon his head. The soothsayers were consulted and answered that, if the bird should be allowed to go, the victory would fall to the enemy, but that, if it were killed, the Roman people would prevail, though Gaius and his whole house would perish. Aelius, however, did not hesitate to kill the woodpecker. The Roman army won the day, but Aelius along with fourteen others of the same family, was slain in battle. Certain authorities do not believe that the man referred to was Gaius Caelius, but a certain Laelius, and that they were Laelii, not Caelii, who perished.[465]

[461] Cf. I.V.15 and note.
[462] Cf. I.XI.3 and note.
[463] Cf. Cic. Tusc. V.XIV.42; Val. Max. VI.IV.ext.4; Plut. Apophth. Lacon. Ignot. 50.
[464] Cf. Cic. Tusc. I.XLII.101; Val. Max. III.VII.ext.8
[465] Cf. Plin. H. N. X.XVIII.20. Val. Max. V.VI.4 says that the Aelian family lost seventeen members at the battle of Cannae. The last sentence of this paragraph is undoubtedly an interpolation.

Two Romans bearing the name Publius Decius, first the father, later the son sacrificed their lives to save the State during their tenure of office. By spurring their horses against the foe they won victory for their country.[466]

When waging war against Aristonicus in Asia somewhere between Elaea and Myrina, Publius Crassus fell into the hands of the enemy and was being led away alive. Scorning the thought of captivity for a Roman consul, he used the stick, with which he had urged on his horse, to gouge out the eye of the Thracian by whom he was held captive. The Thracian, infuriated with the pain, stabbed him to death. Thus, as he desired, Crassus escaped the disgrace of servitude.[467]

Marcus, son of Cato the Censor, fell off his horse which had stumbled in battle. Cato picked himself up, but noticing that his sword had slipped out of its scabbard and fearing disgrace, went back among the enemy, and though he received a number of wounds, finally recovered his sword and made his way back to his comrades.[468]

When the inhabitants of Petelia were blockaded by the Carthaginians, they sent away the children and the aged, on account of the shortage of food. They supported their lives on hides, moistened and then dried by the fire, on leaves of trees, and on all sorts of animals, which sustained them during the siege for eleven months.[469]

When the Spaniards were blockaded at Consabra, they endured all these same hardships; neither did they surrender the town to Hirtuleius.[470]

The story is told that when the inhabitants of Casilinum, were blockaded by Hannibal, suffered such shortage of food that a mouse was sold for two hundred denarii,[471] and that the man who sold it died of starvation, while the purchaser lived. Yet the inhabitants persisted in maintaining their loyalty to the Romans.[472]

---

[466] 340 & 295 B.C. Cf. Val. Max. V.VI.5, 6; Cic. de Fin. II.XIX.61, and frequently; Livy VIII.9, X.28.

[467] Crassus escapes the disgrace of servitude: 130 B.C. Crassus was proconsul at the time of his death. Cf. Val. Max. III.II.12; Flor. II.XX.4 5; Oros. V.x.1 4.

[468] Marcus Cato's sword: 168 BCE (alternatively 172 BCE) Battle of Pydna. Cf. Val. Max. III.II.16; Justin. XXXIII.2. Plut. Aemil. 21 gives a slightly different story.

[469] The resolve of the inhabitants of Petelia: 216 B.C. Cf. Livy XXIII.20, 30; Val. Max. VI.VI.ext.2; Appian Hann. 29.

[470] The resolve of the inhabitants of Consabra: 79 75 B.C.

[471] two hundred denarii: about $4,00 in modern value

[472] The mouse of Casilinum: 216 B.C. Cf. Val. Max. VII.VI.2, 3; Plin. H. N. VIII.LVII.82 Livy XXIII.19

When Mithridates was besieging Cyzicus, he paraded the captives from that city and exhibited them to the besieged, thinking thus to force the people of the town to surrender, through compassion for their fellows. However, the townspeople urged the prisoners to meet death with heroism, and persisted in maintaining their loyalty to the Romans.[473]

Viriathus proposed to send them the inhabitants of Segovia back their wives and children, but they preferred to witness the execution of their loved ones rather than to fail the Romans.[474]

The inhabitants of Numantia preferred to lock the doors of their houses and die of hunger rather than surrender.[475]

---

[473] The resolve of the Cyzicenes: 74 B.C. Cf. Appian Mith. 73.
[474] The resolve of the Segovians: 147 139 B.C.
[475] The resolve of the Numantians: 133 B.C. Cf. Livy Per. 59; Val. Max. III.II.ext.7, VII.VI.ext.2; Sen. de Ira i.11.

VI. On Good Will and Moderation

Quintus Fabius,[476] was urged by his son to seize an advantageous position at the expense of losing a few men, asked: "Do you want to be one of those few?"

Xenophon happened to be on horseback and had just ordered the infantry to take possession of a certain eminence, when he heard one of the soldiers muttering that it was an easy matter for a mounted man to order such difficult enterprises. At this Xenophon leaped down and set the man from the ranks on his horse, while he himself hurried on foot with all speed to the eminence he had indicated. The soldier, unable to endure the shame of this performance, voluntarily dismounted amid the jeers of his comrades. It was with difficulty, however, that the united efforts of the troops induced Xenophon to mount his horse and to restrict his energies to the duties which devolved upon a commander.[477]

When Alexander was marching at the head of his troops one winter's day, he sat down by a fire and began to review the troops as they passed by. Noticing a certain soldier who was almost dead with the cold, he bade him sit in his place, adding: "If you had been born among the Persians, it would be a capital crime for you to sit on the king's seat; but since you were born in Macedonia, that privilege is yours.[478]

When the Deified Vespasianus Augustus learned that a certain youth, of good birth, but ill adapted to military service, had received a high appointment because of his straitened circumstances, Vespasian settled a sum of money on him, and gave him an honorable discharge.

---

[476] Cf. Sil. Ital. VII.539 ff. Plut. Apophth. Caec. Metell. relates a similar reply of Metellus.
[477] 401 B.C. Cf. Xen. Anab. III.IV.44 49.
[478] Cf. Val. Max. V.I.ext.1; Curt. VIII.IV.15 17.

VII. On Sundry Maxims and Devices

Gaius Caesar used to say that he followed the same policy towards the enemy as did many doctors when dealing with the physical ailments; namely, that of conquering the foe by hunger rather than by steel.[479]

Domitius Corbulo used to say that the pick was the weapon with which to beat the enemy.

Lucius Paulus used to say that a general ought to be an old man in character, meaning thereby that moderate counsels should be followed.[480]

When people said that Scipio Africanus lacked aggressiveness, he is reported to have answered: "My mother bore me a general, not a warrior."

When a Teuton challenged Gaius Marius and called upon him to come forth, Marius answered that if the man was desirous of death, he could end his life with a halter. Then, when the fellow persisted, Marius confronted him with a gladiator of despicable size, whose life was almost spent, and told the Teuton that, if he would first defeat this gladiator, he himself would then fight with him.

After Quintus Sertorius learned by experience that he was by no means a match for the whole Roman army, and wished to prove this to the barbarians also, who were rashly demanding battle, he brought two horses into their presence; one very strong, the other very feeble. Then, he brought up two youths of corresponding physique; one robust, the other slight. The stronger youth was commanded to pull out the entire tail of the feeble horse, while the slight youth was commanded to pull out the hairs of the strong horse, one by one. Then, when the slight youth had succeeded in his task, while the strong one was still struggling vainly with the tail of the weak horse, Sertorius observed: "By this illustration I have exhibited to you, my men, the nature of the Roman cohorts. They are invincible to him who attacks them in a body; yet he who assails them by groups will tear and rend them."[481]

---

479 Cf. Veget. III.26; Appian Hisp. 87.
480 Cf. Livy XLIV.36; Gell. XIII.III.6; Plut. Apophth. Aemil. 5.
481 This was previously mentioned in Book 1

The consul Valerius Laevinus, caught a spy within his camp, and having entire confidence in his own forces, ordered the man to be led around. He did this for the sake of terrifying the enemy; his army was open to inspection by the spies of the enemy, as often as they wished.[482]

Caedicius wasa centurion of the first rank, who acted as leader in Germany, when, after the Varian disaster,[483] the Romans were beleaguered, as well as afraid that the barbarians would bring up to the fortifications the wood which they had gathered, and set fire to his camp. He therefore pretended to be in need of fuel, and sent out men in every direction to steal it. In this way he caused the Germans to remove the whole supply of felled trees.[484]

In a naval battle, Gnaeus Scipio had jars filled with pitch and rosin among the vessels of the enemy, in order that damage might result both from the weight of the missiles and from the scattering of their contents, which would serve as fuel for a conflagration.

Hannibal suggested to King Antiochus that he hurl jars filled with vipers among the ships of the enemy, in order to cause fear among the crews to keep them from fighting and from performing their nautical duties.[485]

Prusias did the same, when his fleet was in the brink of retreating.[486]

Marcus Porcius Cato boarded the ships of the enemy and drove the Carthaginians from them. Then, having distributed their weapons and insignia among his own men, he sank many enemy ships by deceiving them with their own equipment.

Inasmuch as the Athenians had been subject to repeated attacks by the Spartans, on one occasion, in the course of a festival which they were celebrating outside the city in honor of Minerva, they studiously affected the role of worshippers, with weapons concealed beneath their clothing. When the ceremony was over, they did not immediately return to Athens, but marched at once upon Sparta at a time when they were least feared, and devastated the lands of an enemy whose victims they had often been.

---

[482] 280 B.C. Cf. Eutrop. II.11; Zonar. VIII.3. Livy XXX.29, Appian Pun. 39 and Polyaen. VIII.XVI.8 attributes° a similar stratagem to Scipio.
[483] The Varian disaster: The defeat of Varus by Arminius in the Teutoburg Forest in 9 A.D.
[484] Cf. Vell. II.120.
[485] Justin. XXXII.4 and Nep. Hann. 10 represent Hannibal as suggesting this device to Prusias.
[486] 48 B.C. Cf. Caes. B.C. III.101

Cassius set fire to some transports which were of no great use for anything else, and sent them with a fair wind against the fleet of the enemy, destroying it with fire.

When Marcus Livius routed Hasdrubal, and certain persons urged him to pursue the enemy to annihilation, he answered: "Let some survive to carry the tidings of our victory to the enemy!"[487]

Scipio Africanus used to say that a road not only ought to be afforded the enemy for flight, but that it ought to be paved.[488]

Paches, the Athenian, declared on one occasion that the enemy would be spared, if they put aside their steel. When they had all complied with these terms, by placing aside their weapons he ordered the entire number to be executed, since they had steel brooches on their cloaks.[489]

When Hasdrubal had invaded the territory of the Numidians with the purpose of subduing them, and they were preparing to resist, he declared that he had come to capture elephants, an animal in which Numidia abounds. For this privilege they demanded money, and Hasdrubal promised to pay it. Having by these representations thrown them off the scent, he attacked them and brought them under his power.

In order to more easily make a surprise attack on a supply convoy of the Thebans, Alcetas, the Spartan, got ready his ships in a secret place and exercised his rowers by turns on a single galley, as though that was all he had. Then at a designated time, as the Theban vessels were sailing past, he sent all his ships against them and captured their supplies.[490]

When Ptolemy fought with a weak force against Perdiccas's powerful army, he arranged for a few horsemen to drive along animals of all sorts, with brush fastened to their backs for them to trail behind them. He himself went ahead with the forces which he had. As a consequence, the dust raised by the animals produced the appearance of a mighty army following, and the enemy, terrified by this impression, was defeated.[491]

---

[487] Marcus Livius leaves a few enemies alive: 207 B.C. Cf. Livy XXVII.49. The Parthians did the same to the Romans in 54 B.C., Plut. Crassus, 28,

[488] Scipio Africanus' paved road: Cf. Veget. III.21.

[489] Paches' steel: Thuc. III.34 and Polyaen. III.2 cite another instance of the cunning treachery of Paches in 427 B.C.

[490] Alcetas' single galley: 377 B.C. Cf. Polyaen. II.7. Caes. B.C. III.24 relates a similar stratagem employed by Antony.

[491] Ptolemy's dust-raising animals: 321 B.C. Cf. Polyaen. IV.19. Front. II.IV.1 relates a somewhat similar device of Papirius Cursor.

Myronides, the Athenian, was about to fight on an open plain against the Thebans, who were very strong in cavalry, and warned his troops that if they stood their ground, there was some hope of safety; however, if they gave way, destruction was absolutely certain. In this way, he encouraged his men and won the victory.[492]

When Gaius Pinarius was in charge of the garrison of Henna in Sicily, the magistrates of the city demanded the keys of the gates, which he had in his keeping. Suspecting that they were preparing to go over to the Carthaginians, he asked for the space of a single night to consider the matter; and, revealing to his soldiers the treachery of the Greeks, he instructed them to get ready and wait for his signal on the morrow. At daybreak, in the presence of his troops, he announced to the people of Henna that he would surrender the keys, if all the inhabitants of the town should be agreed in their view. When the entire populace assembled in the theatre to settle this matter, and, with the obvious purpose of revolting, made the same demand, Pinarius gave the signal to his soldiers and murdered all the people of Henna.[493]

The Athenian general, Iphicrates, once rigged up his fleet in the style of the enemy, and sailed away to a certain city whose people he viewed with suspicion. Being welcomed with unrestrained enthusiasm, he thus discovered their treachery and sacked their town.[494]

When Tiberius Gracchus had proclaimed that he would confer freedom on volunteer slaves that showed great courage, but would crucify the cowards, some four thousand men who had fought rather listlessly, gathered on a fortified hill in fear of punishment. Thereupon, Gracchus sent men to tell them that in his opinion the whole force of volunteer slaves had shared in the victory, since they had routed the enemy. By this expression of confidence, he freed them from their apprehensions and took them back again.[495]

---

[492] Myronides states the odds: 457 B.C. Cf. Polyaen. I.XXXV.2.
[493] 214 B.C. Cf. Livy XXIV.37 39; Polyaen. VIII.21
[494] 390 389 B.C. Cf. Polyaen. III.IX.58.
[495] 214 B.C. Cf. Livy XXIV.14 16

After the battle of Lake Trasimenus, where the Romans suffered great disaster, Hannibal, having brought six thousand of the enemy under his power by virtue of a covenant he had made, generously allowed the allies of the "Latin League"[496] to return to their cities, declaring that he was waging war for the purpose of freeing Italy. As a result, by means of their assistance he received in surrender a number of tribes.[497]

When Locri was blockaded by Crispinus, admiral of the Roman fleet, Mago spread the rumor in the Roman camp that Hannibal had slain Marcellus and was coming to relieve Locri from blockade. Then, secretly sending out cavalry, he commanded them to show themselves on the mountains, which were in view. By doing this, he caused Crispinus, in the belief that Hannibal was at hand, to board his vessels and make off.[498]

Scipio Aemilianus, in the operations before Numantia, distributed archers and slingers not only among all his cohorts, but even among all the centuries.[499]

When Pelopidas, the Theban, had been put to flight by the Thessalians and had crossed the river over which he had constructed an emergency bridge, he ordered his rearguard to burn the bridge, so that it might not serve also as a means of passage to the enemy who were following him.[500]

When the Romans in certain operations were no match for the Campanian cavalry, Quintus Naevius, a centurion in the army of the proconsul Fulvius Flaccus, conceived the plan of picking the men who seemed swiftest of foot and of medium stature from the whole army, arming them with small shields, helmets, and swords, and giving to each man seven spears that were about four feet in length. He attached these men to the cavalry, and commanded them to advance up to the walls, and then, taking their position at that point, to fight amidst the enemy cavalry, when our cavalry retreated. By this means, the Campanians and especially their horses, suffered severely. When these were thrown into confusion, victory became easy for our troops.[501]

---

[496] The "Latin Name": i.e. the Latin League. The cities of Latium were from very early times united in an alliance with Rome. At first this bond was of a political nature, on a basis of perfect equality; later Rome became the leading power and assumed the supremacy.
[497] 217 B.C. Cf. Livy XXII.6, 7, 13; Polyb. III.77, 84 85.
[498] 208 B.C. Cf. Livy XXVII.28.
[499] 133 B.C. Veget. I.15 narrates instances of the important part played in Roman battles by archers and javelin throwers, and emphasizes the necessity of training in archery.
[500] 369 364 B.C.
[501] 211 B.C. Cf. Livy XXVI.4; Val. Max. II.III.3.

Publius Scipio was in Lydia and observed that the army of Antiochus was demoralized by the rain, which fell day and night without cessation, and when he further noted that not only were men and horses exhausted, but that even the bows were rendered useless from the effect of the dampness on their strings, he urged his brother to engage in battle on the following day, although it was consecrated to religious observance. The adoption of this plan was followed by victory.[502]

When Cato was ravaging Spain, the envoys of the Ilergetes, a tribe allied with the Romans, came to him and begged for assistance. Cato, unwilling either to alienate his allies by refusing aid, or to diminish his own strength by dividing his forces, ordered a third part of his soldiers to prepare rations and embark on their ships, directing them to return and to allege head winds as the reason for this action. Meanwhile, the report of approaching aid went on before them, raising the hopes of the Ilergetes, and shattering the plans of the enemy.[503]

In Pompey's army there was a large force of Roman cavalry, which by its skill in arms wrought havoc among the soldiers of Gaius Caesar. The latter ordered his troops to aim with their swords at the faces and eyes of the enemy which forced the enemy to avert their faces and retire.[504]

When the Voccaei were hard pressed by Sempronius Gracchus in a pitched battle, they surrounded their entire force with a ring of carts, which they had filled with their bravest warriors dressed in women's clothes. Sempronius rose up with greater daring to assault the enemy, because he imagined himself proceeding against women, whereupon those in the carts attacked him and put him to flight.[505]

When Eumenes of Cardia, one of the successors of Alexander, was besieged in a certain stronghold, and was unable to exercise his horses, he had them suspended during certain hours each day in such a position that, resting on their hind legs and with their fore feet in the air, they moved their legs till the sweat ran, in their efforts to regain their natural posture.[506]

---

[502] 190 B.C. Cf. Livy XXXVII.37, 39; Flor. II.VIII.17
[503] 195 B.C. Cf. Livy XXXIV.11 13.
[504] 48 B.C. Cf. Plut. Caes. 44 45, Pomp. 69; Polyaen. VIII.XXIII.25.
[505] 179 178 B.C.
[506] 320 B.C. Cf. Nep. Eumen. 5; Plut. Eumen. 11; Diodor. XVIII.42.

Certain barbarians promised Marcus Cato guides for his route of march as well as reinforcements, provided they received a large sum of money, he did not hesitate to make the promise, since, if they won, he could reward them from the spoils of the enemy, while, if they were slain, he would be released from his pledge.[507]

When a certain Statilius, a knight of distinguished record, gave an indication that he might desert to the enemy, Quintus Maximus ordered him to be summoned to his presence, and apologized for not having known until then the real merits of Statilius, owing to the jealousy of his fellow-soldiers. Then, giving Statilius a horse and bestowing a large gift of money besides, he succeeded in sending away rejoicing a man who, when summoned, was conscience-stricken; he succeeded also in securing for the future a loyal and brave knight in place of one whose fealty was in doubt.[508]

Philip,[509] heard that a certain Pythias, an excellent warrior, had become estranged from him because he was too poor to support his three daughters and was not assisted by the king, and having been warned by certain persons to be on his guard against the man, replied: "What! If part of my body were diseased, should I cut it off, rather than give it treatment?" Then, quietly drawing Pythias aside for a confidential talk, and learning the seriousness of his domestic embarrassments, he supplied him with funds, and found in him a better and more devoted adherent than before the estrangement.

After an unsuccessful battle with the Carthaginians, in which he had lost his colleague Marcellus, Titius Quinctius Crispinus, learned that Hannibal was in possession of the ring of the slain hero, and sent letters among all the municipal towns of Italy, warning the inhabitants to give credit to no letters which should be brought sealed with the ring of Marcellus. As a result of this advice, Salapia and other cities were assailed in vain by Hannibal's insidious efforts.[510]

---

[507] 320 B.C. Cf. Nep. Eumen. 5; Plut. Eumen. 11; Diodor. XVIII.42.
[508] Cf. III.XVI.1 and note; Plut. Fab. 20.
[509] Philip: The father of Alexander.
[510]: 208 B.C. Cf. Livy XXVII.28.

After the disaster at Cannae, when the Romans were so terror-stricken that a large part of survivors thought of abandoning Italy with the endorsement of nobles of the highest standing, Publius Scipio, then extremely young, in the very assembly where such a course was being discussed, proclaimed with great vehemence that he would slay whoever refused to declare on oath that he cherished no purpose of abandoning the State with his own hand. Having first bound himself with such an oath, he drew his sword and threatened death to one of those standing near unless he too should take the oath. This man was constrained by fear to swear allegiance; the rest were compelled by the example of the first.[511]

The camp of the Volscians had been pitched near bushes and woods, so Camillus set fire to everything which could carry the flames, once started, up to the very fortifications. In this way, he deprived the enemy of their camp.[512] In the Social War, Publius Crassus was cut off in almost the same way with all his troops.[513]

When Quintus Metellus was about to break camp in Spain and wished to keep his soldiers in line, he proclaimed that he had discovered that an ambush had been laid by the enemy; therefore the soldiers should not quit the standards nor break ranks. Though he had done this merely for purposes of discipline, yet happening to meet with an actual ambuscade, he found his soldiers unafraid, since he had given them warning.[514]

---

[511] 216 B.C. Cf. Livy XXII.53; Val. Max. V.VI.7; Sil. Ital. X.426 ff.
[512] 389 B.C. Cf. Livy VI.II.9 11; Plut. Cam. 34.
[513] Crassus' camp burned down: 90 B.C.
[514] 143 142 B.C.

De Rei Militari (On Military Matters)

By Flavius Vegetius Renatus

Introduction⁵¹⁵

The most influential military treatise in the western world from Roman times to the 19th Century was Vegetius' DE RE MILITARI, which has been translated as "On Military Matters" or "The Military Institutions". Its impressions on our own traditions of discipline and organization are everywhere evident.

As late as 1770, The Austrian Field Marshal, Prince de Ligne called it a golden book and wrote: "A God, said Vegetius, inspired the legion, but for myself, I find that a God inspired Vegetius." Richard Coeur de Lion carried DE RE MILITARI everywhere with him in his campaigns, as did his father, Henry II of England. Around 1000 A. D. Vegetius was the favorite author of Foulques the Black, the able and ferocious Count of Anjou. Numerous manuscript copies of Vegetius circulated in the time of Charlemagne and one of them was considered a necessity of life by his commanders. A manuscript Vegetius was listed in the will of Count Everard de Frejus, about 837 A. D., in the time of Ludwig the Just.

In his Memoirs, Montecuculli, the conqueror of the Turks at St. Gotthard, wrote: "However, there are spirits bold enough to believe themselves great captains as soon as they know how to handle a horse, carry a lance at charge in a tournament, or as soon as they have read the precepts of Vegetius." Such was the reputation of Vegetius for a thousand years.

There are approximately 150 copies of the manuscript copies dating from the 10th to the 15th centuries. DE RE MILITARI was translated into English, French, and Bulgarian before the invention of printing. The first printed edition was made in Utrecht in 1473. It was followed in quick succession by editions in Cologne, Paris and Rome. It was first published in English by Caxton, from an English manuscript copy, in 1489.

---

⁵¹⁵ This introduction is based on a 1940 edition edited by Thomas Phillips

Flavius Vegetius Renatus was a high ranking Roman. In some manuscripts he is given the title of count. Raphael of Volterra calls him a Count of Constantinople. Little is known of his life, but it is apparent from his book that he did not have extensive practical experience as a soldier. He states quite frankly that his purpose was to collect and synthesize the military customs and wisdom from ancient manuscripts and regulations that made ancient Rome great. According to his statement, his principal sources were Cato the Elder, Cornelius Celsus, Paternus, Frontinus, and the regulations and ordinances of Augustus, Trajan and Hadrian.

The Emperor Valentinian, to whom the book is dedicated, is believed to be the second emperor of that name. He evidently was not Valentinian I (364 – 375 AD) since his successor, Gratian, is named in the book. Between the reign of Valentinian II (375-392 AD) and Valentinian III (425 – 455 AD), Rome was taken and burned by Alaric, King of the Goths, an event that unquestionably would have been mentioned had it occurred before the book was written. Vegetius mentions the defeat of the Roman armies by the Goths, but probably refers to the battle of Adrianople (378 AD) where Valens, the colleague of Valentinian I, was killed.

It is a paradox that DE RE MILITARI, which was to become a military bible for innumerable generations of European soldiers, was little used by the Romans for whom it was written. The decay of the Roman armies had progressed too far to be arrested by Vegetius' pleas for a return to the virtues of discipline and courage of the ancients. At the same time Vegetius' hope for a revival of the ancient organization of the legion was impracticable. Cavalry had adopted the armor of the foot soldier and was just commencing to become the principal arm of the military forces. The heavy armed foot-soldier, formerly the backbone of the legion, was falling a victim of his own weight and immobility, and the light-armed infantry, unable to resist the shock of cavalry, was turning more and more to missile weapons. By one of the strange mutations of history, when the cross-bow and gun-powder later deprived cavalry of its shock-power, the tactics of Vegetius again became ideal for armies, as they had been in the times from which he drew his inspiration.

Vegetius unceasingly emphasized the importance of constant drill and severe discipline and this aspect of his work was very tiresome to the soldiers of the middle ages, the feudal system lending itself poorly to discipline. "Victory in war," he states in his opening sentence, "does not depend entirely upon numbers or mere courage; only skill and discipline will insure it." His first book is devoted to the selection, training and discipline of recruits. He insists upon the utmost meticulousness in drill. "No part of drill is more essential in action than for soldiers to keep their ranks with the greatest exactness." His description of the many arms which the Roman soldier was required to become expert in reminds one of the almost innumerable duties of the present day infantryman. Recruits were to be hardened in order to be able to march twenty miles in half a summer's day at ordinary step and twenty-four miles at quick step. It was the ancient regulation that practice marches of this distance must be made three times a month.

The second book deals with the organization and officers of the legion, the ancient system of promotion, and how to form the legion for battle. We find the Romans provided for soldier's deposits, just as is done in the American army today; that guard and duty rosters were kept in those days as now; and that the Roman system of guard duty is only slightly different from our manual for interior guard duty. The field music is described and is an ornamental progenitor of that in use in United States. The legion owed its success, according to Vegetius, to its arms and its machines, as well as to the bravery of its soldiers. The legion had fifty-five ballista for throwing darts and ten onagri, drawn by oxen, for throwing stones. Every legion carried its pontoon equipment, "small boats hollowed out of a single piece of timber, with long cables or chains to fasten them together." In addition were "whatever is necessary for every kind of service, that the encampments may have all the strength and conveniences of a fortified city." Trains of workmen were provided to perform all the duties now performed by the various services in armies.

The third book deals with tactics and strategy and it was this portion of Vegetius that influenced war in the Middle Ages so greatly. He explains the use of reserves, attributing this invention to the Spartans, from whom the Romans adopted it. "It is much better to have several bodies of reserves than to extend your front too much" - an injunction as good today as when it was written. Encircling pursuit is described and terrain is not overlooked. "The nature of the ground is often of more consequence than courage." The enemy should be estimated carefully. "It is essential to know the character of the enemy and of their principal officers-whether they be rash or cautious, enterprising or timid, whether they fight from careful calculation or from chance."

Vegetius' work is filled with maxims that have become a part of our everyday life. "He, therefore, who aspires to peace should prepare for war." "The ancients preferred discipline to numbers." "In the midst of peace, war is looked upon as an object too distant to merit consideration." "Few men are born brave; many become so through training and force of discipline."

Vegetius was a reformer who attempted to restore the degenerate Romans of the 4th Century to the military virtues of the ancients, whom he never ceases to laud. His little book was made short and easy to read, so as not to frighten, by a too arduous text, the readers whom he hoped to convince. He constantly gives the example of the "Ancients" to his contemporaries. The result is a sort of perfume of actuality, which had much to do with his success. It still is interesting reading and still is the subject of modern commentaries. No less than forty have appeared in Germany in the 19th and 20th centuries. *Revue Mititare Generate* (France) and our own *Infantry Journal* carried articles on Vegetius in 1938. Dankfried Schenk published an interesting article in *Klio* in 1930, which gives Vegetius the highest place among the writers of his time.

The present edition includes the first three books of Vegetius' work, omitting only repetitions. The fourth and fifth books, both very brief, deal with the attack and defense of fortified places and with naval operations. These are of interest only to military antiquarians and for that reason have not been included. The present translation was made by Lieutenant John Clarke and published in London in 1767. It is the best available in English and has been edited only to the minimum extent necessary to conform to modern usage.

An excellent discussion of Vegetius can be found in *Warfare*, by Spaulding, Nickerson and Wright, page 294, et sequens, Harcourt Brace & Co., 1925. Delpech, *La Tactique* au 13me Siecte, Paris, 1886, gives the best account of the influence of Vegetius on European military thought. Hans Delbruck's discussion of Vegetius in *Geschichte der Kriegskunft*, Vol. II, Berlin, 1921, although brief, is very acute.

Gallo-Roman Helmet 1st Century AD (Mathias Kabel)

Preface to Book I – On Military Matters

To the Emperor Valentinian

It has been an old custom for authors to offer to their rulers the fruits of their studies in belles letters, from a persuasion that no work can be published with propriety but under the auspices of the Emperor, that the knowledge of a ruler should be more general, and of the most important kind, as its influence is felt so keenly by all his subjects. We have many instances of the favorable reception which Augustus and his illustrious successors conferred on the works presented to them; and this encouragement of the Sovereign made the sciences flourish. The consideration of Your Majesty's superior indulgence for attempts of this sort, induced me to follow this example, and makes me at the same time almost forget my own inability when compared with the ancient writers. One advantage, however, I derive from the nature of this work, as it requires no elegance of expression, or extraordinary share of genius, but only great care and fidelity in collecting and explaining, for public use, the instructions and observations of our old historians of military affairs, or those who wrote expressly concerning them.

My objective in this treatise is to exhibit in some order the peculiar customs and usages of the ancients in the choice and discipline of their new levies. I do not presume to offer this work.to Your Majesty from a supposition that you are not acquainted with every part of its contents; but that you may see that the same salutary dispositions and regulations which your own wisdom prompts You to establish for the happiness of the Empire, were formerly observed by the founders thereof; and that Your Majesty may find with ease in this abridgement whatever is most useful on so necessary and important a subject.

Book I: The Selection and Training of New Levies

THE ROMAN DISCIPLINE THE CAUSE OF THEIR GREATNESS

Victory in war does not depend entirely upon numbers or mere courage; only skill and discipline will insure it. We find that the Romans owed the conquest of the world to no other cause than continual military training, exact observance of discipline in their camps and unwearied cultivation of the other arts of war. Without these, what chance would the inconsiderable numbers of the Roman armies have had against the multitudes of the Gauls? Or with what success would their small size have been opposed to the prodigious stature of the Germans? The Spaniards surpassed us not only in numbers, but in physical strength. We were always inferior to the Africans in wealth and unequal to them in deception and stratagem. And the Greeks, indisputably, were far superior to us in skill in arts and all kinds of knowledge.

But to all these advantages the Romans opposed them in unusual care in the choice of their levies and in their military training. They thoroughly understood the importance of hardening them by continual practice, of training them to every maneuver that might happen in the line and in action. Nor were they less strict in punishing idleness and sloth. The courage of a soldier is heightened by his knowledge of his profession, and he only wants an opportunity to execute what he is convinced he has been perfectly taught. A handful of men, inured to war, proceed to certain victory, while on the contrary numerous armies of raw and undisciplined troops are but multitudes of men dragged to slaughter.

THE SELECTION OF RECRUITS

To treat our subject with methodically, we shall first examine what provinces or nations are to be preferred for supplying the armies with recruits. It is certain that every country produces both brave men and cowards; but it is equally as certain that some nations are naturally more warlike than others, and that courage, as well as strength of body, depends greatly upon the influence of the different climates.

We shall next examine whether the city or the country produces the best and most capable soldiers. No one, I imagine, can doubt that the peasants are the most fit to carry arms for they from their infancy have been exposed to all kinds of weather and have been brought up to the hardest labor. They are able to endure the greatest heat of the sun, are unacquainted with the use of baths, and are strangers to the other luxuries of life. They are simple, content with little, inured to all kinds of fatigue, and prepared in some measure for a military life by their continual employment in their country-work, in handling the spade, digging trenches and carrying burdens. In cases of necessity, however, they are sometimes obliged to make levies in the cities. And these men, as soon as enlisted, should be taught to work on entrenchments, to march in ranks, to carry heavy burdens, and to bear the sun and dust. Their meals should be coarse and moderate; they should be accustomed to lie sometimes in the open air and sometimes in tents. After this, they should be instructed in the use of their arms. And if any long expedition is planned, they should be encamped as far as possible from the temptations of the city. By these precautions their minds, as well as their bodies, will properly be prepared for the service.

I realize that in the first ages of the Republic, the Romans always raised their armies in the city itself, but this was at a time when there were no pleasures, no luxuries to distract them. The Tiber was then their only bath, and in it they refreshed themselves after their exercises and fatigues in the field by swimming. In those days the same man was both soldier and farmer, but a farmer who, when occasion arose, laid aside his tools and put on the sword. The truth of this is confirmed by the instance of Quintius Cincinnatus, who was following the plow when they came to offer him the dictatorship. The chief strength of our armies, then, should be recruited from the country. For it is certain that the less a man is acquainted with the sweets of life, the less reason he has to be afraid of death.

THE PROPER AGE FOR RECRUITS

If we follow the ancient practice, the proper time for enlisting youth into the army is at their entrance into the age of puberty. At this time instructions of every kind are more quickly absorbed and more lastingly imprinted on the mind. Besides this, the indispensable military exercises of running and leaping must be acquired before the limbs are too much stiffened by age. This activity is improved by continual practice, which useful and good for a soldier. Formerly, says Sallust, the Roman youth, as soon as they were of an age to carry arms, were trained in the strictest manner in their camps to all the fatigues and exercises of war. For it is certainly better that a soldier, perfectly disciplined, should, through emulation, lament at his not having arrived at a proper age for action, than have the mortification of knowing it is past. A sufficient time is also required for his instruction in the different branches of the service. It is no easy matter to train the horse or foot archer, or to form the legionary soldier to every part of the drill, to teach him not to quit his post, to keep ranks, to take a proper aim and throw his missile weapons with force, to dig trenches, to plant palisades, how to manage his shield, deflect the blows of the enemy, and how to parry a stroke with dexterity. A soldier, thus perfect in his business, so far from showing any backwardness to engage, will be eager for an opportunity of signaling himself.

THEIR SIZE

We find the ancients very fond of procuring the tallest men they could for the service, since the standard for the cavalry of the wings and for the infantry of the first legionary cohorts was fixed at six feet, or at least five feet ten inches[516]. These requirements might easily be kept up in those times when such numbers followed the profession of arms and before it was the fashion for the flower of Roman youth to devote themselves to the civil offices of state. But when necessity requires it, the height of a man is not to be regarded so much as his strength; and for this we have the authority of Homer, who tells us that the deficiency of stature in Tydeus was amply compensated by his vigor and courage.

---

[516] More recently this height is shown to be false with the average height about five feet five inches.

SIGNS OF DESIRABLE QUALITIES

Those employed to oversee new levies should be particularly careful in examining the features of their faces, their eyes, and the make of their limbs, to enable them to form a true judgment and choose such as are most likely to prove good soldiers. Experience has shown us that men, as well as horses and dogs, show certain signs by which their virtues may be discovered. The young soldier, therefore, ought to have a lively eye, carry his head erect, his chest should be broad, his shoulders muscular and brawny, his fingers long, his arms strong, his waist small, his shape easy, his legs and feet rather nervous than fleshy. When all these marks are found in a recruit, a little height may be dispensed with, since it is of much more importance that a soldier should be strong than tall.

TRADES PROPER FOR NEW LEVIES

Regard should be given to their trade of those chosen as recruits. Fishermen, fowlers, confectioners, weavers, and in general all whose professions more properly belong to women should, in my opinion, by no means be admitted into the service. On the contrary, smiths, carpenters, butchers, and huntsmen are the most proper to be taken into it. The welfare of the Republic depends on the careful choice of soldiers. The very essence of the Roman Empire and its power is so inseparably connected that its great importance should not to be entrusted indiscriminately, but only to persons whose fidelity can be relied on. The ancients considered Sertorius'[517] care in this point as one of the most eminent of his military qualifications. The soldiery to whom the defense of the Empire is consigned and in whose hands is the fortune of war, should, if possible, be of reputable families and unexceptionable in their manners. Such sentiments as may be expected in these men will make good soldiers. A sense of honor, by preventing them from behaving ill, will make them victorious.

---

[517] Roman General Quintus Sertorius. See Appendix of People Mentioned

No good can be expected from a man who is by nature a coward, though well-disciplined or that he has served many campaigns. An army raised without proper regard to the choice of its recruits was never yet made good by length of time; and we are now convinced by fatal experience that this is the source of all our misfortunes. So many defeats can only be imputed to the effects of a long peace which has made us negligent and careless in the choice of our levies while the inclination now prevalent among the better sort in preferring civil posts of the government to the profession of arms. Likewise, the shameful conduct of the superintendents, who, through interest or connivance, accept many men which those who are obliged to furnish substitutes for the army choose to send, and admit such men into the service as the masters themselves would not even keep for servants. Thus it appears that a trust of such importance should be committed to none but men of merit and integrity.

THE MILITARY MARK

The recruit, however, should not receive the military mark[518] as soon as enlisted. First he must be tested to see if he is fit for service; whether he has sufficient stamina and strength; if he has capacity to learn his duty; and whether he possesses the proper degree of military courage. Many a man promising enough in appearance, are found very unfit upon trial. These should be rejected and replaced by better men; it is not numbers, but bravery which carries the day.

After their examination, the recruits should then receive the military mark, and be taught the use of their arms by constant and daily exercise. This essential custom has been abolished by the relaxation introduced by a long peace. We cannot now expect to find a man to teach what he never learned himself. The only method, therefore, that remains of recovering the ancient customs is by books, and by consulting the old historians. These histories are of little service to us in this respect, as they only relate the exploits and events of wars, and take no notice of the objects of our present enquiries, which are considered as universally known.

---

[518] This mark was imprinted on the hands of the soldiers, either with a hot iron, or in some other manner. It was indelible.

INITIAL TRAINING

The first thing the soldiers should be taught is the military step, which can only be acquired by constant practice of marching quick and together. Nothing is of more consequence either on the march or in the line than that they should keep their ranks with the greatest exactness. Troops who march in an irregular and disorderly manner are always in great danger of being defeated. They should march with the common military step twenty miles in five summer-hours, and with the full step, which is quicker, twenty-four miles in the same number of hours. If they exceed this pace, they no longer march but run, and no certain rate can be assigned.

The young recruits in particular must be exercised in running, in order to charge the enemy with great vigor; occupy, on occasion; an advantageous post with greater dispatch, and prevent the enemy in their designs upon the same. They may, when sent to reconnoiter, advance with speed, return with greater haste and more easily come up with the enemy in a pursuit.

Leaping is another important exercise, to enable soldiers to pass ditches or embarrassing encumbrances of any kind without trouble or difficulty. There is also another very material advantage to be derived from these exercises in time of action; for a soldier who advances with his javelin, running and leaping, dazzles the eyes of his adversary, strikes him with terror, and gives him the fatal stroke before he has time to put himself on his defense. Sallust, speaking of the excellence of Pompey the Great in these particulars, tells us that he disputed the superiority in leaping with the most active, in running with the swiftest, and in exercises of strength with the most robust. Nor would he ever have been able to have opposed Serrorius with success, if he had not prepared both himself and his soldiers for action by continual exercises of this sort.

TO LEARN TO SWIM

Every young soldier, without exception, should be taught to swim in the summer months; for it is sometimes impossible to pass rivers on bridges, but the retreating and pursuing armies are often both obliged to swim over them. A sudden melting of snow or fall of rain often makes them overflow their banks, and in such a situation, the danger is as great from ignorance in swimming as from the enemy. The ancient Romans, therefore, perfected every branch of the military arts by a continual series of wars and battles. The Field of Mars was the most commodious for their exercises on account of its vicinity to the Tiber that the youth might therein wash off the sweat and dust, and refresh themselves after their fatigues by swimming. The cavalry as well as the infantry, with the horses and the servants of the army should be accustomed to this exercise, as they are all equally liable to the same accidents.

THE POST EXERCISE

We are informed by the writings of the ancients that, among their other exercises, they had that of the post. They gave their recruits round bucklers woven with willows, twice as heavy as those used on real service, and wooden swords double the weight of the common ones. They exercised them with these at the post both morning and afternoon.

This is an invention of the greatest use, not only to soldiers, but also to gladiators. No man of either profession ever distinguished himself in the circus or field of battle, who was not perfect in this kind of exercise. Every soldier, therefore, fixed a post firmly in the ground, about the height of six feet. Against this, as against a real enemy, the recruit was exercised with the above mentioned arms, as it were with the common shield and sword, sometimes aiming at the head or face, sometimes at the sides, at others endeavoring to strike at the thighs or legs. He was instructed how to advance and retire - in short how to take every advantage of his adversary. Above all he was particularly cautioned not to lay himself open to his antagonist while aiming his stroke at him.

NOT TO CUT, BUT TO THRUST WITH THE SWORD

They were likewise taught not to cut but to thrust with their swords. For the Romans not only made a jest of those who fought with the edge of that weapon, but always found them an easy conquest. A stroke with the edges, though made with ever so much force, seldom kills, as the vital parts of the body are defended both by the bones and armor. On the contrary, a stab, though it penetrates but two inches, is generally fatal. Besides in the attitude of striking, it is impossible to avoid exposing the right arm and side; but on the other hand, the body is covered while a thrust is given, and the adversary receives the point before he sees the sword. This was the method of fighting principally used by the Romans, and their reason for exercising recruits with arms of such a weight at first was, that when they came to carry the common ones so much lighter, the greater difference might enable them to act with greater security and alacrity in time of action.

THE DRILL CALLED ARMATURA

The new levies also should be taught by the masters at arms the system of drill called armatura, as it is still partly kept up among us. Experience convinces us that soldiers, who perfect their drill, are the most useful in engagements and they afford proof of the importance and effects of discipline. We plainly see the difference between those properly trained in this branch of drill and the other troops. The old Romans were so conscious of its usefulness that they rewarded the masters at arms with a double allowance of provision. The soldiers who were deficient in this drill were punished by having their allowance in barley[519]. They did not receive the usual wheat ration until they had, in the presence of the prefect, tribunes, or other principal officers of the legion, showed sufficient proofs of their knowledge of every part of their drills.

---

[519] Barley rations was given as a punishment, instead of corn or wheat.

No state can either be happy or secure that is remiss and negligent in the discipline of its troops. It is not profusion of riches or excess of luxury that can influence our enemies to court or respect us. This can only be affected by the terror of our arms. Cato observed that. misconduct in the common affairs of life may be redeemed, but that it is quite otherwise in war, where errors are fatal and without remedy, and should be followed by immediate punishment. The consequence of engaging an enemy, without skill or courage, is that part of the army is left on the field of battle, and those who remain receive so shaken from their defeat that they dare not look the enemy in the face afterwards.

THE USE OF MISSILE WEAPONS

Besides the aforementioned exercise of the recruits at the post, they were furnished with javelins of greater weight than common, which they were taught to throw at the same post. The masters at arms were very careful to instruct them how to cast them with a proper aim and force. This practice strengthens the arm and makes the soldier a good marksman.

THE USE OF THE BOW

A third or fourth of the youngest and fittest soldiers should also exercise at the post with bows and arrows made for that purpose only. The masters for this branch must be chosen with care and must apply themselves diligently to teach the men to hold the bow in a proper position, to bend it with strength, to keep the left hand steady, to draw the right with skill, to direct both the attention and the eye to the object, and to take their aim with equal certainty either on foot or on horseback. This skill is not acquired without great practice, nor will it be retained without daily exercise and practice.

The utility of good archers in action is evidently demonstrated by Cato in his treatise on military discipline. The use of troops of this sort gave Claudius[520] victory over an enemy who, till that time, had constantly been superior to him. Scipio Africanus, before his battle with the Numantines, who had made a Roman army ignominiously pass under the yoke, thought he could not succed except by mingling a number of select archers with every century.

THE SLING

Recruits should be taught the art of throwing stones both with the hand and sling. The inhabitants of the Balearic Islands are said to have been the inventors of slings, and have managed to use them with surprising dexterity, owing to the manner of bringing up their children. The children were not allowed to have their food by their mothers till they had first struck it with their sling. Soldiers, notwithstanding their defensive armor, are often more annoyed by the round stones from the sling than by all the arrows of the enemy. Stones kill without mangling the body, and the contusion is mortal without loss of blood. It is universally known the ancients employed slingers in all their engagements. There is the greater reason for instructing all troops, without exception, in this exercise, as the sling cannot be reckoned any encumbrance, and often is of the greatest service, especially when they are obliged to engage in stony places, to defend a mountain or an eminence, or to repulse an enemy at the attack of a castle or city.

---

[520] Claudius II, Gothicus (268 – 270 AD) who defeated the Goths at Naissus in 268/9 AD

THE LOADED JAVELIN

The exercise of the loaded javelins, called martiobarbuli, must not be omitted. We formerly had two legions in Illyricum, consisting of six thousand men each, which from their extraordinary dexterity and skill in the use of these weapons were distinguished by the same appellation. For a long time the weight of all the wars fell on them and they distinguished themselves so remarkably that the Emperors Diocletian and Maximian on their accession honored them with the titles of Jovian and Herculean and preferred them before all the other legions. Every soldier carries five of these javelins in the hollow of his shield. And thus the legionary soldiers seem to supply the place of archers, for they wound both the men and horses of the enemy before they come within reach of the common missile weapons.

TO BE TAUGHT TO VAULT

The ancients required both the veteran soldiers and recruits to a constant practice of vaulting. It has become one of our faults, although little regard is paid to it at present. They had wooden horses for that purpose placed in winter under cover and in summer in the field. The young soldiers were taught to vault on them at first without arms, afterwards completely armed. And such was their attention to this exercise that they were accustomed to mount and dismount on either side indifferently, with their drawn swords or lances in their hands[521]. By diligent practice in the leisure of peace, their cavalry was brought to such perfection of discipline that they mounted their horses in an instant even amidst the confusion of sudden and unexpected alarms.

---

[521] Keep in mind this was before the use of stirrups, so an exercise such as this would be very useful.

AND TO CARRY BURDENS

To accustom soldiers to carry burdens was also an essential part of discipline. Recruits in particular should be obliged frequently to carry a weight of not less than sixty pounds (exclusive of their arms), and to march with it in the ranks. This is because on difficult expeditions they often find themselves under the necessity of carrying their provisions as well as their arms. Nor will they find this troublesome when they become used to it, which makes everything easy. Our troops in ancient times were a proof of this, and Virgil has remarked it in the following lines:

> *The Roman soldiers, bred in war's alarms,*
> *Bending with unjust loads and heavy arms,*
> *Cheerful their toilsome marches undergo,*
> *And pitch their sudden camp before the foe.*

THE ARMS OF THE ANCIENTS

Next under consideration comes the manner of arming the troops. The organization of the ancients is no longer being followed. Following the example of the Goths, the Alans and the Huns, we have made some improvements in the arms of the cavalry, yet it is plain that the infantry are entirely defenseless. From the foundation of the city till the reign of the Emperor Gratian, the foot wore cuirasses and helmets. But negligence and sloth were introduced by degree to a total relaxation of discipline; the soldiers began to think their armor too heavy, as they seldom put it on. At first they asked permission from the Emperor to lay aside the cuirass and afterwards the helmet. In consequence of this, in their engagements with the Goths our troops were often overwhelmed with their showers of arrows. Nor was the necessity of obliging the infantry to resume their cuirasses and helmets discovered, notwithstanding such repeated defeats, which brought on the destruction of so many great cities.

Troops that are defenseless and exposed to all the weapons of the enemy, are more disposed to fly than fight. Nothing can be expected from a foot-archer without cuirass or helmet, who cannot hold both his bow and shield; or from the ensigns whose bodies are naked, and who cannot at the same time carry a shield and the colors? The foot soldier finds the weight of a cuirass and even of a helmet intolerable. This is because he is so seldom exercised and rarely puts them on.

The case would be quite different; however, if they were even heavier than they are and by constant practice became accustomed to wear them. It seems that these very men, who cannot support the weight of the ancient armor, think nothing of exposing themselves without defense to wounds and death, or, worse, the shame of being made prisoners, or of betraying their country by flight. By trying to avoid an inconsiderable share of exercise and fatigue, they suffer ignominiously to be cut in pieces. With assurance the ancients could call the infantry a wall, and in some measure they resembled it by the complete armor of the legionary soldiers who had shields, helmets, cuirasses, and greaves of iron on the right leg; and the archers who had gauntlets on the left arm. These were the defensive arms of the legionary soldiers. Those who fought in the first line of their respective legions were called principes, in the second hastati, and in third triarii[522].

The triarii, according to their method of discipline, rested in time of action on one knee, under cover of their shields, so that in this position they might be less exposed to the darts of the enemy than if they stood upright; and also, when there was a necessity for bringing them up, that they might be fresh, in full vigor and charge with the greater impetuosity. There have been many instances of their gaining a complete victory after the entire defeat of both the principes and hastati.

The ancients had likewise a body of light infantry, slingers, and ferentarii (the light troops), who were generally posted on the wings and began the engagement. The most active and best disciplined men were selected for this service; and as their number was not very great, they easily retired in case of a repulse through the intervals of the legion, without creating disorder in the line.

---

[522] This reference is from the re-Marius reforms in 107 BCE.

The Pamonian leather caps worn by our soldiers were formerly introduced with a different design. The ancients obliged the men to wear them at all times so that being constantly accustomed to have the head covered they might be less sensible of the weight of the helmet.

The missile weapons of the infantry were javelins headed with a triangular sharp iron, eleven inches or a foot long, and were called pilum. Once they were thrown and fixed in the shield it was impossible to draw them out. If they were thrown with force and skill, they could penetrate the cuirass without difficulty. At present they are seldom used by the Roman forces, but are the principal weapon of the barbarian heavy-armed foot. They call them bebrae, and every man carries two or three of them to battle.

It must be observed that when the soldiers engage with the javelin, the left foot should be advanced, as the proper stance required for throw it for increased distance. Alternately, when they are close enough to use their pilum and swords, the right foot should be advanced, so that the body may present less of a target to the enemy, and the right arm be tight to the body and in a more advantageous position for striking. Hence it appears that it is as necessary to provide soldiers with defensive arms of every kind as to instruct them in the use of offensive ones. It is certain a man will fight with greater courage and confidence when he finds himself properly armed for defense.

ENTRENCHED CAMPS

Recruits should be instructed how to create entrenched camps, there being no discipline as necessary and useful as this. In a camp, well-chosen and entrenched, the troops lie secure within their works both day and night, even in view of the enemy. This type of camp resembles a fortified city which they can build for their safety wherever they please. This valuable art is now entirely lost, it has been a long time since any of our camps have been fortified either with trenches or palisades. By this neglect our forces have been often surprised by day and night from the enemy's cavalry and suffered very severe losses. The importance of this custom not only protects troops from the dangers they are perpetually exposed when encamp without such precautions, but also from the distressful situation of an army that, after receiving a check in the field, finds itself without retreat and consequently at the mercy of the enemy.

A camp, especially in the presence of an enemy, must be chosen with great care. Its situation should be strong by nature, and there should be plenty of wood, forage and water. If the army is to remain in it any considerable time, attention must be had to the favorability of the place. The camp must not be commanded by any higher grounds from where the enemy might harass the defenders, nor must the location be liable to floods which would expose the army to great danger. The dimensions of the camps must be determined by the number of troops and quantity of baggage, that a large army may have room enough, and that a small one may not be obliged to extend itself beyond its proper ground. The form of the camps must be determined by the site of the country, in conformity to which they must be square, triangular or oval. The Praetorian gate should either front the east or the enemy. In a temporary camp it should face the route by which the army is to march. Within this gate the tents of the first centuries or cohorts are pitched, and the dragons[523] and other ensigns planted. The Decumane gate is directly opposite to the Praetorian in the rear of the camp, and through this the soldiers are conducted to the place appointed for punishment or execution.

There are two methods of entrenching a camp. When the danger is not imminent, a slight ditch is created around the whole circuit, only nine feet broad and seven deep. With the turf taken from this they make a kind of wall or breastwork three feet high on the inner side of the ditch. But where there is reason to be apprehensive of attempts of the enemy, the camp must be surrounded with a regular ditch twelve feet broad and nine feet deep perpendicular from the surface of the ground. A parapet is then raised on the side next the camp, of the height of four feet, with hurdles and fascines properly covered and secured by the earth taken out of the ditch. From these dimensions the interior height of the entrenchment will be found to be thirteen feet, and the breadth of the ditch twelve. On the top of the whole are planted strong palisades[524] which the soldiers carry constantly with them for this purpose. A sufficient number of spades, pickaxes, wicker baskets and tools of all kinds are to be provided for these works.

---

[523] The dragon was the particular ensign of each cohort in the late Empire.

[524] This would probably mean the stakes that all legionnaire carried on the march

There is no difficulty in carrying on the fortifications of a camp when no enemy is in sight. But if the enemy is near, all the cavalry and half the infantry are to be drawn up in order of battle to cover the rest of the troops at work on the entrenchments and be ready to receive the enemy if they offer to attack. The centuries are employed by turns on the work and are regularly called to the relief by a crier till the whole is completed. It is then inspected and measured by the centurions, who punish such as have been indolent or negligent. This is a very important point in the discipline of young soldiers, who when properly trained to it will be able in an emergency to fortify their camp with skill and expedition.

EVOLUTIONS

No part of drill is more essential in action than for soldiers to keep their ranks with the greatest exactness, without opening or closing the files too much. Troops who are too crowded can never fight as they ought, and only embarrass one another. If their order is too open and loose, they give the enemy an opportunity of penetrating. Whenever this happens and they are attacked in the rear, universal disorder and confusion are inevitable. Recruits should therefore be constantly in the field, drawn up by the roll and formed at first into a single rank. They should learn to dress in a straight line and to keep an equal and just distance between each man. They must then be ordered to double the rank, which they must perform very quickly, and instantly cover their file leaders. In the next place, they are to double again and form four ranks deep. The next formation is the triangle or, as it is commonly called, the wedge, a disposition found very serviceable in action. They must be taught to form the circle or orb; well-disciplined troops, after being broken by the enemy, have prevented the total rout of the army by throwing themselves into this position. These evolutions, often practiced in the field of exercise, will be found easy in execution on actual service.

MONTHLY MARCHES

It was a ancientt custom among the old Romans, confirmed by the Ordinances of Augustus and Hadrian, to exercise both cavalry and infantry three times in a month by marches of a certain length. The infantry were obliged to march the distance of ten miles from the camp and return completely armed, in the most exact order and with the military step which they changed and quickened on some part of the march. Their cavalry likewise, in troops and properly armed, performed the same marches and were exercised at the same time in their peculiar movement and evolutions; sometimes, as if pursuing the enemy, sometimes retreating and returning again with the greater impetuosity to the charge. These marches not made only over plain and even ground, but both cavalry and infantry were ordered into difficult and uneven places, to ascend or descend mountains, which prepared them for all kinds of accidents and familiarize them with the different maneuvers that the various situations of a country may require.

CONCLUSION

These military maxims and instructions, invincible Emperor, I have carefully collected from the works of all the ancient authors on this subject as a proof of my devotion and zeal for your service. My hope is to point out the certain method of forming good and serviceable armies, which can only be accomplished by an exact imitation of the ancients in their care, in the choices, and in the discipline of their levies. Men are not lacking courage, nor are the countries that produced the Lacedaemonians, the Athenians, the Marsians, the Samnites, the Peligni and even the Romans themselves, yet exhausted. Did not the Epirots acquire in former times a great reputation in war? Did not the Macedonians and Thessalians, after conquering the Persians, penetrate even into India? It is well known that the warlike dispositions of the Dacians, Moesians and Thracians gave rise to the fable that Mars was born among them.

To pretend to calculate the different nations of old which were so formidable, which are all now are subject to the Romans, would be tedious. But the security established by the long peace has altered their dispositions, drawn them off from military to civil pursuits and infused into them a love of idleness and ease. Hence a relaxation of military discipline ensued, then a neglect of it, and finally it sank at last into entire oblivion. It may appear surprising that this alteration should happened in latter times, considering that the peace, which has lasted about twenty years or somewhat more after the first Punic war, debilitated the Romans, who were victorious everywhere, by idleness and neglect of discipline to such a degree, that in the second Punic War they were not able to keep the field against Hannibal. At last, after the defeat of many consuls and the loss of many officers and armies, they were convinced that the revival of discipline was the only road to victory and thereby recovered their superiority. The necessity, therefore, of discipline cannot be too often repeated, as well as the strict attention requisite in the choice and training of new levies. It is also certain that it is a much less expense to a State to train its own subjects to arms than to take foreigners into its pay.

Preface to Book II – On Military Matters

To the Emperor Valentinian

Such a continued series of victories and triumphs proved incontestably Your Majesty's full and perfect knowledge of the military discipline of the ancients. Success in any profession is the most certain mark of skill in it. By the greatness of mind, above human comprehension Your Majesty condescends to seek instruction from the ancients, notwithstanding your own recent exploits surpass antiquity itself. On receiving Your Majesty's orders to continue this abridgement, not so much for your instruction as convenience, I do not know how to reconcile my devotion to your commands with the respect due to Your Majesty. Would it not be the greatest height of presumption to pretend to mention the art of war to the Lord and Master of the world and the Conqueror of all the barbarous nations, unless it was to describe his own actions? Disobedience to the will of so great a Prince would be both highly criminal and dangerous. My obedience, therefore, made me presumptuous, from the apprehensions of appearing more so by a contrary conduct. In this I was greatly encouraged by the late instance of Your Majesty's indulgence. My treatise on the choice and discipline of new levies met with a favorable reception from Your Majesty, and since a work succeeded so well, composed of my own accord, I can have no fears for one undertaken by your own express commands.

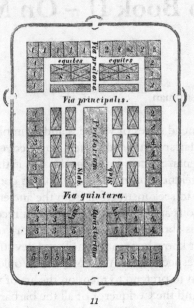

Roman Marching Camp (Bilder Atlas)

Book II: The Organization of the Legion

THE MILITARY ESTABLISHMENT

The military establishment consists of three parts, the cavalry, infantry and marine. The wings of cavalry were so called from their similitude to wings in their extension on both sides of the main body for its protection. They are now called vexillations from the kind of standards peculiar to them. The legionary horse are bodies specifically annexed to each legion, and of a different kind; and on their model were organized the cavalry called Ocreati, from the light boots they wear. The fleet consists of two divisions; the first division was called Liburnae, and the other of armed sloops. The cavalry are designed for plains. Fleets are employed for the protection of seas and rivers. The infantry are proper for the defense of lands, for the garrisons of cities and are equally serviceable in plain and in uneven ground. The latter, therefore, from their facility of acting everywhere, are certainly the most useful and necessary troops to a state exclusively of the consideration of their being maintained at a less expense. The infantry are divided into two corps, the legions and auxiliaries, the latter of which are furnished by allies or confederates. The peculiar strength of the Romans always consisted in the excellent organization of their legions. They were so denominated ab eligendo, from the care and exactness used in the choice of the soldiers. The number of legionary troops in an army is generally much more considerable than those of the auxiliaries.[525]

DIFFERENCE BETWEEN THE LEGIONS AND AUXILIARIES

---

[525] This ratio changed depending on the period. In the early republic auxiliaries outnumbered the Legions

The Macedonians, the Greeks and the Dardanians formed their troops into phalanxes of eight thousand men each. The Gauls, Celtiberians and many other barbarous nations divided their armies into bodies of six thousand each. The Romans have their legions usually six thousand strong, sometimes more.

We will now explain the difference between the legions and the auxiliaries. The latter are hired corps of foreigners assembled from different parts of the Empire, made up of different numbers, without knowledge of one another or any tie of affection. Each nation has its own peculiar discipline, customs and manner of fighting. Little can be expected from forces so dissimilar in every respect, since it is one of the most essential points in military undertakings that the whole army should be put in motion and governed by one and the same order. It is almost impossible for men to act in concert under such varying and unsettled circumstances. They are, however, when properly trained and disciplined, of material service and are always joined as light troops with the legions in the line. Although the legions did not place their principal dependence on them, yet they look on them as a very considerable addition to their strength.[526]

The complete Roman legion, with its own organic cohorts, contains heavy-armed foot as designated: the principes, hastati, triarii, and antefignani, the light-armed foot, consisting of the ferentarii[527], archers, slingers, and balistarii, together with the legionary cavalry incorporated with it. These bodies, all actuated with the same spirit, are uniform in their various dispositions for forming, encamping and fighting. Thus the legion is compact and perfect in all its parts and, without any foreign assistance, has always been superior to any force that could be brought against it. The Roman greatness is a proof of the excellence of their legions, for with them they always defeated whatever numbers of the enemy they thought fit, or their circumstances gave them an opportunity to engage.

---

[526] This is true for the Republic, but under the Empire the Auxilaries were standardized and looked very much like legionaires. (see appendix for more information)

[527] This should be feoderati

CAUSES OF DECAY OF THE LEGION

The name of the legion still remains to this day in our armies, but its strength and substance are gone, since by the neglect of our predecessors, honors and promotions, which were formerly the recompenses of merit and long services, were to be attained only by influence and favor. Care is no longer taken to replace the soldiers, who received their discharges after serving their full time. Vacancies are continually happening because of sickness, discharges, desertion and various other casualties, if not replaced every year or even every month, must in time disable the most numerous army. Another cause of the weakness of our legions is that the soldiers find the duty hard, the arms heavy, the rewards distant and the discipline severe. To avoid these inconveniences, the young men enlist in the auxiliaries, where the service is less laborious and they have reason to expect rewards quicker.

Cato the Elder, who was often Consul and always victorious at the head of the armies, believed he would do his more to help his country by writing on military affairs, than by all his exploits in the field. The consequences of bravery are temporary, while whatever is committed to writing for public good is of lasting benefit. Several others have followed his example, particularly Frontinus, whose elaborate works on this subject were so well received by the Emperor Trajan. These are the authors whose maxims and institutions I have undertaken to abridge in the most faithful and concise manner.

The expense of keeping up good or bad troops is the same; but it depends wholly on you, most August Emperor, to recover the excellent discipline of the ancients and to correct the abuses of recent times. This is a reformation, the advantages of which will be equally felt by ourselves and our posterity.

THE ORGANIZATION OF THE LEGION

All our writers agree that never more than two legions, besides auxiliaries, were sent under the command of each consul against the most numerous armies of the enemies. Such was the dependence on their discipline and resolution that this number was thought sufficient for any war they were engaged in. I shall therefore explain the organization of the ancient legion according to the military constitution. If the description appears obscure or imperfect, it is not to because of me, but to the difficulty of the subject itself, which should therefore be examined with the greater attention. A prince, skilled himself in military affairs, has it in his power to make himself invincible by keeping up whatever number of well-disciplined forces he thinks proper.

The recruits having thus been carefully chosen with proper attention to their persons and dispositions, and having been daily exercised for the space of at least four months, the legion is formed by the command and under the auspices of the Emperor. The military mark, which is indelible, is first imprinted on the hands of the new levies, and as their names are inserted in the roll of the legions they take the usual oath, called the military oath. They swear by God, by Christ and by the Holy Ghost; and by the Majesty of the Emperor who, after God, should be the chief object of the love and veneration of mankind. For when he has received the title of August, his subjects are bound to pay him the most sincere devotion and homage, as the representative of God on earth. Every man, whether in a private or military station, serves God in serving him faithfully who reigns by His authority. The soldiers, therefore, swear they will obey the Emperor willingly and implicitly in all his commands that they will never desert and will always be ready to sacrifice their lives for the Roman Empire.

The legion should consist of ten cohorts, the first of which exceeds the others both in number and quality of its soldiers, who are selected to serve in it as men of some family and education. This cohort has the care of the eagle, the chief ensign in the Roman armies and the standard of the whole legion, as well as of the images of the emperors which are always considered as sacred. It consists of eleven hundred and five foot and one hundred and thirty-two horse cuirassiers, and is distinguished by the name of the Millarian Cohort. It is the head of the legion and is always first formed on the right of the first line when the legion draws up in order of battle.

The second cohort contains five hundred and fifty-five foot and sixty-six horse, and is called the Quingentarian Cohort. The third is composed of five hundred and fifty-five foot and sixty-six horse, generally chosen men, on account of its situation in the center of the first line. The fourth consists of the same number of five hundred and fifty-five foot and sixty-six horse. The fifth has likewise five hundred and fifty-five foot and sixty-six horse, which should be some of the best men, being posted on the left flank as the first cohort is on the right. These five cohorts compose the first line.

The sixth includes five hundred and fifty-five foot and sixty-six horse, which should be the flower of the young soldiers as it draws up in the rear of the eagle and the images of the emperors, and on the right of the second line. The seventh contains five hundred and fifty-five foot and sixty-six horse. The eighth is composed of five hundred and fifty-five foot and sixty-six horse, all selected troops, as it occupies the center of the second line. The ninth has five hundred and fifty-five foot and sixty-six horse. The tenth consists of the same number of five hundred and fifty-five foot and sixty-six horse and requires good men, as it closes the left flank of the second line. These ten cohorts form the complete legions, consisting in the whole of six thousand one hundred foot and seven hundred and twenty-six horses. A legion should never be composed of a less number of men, but it is sometimes stronger by the addition of other Millarian Cohorts.

THE OFFICERS OF THE LEGION

Having shown the ancient establishment of the legion, we shall now explain the names of the principal soldiers or, to use the proper term, the officers, and their ranks according to the present rolls of the legions. The first tribune is appointed by the express commission and choice of the Emperor. The second tribune rises to that rank by length of service. The tribunes are so called from their command over the soldiers, who were at first levied by Romulus out of the different tribes. The officers who in action commanded the orders or divisions are called Ordinarii. The Augustales were added by Augustus to the Ordinarii; and the Flaviales were appointed by Flavius Vespasian to double the number of the Augustales. The eagle-bearers and the image-bearers are those who carry the eagles and images of the Emperors. The Optiones are subaltern officers, so denominated from their being selected by the option of their superior officers, to do their duty as their substitutes or lieutenants in case of sickness or other accident. The ensign-bearers carry the ensigns and are called Draconarii. The Tesserarii deliver the parole and the orders of the general to the different messes of the soldiers.

The Campignei or Antefignani are those whose duty it is to keep the proper exercises and discipline among the troops. The Metatores are ordered before the army to fix on the ground for its encampments. The Beneficiarii are so named from their owing their promotion to the benefit or interest of the Tribunes. The Librarii keep the legionary accounts. The Tubicines, Cornicines, and Buccinatores derive their appellations from blowing the trumpet, cornet, and buccina. Those who, expert in their exercises, receive a double allowance of provisions, are called Armaturae Duplares, and those who have but a single portion, Simplares. The Mensores mark out the ground by measure for the tents in an encampment, and assign the troops their respective quarters in garrison. The Torquati, received their names from the gold collars given them in reward for their bravery, had besides this honor different allowances. Those who received double were called Torquati Duplares, and those who had only single, Simplares. There were, for the same reason, Candidatii Duplares, and Candidatii Simplares. These are the principal soldiers or officers distinguished by their rank and privileges thereto annexed. The rest are called Munifices, or working soldiers, from their being obliged to every kind of military work without exception. Formerly it was the rule that the first Princeps of the legion should be promoted regularly to the rank of Centurion of the Primiple. He not only was entrusted with the eagle but commanded four centuries, that is, four hundred men in the first line. As head of the legion he had appointments of great honor and profit. The first Hastatus had the command of two centuries or two hundred men in the second line, and is now called Ducenarius.

The Princeps of the first cohort commanded a century and a half, that is, one hundred and fifty men, and kept in a great measure the general detail of the legion. The second Hastatus had likewise a century and a half, or one hundred and fifty men. The first Triarius had the command of one hundred men. Thus the ten centuries of the first cohort were commanded by five Ordinarii, who by the ancient establishment enjoyed great honors and emoluments that were annexed to this rank in order to inspire the soldiers of the legions with emulation to attain such ample and considerable rewards. They had also Centurions appointed to each century, now called Centenarii and Decani, who commanded ten men, now called heads of messes. The second cohort had five Centurions; and all the rest to the tenth inclusively the same number. In the whole legion there were fifty-five.

Lieutenants of consular rank were formerly sent to command in the armies under the general, and their authority extended over both the legions and auxiliaries in peace and war. Instead of these officers, civilians of high rank are now substituted with the title of Masters of the Forces. They are not limited to the command of two legions only, but have often a greater number. But the peculiar officer of the legion was the Praefect, who was always a count of the first order. He was given the chief command in the absence of the lieutenant. The Tribunes, Centurions, and all the soldiers in general were under his orders: He provided the parole, orders for the march and for the guards. If a soldier committed a crime, the Tribune by his authority adjudged his punishment. He had charge of the arms, horses, clothing and provisions. It was also his duty to keep both the legionary horse and foot exercised daily and to maintain the strictest discipline. He ought to be a careful and diligent officer with the sole charge of forming the legion to regularity and obedience. He was depended on by the generals for the excellence of the soldiers, due entirely to his own honor and credit.

The Praefect of the camp, though inferior in rank to the former, had an important. The position of the camp, the direction of the entrenchments, the inspection of the tents or huts of the soldiers and the baggage were comprehended in his province. His authority extended over the sick, and the physicians who had the care of them as well as regulating the expenses relative to it. He was in charge of providing carriages, sawhorses, the proper tools for sawing and cutting wood, digging trenches, raising parapets, sinking wells and bringing water into the camp. He likewise had the care of furnishing the troops with wood and straw, as well as the rams, onagri, balistae and all the other engines of war under his direction. This post was always conferred on an officer of great skill, experience and long service, who was capable of instructing others in those branches of the profession in which he had distinguished himself.

THE PRAEFECT OF THE WORKMEN

The legion had a train of joiners, masons, carpenters, smiths, painters, and workmen of every kind for the construction of barracks in the winter-camps and for making or repairing the wooden towers, arms, carriages and the various sorts of machines and engines for the attack or defense of places. They had also traveling workshops in which they made shields, cuirasses, helmets, bows, arrows, javelins and offensive and defensive arms of all kinds. The ancients made it their chief care to have everything for the service of the army within the camp. They even had a body of miners who, by working under ground and piercing the foundations of walls, according to the practice of the Beffi, penetrated into the body of a place. All these were under the direction of the officer called the Praefect of the Workmen.

THE TRIBUNE OF THE SOLDIERS

We have observed that the legions had ten cohorts, the first of which, called the Millarian Cohort, was composed of men selected on account of their circumstances, birth, education, person and bravery. The tribune who commanded them was likewise distinguished for his skill in his exercises, for the advantages of his person and the integrity of his manners. The other cohorts were commanded, according to the Emperor's pleasure, either by tribunes or other officers commissioned for that purpose. In former times the discipline was so strict that the tribunes or officers abovementioned not only caused the troops under their command to be exercised daily in their presence, but were themselves so perfect in their military exercises as to set them the example. Nothing does so much honor to the abilities or application of the tribune as the appearance and discipline of the soldiers, when their apparel is neat and clean, their arms bright and in good order and when they perform their exercises and evolutions with dexterity.

CENTURIES AND ENSIGNS OF THE FOOT

The chief ensign of the legion is the eagle and is carried by the eagle-bearer. Each cohort has also its own peculiar ensign, the Dragon, carried by the Draconarius. The ancients, knowing the ranks were easily disordered in the confusion of action, divided the cohorts into centuries and gave each century an ensign inscribed with the number both of the cohort and century so that the men keeping it in sight might be prevented from separating from their comrades in the greatest fighting. The centurions, now called centenarii, were distinguished by different crests on their helmets, to be easily recognizable by the soldiers of their respective centuries. These precautions prevented any mistake, as every century was guided not only by its own ensign but likewise by the peculiar form of the helmet of its commanding officers. The centuries were also subdivided into messes of ten men each who lay in the same tent and were under orders and inspection of a Decanus or head of the mess. These messes were also called Maniples from their constant custom of fighting together in the same company or division.

LEGIONARY TROOPS OF HORSE

As the divisions of the infantry are called centuries, so those of the cavalry are called troops. A troop consists of thirty-two men and is commanded by a Decurion. Every century has its ensign and every troop its Standard. The centurion in the infantry is chosen for his size, strength, dexterity in throwing missile weapons and for his skill in the use of his sword and shield; in short for his expertness in all the exercises. He should be vigilant, temperate, active and ready to execute the orders he receives at once. He must be strict in exercising, keeping up proper discipline among his soldiers, in obliging them to appear clean and well-dressed and to have their arms constantly polished and bright. In like manner the Decurion in command of a troop should be known for his activity and ability in mounting his horse completely armed; his skill in riding and in the use of the lance and bow; for his attention in forming his men to all the evolutions of the cavalry; and for his care in obliging them to keep their cuirasses, lances and helmets always bright and in good order. The splendor of the arms has a great effect in striking terror into an enemy. Can that man be reckoned a good soldier who through negligence suffers his arms to be spoiled by dirt and rust? In short, it is the duty of the Decurion to be attentive to whatever concerns the health or discipline of the men or horses in his troop.

DRAWING UP A LEGION IN ORDER OF BATTLE

We shall illustrate the manner of drawing up an army in order of battle in the instance of one legion, which may serve for any number. The cavalry are posted on the wings. The infantry begin to form on a line with the first cohort on the right. The second cohort draws up on the left of the first; the third occupies the center; the fourth is posted next; and the fifth closes the left flank. The ordinarii, the other officers and the soldiers of the first line, ranged before and round the ensigns, were called the Principes. They were all heavily armed troops with helmets, cuirasses, greaves, and shields. Their offensive weapons were large swords, called spathae, and smaller ones called semispathae together with five loaded javelins in the concavity of the shield, which they threw at the first charge. They had likewise two other javelins, the largest of which was composed of a staff five feet and a half long and a triangular head of iron nine inches long. This was formerly called the pilum, but now it is known by the name of spiculum. The soldiers were familiar with the use of this weapon, because when thrown with force and skill it often penetrated the shields of the foot and the cuirasses of the horse. The other javelin was of smaller size; its triangular point was only five inches long and the staff three feet and one half. It was anciently called verriculum but now verutum.

The first line, as I said before, was composed of the Principes; the Hastati formed the second and were armed in the same manner. In the second line the sixth cohort was posted on the right flank, with the seventh on its left; the eighth drew up in the center; the ninth was the next; and the tenth always closed the left flank. In the rear of these two lines were the ferentarii, light infantry and the troops armed with shields, loaded javelins, swords and common missile weapons, much in the same manner as our modern soldiers. This was also the post of the archers who had helmets, cuirasses, swords, bows and arrows; of the slingers who threw stones with the common sling or with the fustibalus; and of the tragularii who annoyed the enemy with arrows from the manubalistae or arcubalistae.

In the rear of all the lines, the triarii, completely armed, were drawn up. They had shields, cuirasses, helmets, greaves, swords, daggers, loaded javelins, and two of the common missile weapons. They rested during the acnon on one knee, so that if the first lines were obliged to give way, they might be fresh when brought up to the charge, and thereby retrieve what was lost and recover the victory. All the ensigns though, of the infantry, wore cuirasses of a smaller sort and covered their helmets with the shaggy skins of beasts to make themselves appear more terrible to the enemy. But the centurions had complete cuirasses, shields, and helmets of iron, the crest of which, placed transversely thereon, were ornamented with silver that they might be more easily distinguished by their respective soldiers.

The following disposition deserves the greatest attention. In the beginning of an engagement, the first and second lines remained immovable on their ground, and the triarii in their usual positions. The light-armed troops, composed as above mentioned, advanced in the front of the line, and attacked the enemy. If they could make the enemy give way, the light troops pursued them; but if they were repulsed by superior bravery or numbers, they retired behind their own heavy armed infantry, which appeared like a wall of iron and renewed the action, at first with their missile weapons, then sword in hand. If they broke the enemy they never pursued them, least they should break their ranks or throw the line into confusion, and lest the enemy, taking advantage of their disorder, should return to the attack and destroy them without difficulty. The pursuit therefore was entirely left to the light-armed troops and the cavalry. Through these precautions and dispositions the legion was victorious without danger, or if the contrary happened, was preserved without any considerable loss, for as it is not calculated for pursuit, it is likewise not easily thrown into disorder.

NAMES OF SOLDIERS INSCRIBED ON THEIR SHIELDS

Lest in the confusion of battle the soldiers should be separated from their comrades, every cohort had its shields painted in a manner peculiar to itself. The name of each soldier was also written on his shield, together with the number of the cohort and century to which he belonged. From this description we may compare a legion in proper order, to a well-fortified city as containing everything requisite in war, wherever it moved. It was secure from any sudden or surprise attacks of an enemy by its expeditious method of entrenching their camp even in the open plains and it was always provided with troops and arms of every kind. To be victorious over our enemies in the field, therefore, we must unanimously pray heaven that the Emperor is amenable to reform the abuses in raising our levies and to recruit our legions after the method of the ancients. The same care in choosing and instructing our young soldiers in all military exercises and drills will soon make them equal to the old Roman troops who subdued the whole world. This alteration and loss of ancient discipline should not affect Your Majesty, since it is a happiness reserved for You alone both to restore the ancient ordinances and establish new ones for the public welfare. The start of any endeavor carries an appearance of difficulty; but in this case, if the levies are careful chosen, led by experienced officers, an army may be raised, disciplined and rendered fit for service in a very short time. Once the necessary expenses are provided, diligence soon effects whatever it undertakes.

RECORDS AND ACCOUNTS

Several posts in the legion require men of some education. The superintendents of the levies should select some recruits for their skill in writing and accounts, besides the general qualifications such as size, strength and proper disposition for the service. The detailed information of the legion, including the lists of the soldiers exempted from duty on private accounts, the rosters for their tour of military duties and their pay lists, is entered daily in the legionary books and kept we may confidently say, with greater exactness than the regulations of provisions or other civil matters in the registers of the police. The rolls are punctually kept for this purpose; in time of peace, the daily guards, the advanced guards and outposts in time of war, are mounted regularly by the centuries and messes in their turns, with the name of each soldier whose tour is past, so that no one may have injustice done him or be excused from his duty by favor.

The superintendents are also exact in entering the time and limitation of furloughs, which formerly were never granted without difficulty and only on real and urgent business. They don't allow the soldiers to attend on any private person or to concern themselves in private occupations, thinking it absurd and improper that the Emperor's soldiers, clothed and subsisted at the public expense, should follow any other profession. Some soldiers, however, were allowed for the service of the Praefects, Tribunes and other officers, out of the number of the accensi or such as were raised after the legion was complete. These latter are now called supernumeraries. The regular troops were obliged to carry their wood, hay, water and straw into the camp themselves. From such kind of services they were called munifices.

SOLDIER'S DEPOSITS

The institution of the ancients which obliged the soldiers to deposit half of every donative they received at the colors was wise and judicious; the intent was to preserve it for their use so that they might not squander it in extravagance or idle expense. For most men, particularly the poorer sort, soon spend whatever they can get. A reserve of this kind therefore is evidently of the greatest service to the soldiers themselves; since they are maintained at the public expense; their military stock by this method is continually increasing. The soldier who knows all his fortune is deposited at his colors, entertains no thoughts of desertion, experiences greater loyalty for them and fights with greater intrepidity in their defense. He is also prompted by funds, the most prevailing consideration among men. This money was contained in ten bags, one for each cohort. There was an eleventh bag also for a small contribution from the whole legion, as a common fund to defray the expense of burial of any of their deceased comrades. These collections were kept in baskets in the custody of the ensigns, chosen for their integrity and capacity, and answerable for the trust and obliged to account with every man for his own proportion.

PROMOTION IN THE LEGION

Heaven certainly inspired the Romans with the organization of the legion, so superior does it seem to human invention. Such is the arrangement and disposition of the ten cohorts that compose it, as to appear one perfect body and form one complete whole. As he advances in rank, a soldier proceeds as it were, by rotation through the different degrees of the several cohorts in such a manner that one who is promoted passes from the first cohort to the tenth, and returns again regularly through all the others with a continual increase of rank and pay to the first. Thus the centurion of the Principe, after having commanded in the different ranks of every cohort, attains that great dignity in the first with infinite advantages from the whole legion. The chief Praefect of the Praetorian Guards rises by the same method of rotation to that lucrative and honorable rank. Thus the legionary cavalry contract affection for the foot of their own cohorts, notwithstanding the natural antipathy existing between the two corps. This connection establishes a reciprocal attachment and union between all the cohorts and the cavalry and infantry of the legion.

LEGIONARY MUSIC

The music of the legion consists of trumpets, cornets and buccinae. The trumpet sounds the charge and the retreat. The cornets are used only to regulate the motions of the colors; the trumpets serve when the soldiers are ordered out to any work without the colors; but in time of action, the trumpets and cornets sound together. The classicum, which is a particular sound of the buccina or horn, is appropriated to the commander-in-chief and is used in the presence of the general, or at the execution of a soldier, as a mark of its being done by his authority. The ordinary guards and outposts are always mounted and relieved by the sound of trumpet, which also directs the motions of the soldiers on working parties and on field days. The cornets sound whenever the colors are to be struck or planted. These rules must be punctually observed in all exercises and reviews so that the soldiers may be ready to obey them in action without hesitation according to the general's orders either to charge or halt, to pursue the enemy or to retire. Reason convinces us that what is necessary to be performed in the heat of action should constantly be practiced in the leisure of peace.

THE DRILLING OF THE TROOPS

The organization of the legion being explained let us return to the drills. The younger soldiers and recruits went through all of their drills every morning and afternoon, while the veterans and experienced troops did so regularly once a day. Length of service or age alone will never form a military man, because after serving many years an undisciplined soldier is still a novice in his profession. Not only those under the masters at arms, but all the soldiers, were previously trained incessantly in those drills which now are only exhibited as shows in the circus for particular solemnities. Only by practice can agility of body be acquired and the skill requisite to engage an enemy with advantage, especially in close fight. The most essential point of all these exercise is to teach soldiers to keep their ranks and never abandon their colors in the most difficult circumstances. Men trained in this manner are never at a loss amidst the greatest confusion of numbers.

The recruits likewise are to be exercised with wooden swords at the post, to be taught to attack this imaginary antagonist on all sides while aiming at the sides, feet or head, both with the point and edge of the sword. They must be instructed how to spring forward to give the blow, to rise with a bound above the shield and then to sink down and shelter themselves under cover of it, and how to advance and retire. They must also throw their javelins at the post from a considerable distance in order to acquire a good aim and strengthen the arm.

The archers and slingers set up bundles of twigs or straw for marks, and generally strike them with arrows and stones from the fustiablus at the distance of six hundred feet. They acquired coolness and exactness in action from familiar custom and exercise in the field. The slingers should be taught to whirl the sling only once over their head before they cast the stone. Formerly all soldiers were trained to the practice of throwing stones of a pound weight with the hand, as this was thought a readier method since it did not require a sling. The use of the common missile weapons and loaded javelins was another part of the drill strictly attended to.

To continue this drill without interruption during the winter, they erected porticos or riding halls covered with tiles or shingles for the cavalry, and if they were not able to build these, with reeds, rushes or thatch. Large open halls were likewise constructed in the same manner for the use of the infantry. By these means the troops were provided with places of drill sheltered from bad weather. But in winter, if it did not rain or snow, they were obliged to perform their drills in the field, lest an omission of discipline should affect both the courage and constitution of the soldier. In short, both legionary and auxiliary troops should continually be drilled in cutting wood, carrying burdens, passing ditches, swimming in the sea or in rivers, marching in the full step and even running with their arms and baggage, so that, used to labor in peace, they may find no difficulty in war. The well trained soldier is eager for action, just as the untaught fear it. In war discipline is superior to strength; but if that discipline is neglected, there is no longer any difference between the soldier and the peasant. The old maxim is certain that the very essence of an art consists in constant practice.

MACHINES AND TOOLS OF THE LEGION

The legion owes its success to its arms and machines, as well as to the number and bravery of its soldiers. In the first place every century has a balista mounted on a carriage drawn by mules and served by a unit that is ten men from the century to which it belongs. The larger these engines are, the greater distance they carry and with the greater force. They are used not only to defend the entrenchments of camps, but are also placed in the field in the rear of the heavily armed infantry. Such is the violence with which they throw the darts that neither the cuirasses of the horse nor shields of the foot can resist them. There are fifty-five of these engines in a legion. Besides these there are ten onagri, one for each cohort; which are drawn ready armed on carriages by oxen; in case of an attack, they defend the works of the camp by throwing stones as the balistae do darts.

The legion carries a number of small boats with it; each hollowed out of a single piece of timber, with long cables and sometimes iron chains to fasten them together. These boats, joined and covered with planks, serve as bridges over unfordable rivers, on which both cavalry and infantry pass without danger. The legion is provided with iron hooks, called wolves, and iron scythes fixed to the ends of long poles along with forks, spades, shovels, pickaxes, wheelbarrows and baskets for digging and transporting earth; together with hatchets, axes and saws for cutting wood. In addition, a train of workmen are furnished with all instruments necessary for the construction of tortoises, musculi, rams, vines, moving towers and other machines for the attack of places. As the detail of all the particulars of this sort would be too tedious, I shall only observe that the legion should carry with it wherever it moves, whatever is necessary for every kind of service so that the encampments may have all the strength and conveniences of a fortified city.

Preface to Book III – On Military Matters

To the Emperor Valentinian

History informs us that the Athenians and Lacedaemonians were masters of Greece before the Macedonians. The Athenians excelled not only in war but in other arts and sciences. The Lacedaemonians made war their chief study. They are pronounced to be the first people who studied the outcome of battles and committed their observations to writing with such success as to reduce the military art, before considered as totally dependent on courage or fortune, to certain rules and fixed principles. As a consequence they established schools of tactics for the instruction of youth in all the maneuvers of war. These people are worthy of admiration for applying themselves to the study of an art, without which no other art can possibly exist. The Romans followed their example, and both practiced their institutions in their armies and preserved them in their writings. These are the maxims and instructions dispersed through the works of different authors, which Your Majesty has ordered me to abridge, since the perusal of the whole would be too tedious, and the authority of only a part unsatisfactory. The effect of the Lacedaemonian skill in dispositions for general actions appears evidently in the single instance of Xantippus, who assisted the Carthaginians after the repeated ruin of their armies. Superior skill and conduct alone defeated Attilius Regulus at the head of a Roman army, till that time always victorious. Xantippus took him prisoner and thus terminated the war by a single action. Before he set out on his expedition into Italy, Hannibal also chose a Lacedaemonian for his counselor in military operations; and by his advice, though they were inferior to the Romans both in number and strength, overthrew so many consuls and such mighty legions. Therefore, he who desires peace, should prepare for war. He who aspires to victory, should spare no pains to form his soldiers. And he who hopes for success, should fight on principle, not chance. No one dares to offend or insult a power of known superiority in action.

Roman Siege (Bilder Atlas)

Book III: Dispositions for Action

THE NUMBER WHICH SHOULD COMPOSE AN ARMY

The first book covers the selection and exercise of new levies; the second explains the establishment of the legion and the method of discipline; and the third contains the dispositions for action. By this methodical progression, the following instructions on general actions and means of victory will be better understood and of greater use. By the term an army I mean a number of troops, legions, auxiliaries, cavalry and infantry, assembled to make war. This number is limited by judges of the profession. The defeats of Xerxes, Darius, Mithridates and other monarchs, who brought innumerable multitudes into the field, plainly show that the destruction of such prodigious has more to do with their own numbers than to the bravery of their enemies. An army too numerous is subject to many dangers and inconveniences. Its bulk makes it slow and unwieldy in its motions; and as it is obliged to march in columns of great length, it is exposed to the risk of being continually harassed and insulted by small groups of the enemy. The encumbrance of the baggage is often an occasion of its being surprised in its passage through difficult places or over rivers. The difficulty of providing forage for such numbers of horses and other beasts of burden is very great. Besides, scarcity of provisions, which should be carefully guarded on all expeditions, soon ruins such large armies where the consumption is so great. All the above notwithstanding, the greatest care should be taken in filling the magazines because they will begin to fail after a short time. Sometimes they will unavoidably be distressed from lack of water. But, if this immense army should unfortunately be defeated, the numbers lost would probably be very great, and the remainder, who save themselves by flight, would be too dispirited to be brought again to action.

The ancients taught by experience, preferring discipline to numbers. In wars of lesser importance they thought one legion with auxiliaries, that is, ten thousand foot and two thousand cavalry was sufficient. They often gave command of this force to a praetor as a general of the second rank. While preparations of the enemy were developing, they sent a general of consular dignity with twenty thousand foot and four thousand horse after them. In our times this command was given to a count of the first order. In those emergencies when the army faced any dangerous insurrection supported by infinite multitudes of fierce and barbarous nations, they took the field with two armies under two consuls, who were charged, both singly and jointly, to take care to preserve the Republic from danger. By managing the forces in this manner, the Romans, almost continually engaged in war with different nations in different parts of the world, found themselves able to oppose them in every quarter. The excellence of their discipline made their small armies sufficient to encounter all their enemies with success. It was an invariable rule in their armies that the number of allies or auxiliaries should never exceed that of the Roman citizens[528].

MEANS OF PRESERVING IT IN HEALTH

The next article is of the greatest importance: the means of preserving the health of the troops. Much of this depends on the site of the camp, the water supply, the season of the year, medicine, and exercise. As to the situation, the army should never continue in the neighborhood of unwholesome marshes any length of time, on dry plains or a position without some sort of shade or shelter. In the summer, the troops should never encamp without tents. On their marches, in the summer when the heat is excessive, should begin by break of day so that they may arrive at the place of destination in good time; otherwise they will contract diseases from the heat of the weather and the fatigue of the march. In severe time of winter they should never march at night in frost and snow, or be exposed to want of wood or clothes. A soldier, starved with cold, can neither be healthy nor fit for service. The water must be wholesome and not marshy. Bad water is a kind of poison and the cause of epidemic distempers.

---

[528] We don't know what sources Vegetius is working from, but this does not seem to bear out according to modern studies of the Roman Army during the early Empire.

It is the duty of the officers of the legion, of the tribunes, and even of the commander-in-chief himself, to take care that the sick soldiers are supplied with proper diet and diligently attended by the physicians. Little can be expected from men who have both the enemy and diseases to struggle with. The best judges of the service, however, have always been of the opinion that daily practice of the military exercises is much more effective towards the health of an army than all the art of medicine. This is the reason they exercised their infantry without intermission. If it rained or snowed, they performed under cover; and fine weather, in the field. They also were diligent in exercising their cavalry, not only on plains, but also on difficult terrain, broken and cut with ditches. The horses as well as the men were trained in this manner, both on the above mentioned account and to prepare them for action. Hence we understand the importance and necessity of a strict observance of the military exercises in an army, since health in the camp and victory in the field depend on them. If a large army stays in one place for too long in the summer or in the autumn, the waters become corrupt and the air infected. Malignant and fatal distempers proceed from this and can be avoided only by frequent changes of encampments[529].

CARE TO PROVIDE FORAGE AND PROVISIONS

Famine wreaks more havoc in an army than the enemy, and is more terrible than the sword. Time and opportunity may help to retrieve other misfortunes, but where forage and provisions have not been carefully provided, the evil is without remedy. The main and principal point in war is to secure plenty of provisions and to destroy the enemy by famine. An exact calculation must therefore be made before the commencement of the war as to the number of troops and the expenses required of them, so that the provinces may have sufficient time to furnish the forage, corn, and all other kinds of provisions demanded of them to be transported. They must be in more than sufficient quantity, and gathered into the strongest and most convenient cities before the opening of the campaign. If the provinces cannot raise their quotas in kind, they must provide sufficient money to be employed in procuring all things requisite for the service. The possessions of the subjects cannot otherwise be kept secure than by the defense of arms.

---

529 Even at this time they realized sanitation was important even if they didn't know why. This aspect of military camps was overlooked until late in the 19th century.

These precautions often become doubly necessary as a siege is sometimes protracted beyond expectation as the besiegers are resolved to steel themselves against all the inconveniences of want sooner than raise the siege, if they have any hopes of reducing the place by famine. Edicts should be issued requiring the country people to bring their cattle, grain, wine and all kinds of provisions that may be of service to the enemy, into garrisoned fortresses or into the safest cities. If they do not comply with the order, proper officers are to appointed to compel them to do it. The inhabitants of the province must likewise be obliged to retire with their effects into some fortified place before the irruption of the enemy. The fortifications and all the different kinds of machines must be examined and repaired in time. If you are surprised by the enemy before you have prepared for defense, you will be thrown into irrecoverable confusion, and no longer draw any assistance from the neighboring places, all communication with them will be cut off. If proper precautions taken from the beginning a faithful management of the magazines combined with a frugal distribution of the provisions, will insure sufficient supplies. When provisions once begin to fail, being thrifty is ill-timed and comes too late.

On difficult expeditions the ancients distributed the provisions at a fixed allowance to each man without distinction of rank; and when the emergency was past, the government accounted for the full proportions. The troops should never want wood and forage in winter or water in summer. They should have corn, wine, vinegar, and even salt, in plenty at all times. Cities and fortresses are garrisoned by such men as are least fit for the service of the field. They are provided with all sorts of arms, arrows, fustibali, slings, stones, onagri and balistae for their defense. Great caution is required that the simplicity of the inhabitants lead to treachery or perjury at the hands of the enemy, for pretended conferences and deceitful truces have often been more fatal than force. By observing the foregoing precautions, the besieged may have it in their power to ruin the enemy by famine, if he keeps his troops together, and if he divides them, by frequent sallies and surprises.

METHODS TO PREVENT MUTINY IN AN ARMY

An army drawn together from different areas of the empire is sometimes disposed to mutiny. Likewise, troops, though not inclined to fight, can pretend to be angry at not being led against the enemy. Such seditious dispositions principally show themselves in those who have lived in their quarters in idleness and effeminacy. These men, unaccustomed to the necessary fatigue of the field, are disgusted at its severity. Their ignorance of discipline makes them afraid of action and inspires them with insolence.

There are several remedies for this evil. While the troops are yet separated and each corps continues in its respective quarters, let the tribunes, their lieutenants and the officers in general make it their business to keep up so strict a discipline as to leave them no room to harbor any thoughts but of submission and obedience. Let them be constantly employed either in field days or in the inspection of their arms. They should not be allowed to be absent on furlough. They should be frequently called by roll and trained to be exact in the observance of every signal. Let them be exercised in the use of the bow, in throwing missile weapons and stones, both with the hand and sling, and with the wooden sword at the post; let all this be continually repeated and let them be often kept under arms till they are tired. Let them be exercised in running and leaping to facilitate the passing of ditches. And if their quarters are near the sea or a river, let them all, without exception, be obliged in the summer to have the frequent swimming practice. Let them be accustomed to marching through thickets, enclosures and broken grounds, to fell trees and cut out timber, to break ground and to defend a post against their comrades who are to trying to overcome them; and in the encounter each party should use their shields to dislodge and bear down against their antagonists. All the different kinds of troops trained in this manner and exercised in their quarters will find themselves inspired to seek glory and eagerness for action when they come to take the field. In short, a soldier who has proper confidence in his own skill and strength entertains no thought of mutiny.

A general should be attentive to discover the turbulent and seditious soldiers in the army, legions or auxiliaries, cavalry or infantry. He should endeavor to procure his intelligence not from informers, but from the tribunes, their lieutenants and other officers of undoubted veracity. It would then be prudent of him to separate them from the rest under pretense of some service agreeable to them, or detach them to garrison cities or castles, but with such address that though he wants to get rid of them, they may think themselves employed by preference and favor. A multitude never broke out into open sedition at once and with unanimous consent. They are prepared and excited by small group of mutineers, who hope to secure impunity for their crimes by the number of their associates. If stopping a mutiny requires violent remedies, then it is advisable, after the manner of the ancients, to punish the ring-leaders only in order that, though few suffer, all may be terrified by the example. It is much more to the credit of a general to form his troops to submission and obedience by habit and discipline than to be obliged to force them to their duty by the terror of punishment.

MARCHES IN THE NEIGHBORHOOD OF THE ENEMY

It has been asserted by those who have made the profession their study that an army is exposed to more danger on marches than in battles. In an engagement if men are properly armed, they see their enemies before them and come prepared to fight. But on a march the soldier is less on his guard, does not have his arms always ready and is thrown into disorder by a sudden attack or ambush. A general, therefore, cannot be too careful or diligent in taking necessary precautions to prevent a surprise on the march and in making proper dispositions to repulse the enemy, in case of such accident, without loss.

In the first place, he should have an exact description of the country in which they are fighting, the distances of places specified by the number of miles, the nature of the roads, the shortest routes, by-roads, mountains and rivers, and should be correctly inserted. We are told that the greatest generals carry out their precautions in his head and not satisfied with the simple description of the country where they are engaged, they make maps of it on the spot, in order to regulate their marches by the eye with greater safety. A general should also acquaint himself of all these particulars from people well acquainted with the country by examining them separately at first, and then comparing their accounts in order to ascertain the validity of the descriptions.

If any difficulty arises about the choice of roads, he should procure proper and skillful guides. He should put them under a guard and spare neither promises nor threat to induce them to be faithful. They will acquit themselves well when they know it is impossible to escape and are certain of being rewarded for their fidelity or punished for their perfidy. He must be sure of their capacity and experience that the whole army will not be brought into danger by the errors of two or three persons. Sometimes the local peasants imagine they know what they really do not, and through ignorance promise more than they can perform.

Of all precautions the most important is to keep the way or by what route the army will march completely secret. The security of an expedition depends on the concealment of all motions from the enemy. The figure of the Minotaur was among the most ancient legionary ensigns, signifying that this monster, according to the fable, was concealed in the most secret recesses and windings of the labyrinth, just as the designs of a general should always be impenetrable. When the enemy has no knowledge of a march, it is made with security; but as scouts sometimes either suspect or discover the route, or traitors or deserters give intelligence thereof, it will be proper to mention the method of acting in case of an attack on the march.

Before he puts his troops in motion, the general should send out detachments of trusty and experienced soldiers well mounted, to reconnoiter the places through which he is to march, to the front, the rear, and on the right and left, lest he should fall into ambushes. The night is safer and more advantageous for your spies to do their business in than day, for if they are taken prisoners, you have, as it were, betrayed yourself. After this, the cavalry should march off first, then the infantry; the baggage, bat horses, servants and carriages follow in the center; and part of the best cavalry and infantry come in the rear, since it is oftener attacked on a march than the front. The flanks of the baggage, exposed to frequent ambuscades, must also be covered with a sufficient guard to secure them. Above all, the part of the line where the enemy is most expected must be reinforced with some of the best cavalry, light infantry and foot archers.

If surrounded on all sides by the enemy, you must make dispositions to receive them wherever they come, the soldiers should be cautioned beforehand to keep their arms in their hands, and to be ready in order to prevent the bad effects of a sudden attack. Men are frightened and thrown into disorder by sudden accidents and surprises are of no consequence when forewarned. The ancients were very careful that the servants or followers of the army, if wounded or frightened by the noise of the action, should not disorder the troops while engaged, and also to prevent them either straggling or crowding one another too much, which might inconvenience their own men and give advantage to the enemy. They arranged the baggage, therefore, in the same manner as the regular troops under particular ensigns. They selected from among the servants the most proper and experienced, giving them the command of a number of servants and boys, not exceeding two hundred, and their ensigns directed them where to assemble the baggage. Proper intervals should always be kept between the baggage and the troops, that the latter may not be embarrassed for want of room in case of an attack during the march. The manner and disposition of defense must be varied according to the difference of ground. In an open country you are more liable to be attacked by horse than foot. But in a woody, mountainous or marshy situation, the danger to be apprehended is from foot. Some of the divisions being apt through negligence to move too fast, and others too slow, great care is to be taken to prevent the army from being broken or from running into too great a length, as the enemy would instantly take advantage of the neglect and penetrate without difficulty.

The tribunes, their lieutenants or the masters at arms of most experience, must therefore be posted at proper distances, in order to halt those who advance too fast and quicken those who move too slow. If men are too far in the front, on the appearance of an enemy, they are more likely to fly than to join their comrades. Those too far behind, lacking assistance, are sacrificed to the enemy and their own despair. The enemy, it may be concluded, will either plant ambushes or make his attack by open force, according to the advantage of the ground. Caution in examining the surrounding area will be a security against concealed danger; and an ambush, if discovered and promptly surrounded, will return the intended mischief with interest.

If the enemy prepares to fall upon you by open force in a mountainous country, detachments must be sent forward to occupy the highest eminences, so that on their arrival the enemy would not dare to attack you under such a disadvantage of ground, your troops being posted so much above the enemy and presenting a front ready for their reception. It is better to send men forward with hatchets and other tools in order to open ways that are narrow but safe, without regard to the labor, rather than to run any risk in the finest roads. It is necessary to be well acquainted with the habits of the enemy; so make their attempts in the night, at break of day or in the hours of refreshment or rest; and by knowing their customs to guard against what we find their general practice. We must also learn whether they are stronger in infantry or cavalry; whether their cavalry is chiefly armed with lances or with bows; and whether their principal strength consists in their numbers or the excellence of their arms. All of this will enable us to take the most proper measures to distress them to our advantage. When we have a plan in mind, we must consider whether it is more advisable to begin the march by day or by night; we must calculate the distance of the places we want to reach; and take such precautions that in summer the troops may not suffer for want of water on their march, nor be obstructed in winter by impassable morasses or torrents, as these would expose the army to great danger before it could arrive at the place of its destination. As it highly concerns us to guard against these inconveniences with prudence, so it would be inexcusable not to take advantage of an enemy that fell into them through ignorance or negligence. Our spies should be constantly abroad; we should spare no pains in tampering with their men, and give all manner of encouragement to deserters. By these means we may get intelligence of their present or future designs. And we should constantly keep in readiness some detachments of cavalry and light infantry, to fall upon them when they least expect it, either on the march, or when foraging or marauding.

PASSAGES OF RIVERS

The passage of rivers is very dangerous without great precaution. In crossing broad or rapid streams, the baggage, servants, and sometimes the most indolent soldiers are in danger of being lost. Having first sounded the ford, two lines of the best mounted cavalry are ranged at a convenient distance entirely across the river, so that the infantry and baggage may pass between them. The line above the ford breaks the violence of the stream, and the line below recovers and transports the men carried away by the current. When the river is too deep to be forded either by the cavalry or infantry, the water should be drawn off, if it runs in a plain, by cutting a great number of trenches, and thus it is passed with ease.

Navigable rivers are passed by means of piles driven into the bottom and floored with planks; or in a sudden emergency by fastening together a number of empty casks and covering them with boards. The cavalry, throwing off their accoutrements, make small floats of dry reeds or rushes on which they lay their rams and cuirasses to preserve them from being wet. They themselves swim their horses across the river and draw the floats after them by a leather thong.

The most helpful invention is that of small boats hollowed out of one piece of timber and very light both by their make and the quality of the wood. The army always has a number of these boats upon carriages, together with a sufficient quantity of planks and iron nails. Thus with the help of cables to lash the boats together, a bridge is instantly constructed, which has the solidity of a bridge of stone for a short time.

As the enemy generally endeavor to fall upon an army at the passage of a river either by surprise or ambush, it is necessary to secure both sides with strong detachments so that the troops may not be attacked and defeated while separated by the channel of the river. It is still safer to palisade both the posts, since this will enable you to sustain any attempt without much loss. If the bridge is needed, not only for the present transportation of the troops but also for their return and for convoys, it will be proper to throw up works with large ditches to cover each head of the bridge, with a sufficient number of men to defend them as long as the circumstances of affairs require.

RULES FOR ENCAMPING AN ARMY

An army on the march cannot always expect to find walled cities for quarters, and it is very imprudent and dangerous to encamp in a straggling manner without some sort of entrenchment. It is an easy matter to surprise troops while refreshing themselves or dispersed in the different occupations of the service. The darkness of night, the necessity of sleep and the dispersion of the horses at pasture afford opportunities of surprise. A good situation for a camp is not sufficient; we must choose the very best that can be found lest, having failed to occupy a more advantageous post the enemy should get possession of it to our great detriment.

An army should not encamp in summer near bad waters or far from good ones, nor in winter in a situation without plenty of forage and wood. The camp should not be liable to sudden deluges. The avenues should not be too steep and narrow lest, if invested, the troops should find it difficult to make their retreat; nor should it be commanded by any circumstances from which it may be annoyed by the enemy's weapons.

After these precautions, the camp is formed square, round, triangular or oblong, according to the nature of the ground. The shape of a camp does not make it secure. Those camps, however, are thought best where the length is one third more than the depth. The dimensions must be exactly computed by the engineers, so that the size of the camp may be proportioned to the number of troops. A camp which is too confined will not permit the troops to perform their movements with freedom, and one which is too extensive divides them too much. There are three methods of entrenching a camp. The first is for the case when the army is on the march and will continue in the camp for only one night. They throw up a slight parapet of turf and plant a row of palisades or caltrops of wood in top. The sod is cut with iron instruments. If the earth is strongly held together by the roots of the grass, they are cut in the form of a brick a foot and one half high, a foot broad and a foot and one half long. If the earth is so loose that the turf cannot be cut in this form, they run a slight trench round the camp, five feet broad and three feet deep. The earth taken from the trench forms a parapet on the inside and this secures the army from danger. This is the second method.

Permanent camps in the enemy territory used for summer or winter, are fortified with greater care and regularity. After the ground is marked out by the proper officers, each century receives a certain number of feet to entrench. They then arrange their shields and baggage in a circle about their own colors and, without arms other than their swords, open a trench nine, eleven or thirteen feet broad. If they are concerned about the enemy, they enlarge it to seventeen feet (it being a general rule to observe odd numbers). Within this they construct a rampart with fascines or branches of trees well fastened together with pickets, so that the earth may be better supported. On this rampart they raise a parapet with battlements as in the fortifications of a city. The centurions measure the work with rods ten feet long and examine whether everyone has properly completed the proportion assigned to him. The tribunes likewise inspect the work and should not leave the place till the whole is finished. So that the workmen may not be suddenly interrupted by the enemy, all the cavalry and that part of the infantry are exempted from working, remaining in order of battle in front of the entrenchment ready to repel any assault.

After entrenching the camp, the first thing to be done, is to plant the ensigns, which are held by the soldiers in the highest veneration and respect, in their proper places. After this the praetorium is prepared for the general and his lieutenants, and the tents pitched for the tribunes, with specific soldiers appointed for that service to fetch their water, wood, and forage. Then the legions and auxiliaries, cavalry and infantry, have the areas distributed to them to pitch their tents according to the seniority of the various units. Four infantrymen of each century and four troopers of each troop are on guard every night. It was impossible for a sentinel to remain at his post a whole night; the watches were divided by the hourglass into four parts that each man might stand only three hours. All guards were mounted by the sound of trumpet and relieved by the sound of cornet. The tribunes chose reliable and trusty men to visit the different posts and report to them whatever they find amiss. This is now a military office and the persons appointed to it are called officers of the rounds.

The cavalry furnish the grand guards at night and the outposts by day. They were relieved every morning and afternoon because of the fatigue of the men and horses. It is particularly incumbent upon the general to provide for the protection of the pastures and of the convoys of grain and other provisions either in camp or in garrison, and to secure wood, water and forage against the incursions of the enemy. This can only be achieved by posting detachments advantageously in the cines or walled castles on the roads along which the convoys advance. If no ancient fortifications are found, small forts must be built in proper situations, surrounded with large ditches, for the reception of detachments of horse and foot, so that the convoys will be effectually protected. For an enemy will hardly venture far into a country where he knows his adversary's troops are so disposed as to be ready to encompass him on all sides.

MOTIVES FOR THE PLAN OF OPERATIONS OF A CAMPAIGN

Readers of this military abridgement might be impatient for instructions regarding general engagements. But they should consider that a battle is commonly decided in two or three hours, after which no further hopes are left for the worsted army. Every plan, therefore, should be considered, every expedient tried and every method taken before matters are brought to a general engagement. Good officers decline general engagements where there is common danger, and prefer the employment of stratagem and finesse to destroy the enemy as much as possible in detail and intimidate them without exposing our own forces.

I shall insert some necessary instructions from the collected minds of the ancients. It is the duty and interest of the general to frequently assemble the most prudent and experienced officers of the different corps of the army and consults them on the state both of his own and the enemy's forces. Overconfidence is dangerous in its consequences and must be banished from the planning. He must examine who has the superiority in numbers, whether his or the adversary's troops are best armed, who are in the best condition, best disciplined and most resolute in emergencies. The state of the cavalry of both armies must be examined, but especially those of the infantry because the main strength of an army consists of the latter. In regards to the cavalry, he must endeavor to find out who have the greatest numbers of horse archers or lancers, who has the most cuirassiers and who has the best horses. Lastly, he must consider the field of battle and judge whether the ground is more advantageous for him or his enemy. If we are stronger in cavalry, we should prefer plains and open ground; if superior in infantry, we should choose a situation full of hedges, ditches, morasses, woods, and sometimes mountainous. Plenty or scarcity of supplies in either army are considerations of no small importance, for famine, according to the common proverb, is an internal enemy that makes more havoc than the sword. The most material article, however, is to determine whether it is most proper to temporize or to bring the affair to a speedy decision by action. The enemy sometimes expects an expedition over quickly; and if it is protracted to any length, his troops are either consumed by want, induced to return home by the desire of seeing their families or, having done nothing considerable in the field, disperse themselves from despair of success. Large numbers, suffering from fatigue and disgusted with the service, desert, others betray them and many surrender. Fidelity is seldom found in troops disheartened by misfortunes. In such case an army which was numerous on taking the field insensibly dwindles away to nothing.

It is essential to know the character of the enemy and of their principal officers- whether they are rash or cautious, enterprising or timid, whether they fight on principle or from chance and whether the nations they have been engaged with were brave or cowardly.

We must know how far to depend upon the fidelity and strength of auxiliaries, how the enemy's troops and our own are affected and which appear most confident of success, a consideration of great effect in raising or depressing the courage of an army. A harangue from the general, especially if he shows no fear himself, may reanimate the soldiers if dejected. Their spirits might revive if they gained and advantage either by stratagem or otherwise, if the fortune of the enemy begins to change or if you can contrive to beat some of their weak or poorly-armed detachments.

You must never try to lead a shaky or indifferent army to a general engagement. The difference is great between whether your troops are raw or veterans, whether used to war by recent service or idle for several years. Soldiers unused to fighting for a length of time must be considered in the same light as recruits. As soon as the legions, auxiliaries and cavalry are assembled from their camps, it is the duty of a good general to have every corps instructed separately in every part of the drill by tribunes well respected for that purpose. Afterwards, he should form them into one body and train them in all the maneuvers of the line as for a general action. He must frequently drill them himself to hone their skill and strength, and to see that they perform their drills with proper regularity and are sufficiently attentive to the sound of the trumpets, the motions of the colors and to his own orders and signals. If deficient in any of these particulars, they must be instructed and exercised till perfect.

The troops should be thoroughly disciplined and competent in their field exercises, in the use of the bow and javelin, and in the evolutions of the line, it is not advisable to lead them rashly or immediately to battle. First, a favorable opportunity must be observed, and they must be prepared by frequent skirmishes and slight encounters. Thus, a vigilant and prudent general will carefully take into account the state of his own forces and of those of the enemy, just as a civil magistrate judging between two contending parties. If he finds himself in many respects superior to his adversary, he must by no means defer bringing on an engagement. But, if he knows his forces are inferior, he must avoid general actions and endeavor to succeed by surprises, ambushes and stratagems. When skillfully managed by good generals, they often gain victory over enemies superior both in numbers and strength.

HOW TO MANAGE RAW AND UNDISCIPLINED TROOPS

All arts and trades can be made perfect by continual practice. How much more should this maxim, true in inconsiderable matters, be observed than in affairs of importance! The art of war is superior to all others, by which our liberties are preserved, our dignities perpetuated and the provinces and the whole Empire itself exist. The Lacedaemonians, and after them the Romans, were so aware of this truth that to this science they sacrificed all others. Even today the barbarous nations believe only this art worth attention, believing it includes or confers everything else. In short, it is indispensably necessary for those engaged in war not only to instruct them in the means of preserving their own lives, but how to gain the victory over their enemies.

A commander-in-chief's power and dignity are so great and to whose fidelity and bravery the fortunes of his countrymen, the defense of their cities, the lives of the soldiers, and the glory of the state, are entrusted, should not only consult the good of the army in general, but extend his care to every private soldier in it. When any misfortunes happen to those under his command, they are considered as public losses and imputed entirely to his misconduct. If therefore he finds his army composed of raw troops or if they have long been unaccustomed to fighting, he must carefully study the strength, the spirit, the manners of each particular legion, and of each body of auxiliaries, cavalry and infantry. He must know, if possible, the name and capacity of every count, tribune, subaltern and soldier. He must assume the utmost authority and maintain it by severity. He must punish all military crimes with the greatest rigor of the laws. He must have the character of being adament towards offenders and endeavor to give public examples of these in different places and on different occasions.

Having once firmly established these regulations, he must watch for the opportunity when the enemy, dispersed in search of plunder, think themselves secure, and attack them with detachments of reliable cavalry or infantry, intermingled with young soldiers, or such as are under the military age. The veterans will acquire fresh experience and the others will be inspired with courage by the advantages such opportunities will give him. He should form ambushes with the greatest secrecy to surprise the enemy at the passages of rivers, in the rugged passes of mountains, in defiles in woods and when embarrassed by morasses or difficult roads. He should regulate his march to fall upon them while taking their refreshments or sleeping, or at a time when they suspect no dangers and are dispersed, unarmed and their horses unsaddled. He should continue these kinds of encounters till his soldiers have imbibed a proper confidence in themselves. For troops that have never been in action or have not for some time been used to such spectacles, are greatly shocked at the sight of the wounded and dying; and the impressions of fear they receive dispose them rather to fly than fight.

If the enemy makes excursions or expeditions, the general should attack him after the fatigue of a long march, fall upon him unexpectedly, or harass his rear. He should detach troops to surprise and ambush enemy units separated from the main army for the convenience of forage or provisions. This tactic should be pursued first as it will not harm the morale or position of the attackers if they should not go as planned, but would provide a great advantage to the attacking army if successful. A prudent general will also try to sow dissention among his adversaries, because no nation, though weak in arms can be completely ruined by its enemies unless its fall is facilitated by its own distraction. In civil dissensions men are so intent on the destruction of their private enemies that they ignore the public safety.

One maxim must be remembered throughout this work: no one should ever despair of effecting what has been already performed. It has been questioned in the recent past if our troops fortified their permanent camps with ditches, ramparts or palisades. The answer is plain; if those precautions had been taken, our armies would never have suffered by surprises of the enemy both by day and night. The Persians, after the example of the old Romans, surround their camps with ditches and, as the ground in their country is generally sandy, they always carry empty bags with them to fill with the sand taken out of the trenches and raise a parapet by piling them one on the other. All the barbarous nations range their carriages round them in a circle, a method which bears some resemblance to a fortified camp. They thus pass their nights secure from surprise.

We should be afraid of using what others have learned from us. At present this is only found in books, although it was previously constantly practiced. Inquiries are now no longer made about long neglected customs, because in the midst of peace, war is looked upon as an object too distant to merit consideration. Learning previous practices will convince us that the reestablishment of ancient discipline is by no means impossible, although now so totally lost.

In former ages the arts of war, were often neglected and forgotten, and just as often recovered from books and reestablished by the authority and attention of our generals. When Scipio Africanus took the command of our armies in Spain, they were in bad order and had often been beaten under preceding generals. He soon reformed them by severe discipline and obliged them to undergo the greatest tests of stamina in the different military exercises, reproaching them since they would not wet their hands with the blood of their enemies, nor soil them with the mud of the trenches. In short, he afterwards took the city of Numantia with these very troops and sacked the city with such destructive force that not one of its inhabitants escaped. In Africa an army, which had been forced to pass under the yoke under the command of Albinus, was brought into firm order and discipline by Metellus, by forming it on the ancient model, that they afterwards vanquished those very enemies who had subjected them to that ignominious treatment. The Cimbri defeated the legions of Caepio, Manilus and Silanus in Gaul, but Marius collected their shattered remnants and disciplined them so effectually that he destroyed an innumerable multitude of the Cimbri, Teutones and Ambrones in one general engagement. Nevertheless it is easier to form young soldiers and inspire them with proper notions of honor than to reanimate troops who have been once disheartened.

PREPARATIONS FOR A GENERAL ENGAGEMENT

Having explained the less important branches of the art of war, the order of military affairs naturally leads us to the general engagement. This is a conjuncture full of uncertainty and fatal to kingdoms and nations, for in the decision of a pitched battle consists the fullness of victory. This eventuality above all others requires the exertion of all the abilities of a general, as his good conduct on such an occasion gains him greater glory, or his dangers expose him to greater danger and disgrace. This is the moment in which his talents, skill and experience show themselves in their fullest extent.

In Former days, to enable the soldiers to charge with great energy, it was customary to order them a moderate refreshment of food before an engagement, so that their strength could withstand a long conflict. When the army marches out of a camp or city in the presence of their enemies drawn up and ready for action, great precaution must be observed lest they should be attacked as they defile from the gates and be cut to pieces in detail. Proper measures must therefore be taken so that the whole army might clear of the gates and form in order of battle before the enemy's approach. If they are ready before you can have quitted the place, your design of marching out must either be deferred till another opportunity or at least dissembled, so that when they begin to insult you on the supposition that you dare not appear, or think of nothing but plundering or returning and no longer keep their ranks, you may sally out and fall upon them while in confusion and surprise. Troops must never be engaged in a general action immediately after a long march, when the men are fatigued and the horses tired. The strength required for action is spent in the toil of the march. What can a soldier do who charges when out of breath? The ancients carefully avoided this inconvenience, but in later times some of our Roman generals, without mentioning names, have lost their armies by awkwardly neglected this precaution. Two armies, one tired and spent, the other fresh and in full vigor, are by no means an equal match.

THE SENTIMENTS OF THE TROOPS SHOULD BE DETERMINED BEFORE BATTLE

It is necessary to know the sentiments of the soldiers on the day of an engagement. Their confidence or apprehensions are easily discovered by their looks, their words, their actions and their motions. No great dependence should be placed on the eagerness of young soldiers for action, for fighting has something agreeable in the idea to those who are strangers to it. On the other hand, it would be wrong to hazard an engagement, if the old experienced soldiers display their disinclination to fight. A general, however, may encourage and animate his troops by proper exhortations and harangues, especially if by his account of the approaching action he can persuade them into the belief of an easy victory. With this view, he should lay the cowardice or unskillfulness of their enemies before them and remind them of any former advantages they may have gained over the enemy. He should employ every argument capable of exciting rage, hatred and indignation against the adversaries in the minds of his soldiers.

It is natural for men in general to be affected with some sensations of fear at the beginning of an engagement, but they are without doubt some of a more timorous disposition who are disordered by the very sight of the enemy. To diminish these apprehensions before you venture on action, present your army in order of battle frequently in some safe situation, so that your men may be accustomed to the sight and appearance of the enemy. When opportunity offers, they should be sent to attack the enemy, endeavoring to put them to flight or kill some of their men. Thus they will become acquainted with their customs, arms and horses. Objects with which we are once familiarized are no longer capable of inspiring us with terror.

CHOICE OF THE FIELD OF BATTLE

Good generals are acutely aware that victory depends much on the nature of the field of battle. When you therefore intend to engage, endeavor to draw the chief advantage from your situation. The highest ground is reckoned the best. Weapons thrown from a height strike with greater force; and the party above their antagonists can repulse and bear them down with greater impetuosity, while they who struggle with the ascent have both the ground and the enemy to contend with. There is, however, this difference with regard to place: if you depend on your foot against the enemy's horse, you must choose a rough, unequal and mountainous situation. But if, on the contrary, you expect your cavalry to act with advantage against the enemy's infantry, your ground must indeed be higher, but plain and open, without any obstructions of woods or morasses.

ORDER OF BATTLE

In drawing up an army in order of battle, three things are to be considered: the sun, the dust and the wind. The sun in your face dazzles the sight: if the wind is against you, it turns aside and blunts the force of your weapons, while it assists those of your adversary; and the dust driving in your front fills the eyes of your men and blinds them. Even the most unskilled general can avoid these inconveniences while making their dispositions; but a prudent general should extend his views beyond the present; he should take such measures as not to be inconvenienced in the course of the day by different aspects of the sun or by contrary winds which often rise at a certain hour and might be detrimental during action. Our troops should be placed in the field as to have these issues behind them, while they are directly in the enemy's front.

PROPER DISTANCES AND INTERVALS

Having explained the general disposition of the lines, we now come to the distances and dimensions. One thousand paces contain a single rank of one thousand six hundred and fifty-six foot soldiers, each man being allowed three feet. Six ranks drawn up on the same extent of ground will require nine thousand nine hundred and ninety-six men. To form only three ranks of the same number will take up two thousand paces, but it is much better to increase the number of ranks than to make your front too extensive. We have before observed the distance between each rank should be six feet, one foot of which is taken up by the men. Thus if you form a body of ten thousand men into six ranks they will occupy thirty-six feet in depth and a thousand paces in front. By this calculation it is easy to compute the extent of ground required to form twenty or thirty thousand men. A general, therefore, should not be mistaken when he knows the proportion of ground for any fixed number of men.

If the field of battle is not spacious enough or your troops are very numerous, you may form them into nine ranks or more, because it is more advantageous to engage in close order than to extend your line too much. An army that takes up too much ground in front and too little in depth is quickly penetrated by the enemy's first onset. After this there is no remedy. In regards to posting the different corps in the right or left wing or in the center, it is the general rule to draw them up according to their respective ranks or to distribute them as circumstances or the dispositions of the enemy may require.

DISPOSITION OF THE CAVALRY

The line of infantry is formed in the center, while the cavalry are drawn up in the wings. The heavy horse, that is, the cuirassiers and troopers armed with lances, should be placed with the infantry. The light cavalry, consisting of the archers and those who have no cuirasses, should be placed at some distance in the front. The best and heaviest horse should cover the flanks of the foot, and the light horse are posted as abovementioned to surround and disorder the enemy's wings. A general should know what part of his own cavalry is most proper to oppose any particular squadrons or enemy troops. While not covered here, some types of troops fight better against others, and those who have defeated superior enemies are often overcome by an inferior force.

If your cavalry is not equal to the enemy's it is proper, after the ancient custom, to intermingle it with light infantry armed with small shields and trained to this kind of service. By following this method, even if the flower of the enemy's cavalry should attack you, they will never be able to cope with this mixed disposition. This was the only resource of the old generals to supply the defects of their cavalry, and they inter-mingled the men, used to running and armed for this purpose with light shields, swords and darts, among the horse, placing one of them between two troopers.

RESERVES

The method of having bodies of reserves in rear of the army, composed of elite infantry and cavalry, commanded by the supernumerary lieutenant generals, counts and tribunes, is very judicious and of great aide towards winning a battle. Some reserves should be posted in rear of the wings and some near the center, to be ready to immediately fly to the assistance of any part of the line which is hard pressed, to prevent its being pierced, to supply the gaps made in the line during the action and helps to keep up the courage of their fellow soldiers and check the impetuosity of the enemy. This was an invention of the Lacedaemonians, which was imitated by the Carthaginians. The Romans have since employed it, and indeed no better disposition can be found.

The line is solely designed to repulse, or if possible, break the enemy. If it is necessary to form the wedge or the pincers, it must be done by the supernumerary troops stationed in the rear for that purpose. If the saw[530] is to be formed, it must also be done from the reserves, for if once you begin to draw off men from the line you throw everyone into confusion. If any flying platoon of the enemy should fall upon your wing or any other part of your army, and you have no supernumerary troops to oppose it or if you pretend to detach either horse or foot from your line for that service by endeavoring to protect one part, you will expose the other to greater danger. In armies that are not very numerous, it is much better to contract the front, and to have strong reserves. In short, you must have a reserve of good well-armed infantry near the center to form the wedge in order to pierce the enemy's line; while bodies of cavalry armed with lances and cuirasses and light infantry, near the wings, to surround the flanks of the enemy.

[530] A zig-zag formation

THE POST OF THE GENERAL AND OF THE SECOND AND THIRD IN COMMAND

The post of the commander-in-chief is generally on the right between the cavalry and infantry. From this place in the line he can best direct the motions of the whole army and move elements with the great ease wherever he finds it necessary. It is also the most convenient spot to give his orders to both cavalry and infantry, as well as encouraging them by his presence. It is his duty to surround the enemy's left wing opposed to him with his reserve of horse and light infantry, and attack it in the flank and rear. The second in command is posted in the center of the infantry to encourage and support them. A reserve of good and well-armed infantry is near him and under his orders. With this reserve he can either form the wedge to pierce the enemy's line or, if they form the wedge first, prepares the pincers for its reception. The post of the third in command is on the left. He should be a careful and intrepid officer, because this part of the army is difficult to manage and defective, as it were, from its situation in the line. He should therefore have a reserve of good cavalry and active infantry to enable him always to extend his left in such a manner as to prevent its being surrounded.

The war shout should not be begun till both armies have joined, for it is a mark of ignorance or cowardice to give it at a distance. The effect is much greater on the enemy when they find themselves struck at the same instant with the horror of the noise and the points of the weapons.

You must always endeavor to get your enemy to commit first in drawing up in order of battle, as you will then have it in your power to make your proper dispositions without obstruction. This will increase the courage of your own troops and intimidate your adversaries. A superiority of courage seems to be implied on the side of an army that offers battle, whereas troops begin to be fearful who see their enemies ready to attack them. You will also secure another advantage, by marching up in order and falling upon them while forming and still in confusion. A part of victory consists in throwing the enemy into disorder before you engage them.

MANEUVERS IN ACTION

An able general never loses an opportunity of surprising the enemy either when tired on the march, divided in the passage of a river, tangled in morasses, struggling with the declivities of mountains, when dispersed over the country they think themselves in security or are sleeping in their quarters. In all these cases the adversaries are surprised and destroyed before they have time to put themselves on their guard. But, if they are too cautious to give you an opportunity of surprising or ensnaring them, you are then obliged to engage openly and on equal terms. This is at present, however, foreign to the subject. Military skill is no less necessary in general actions than in carrying on war by subtlety and stratagem.

Your first care is to secure your left wing from being surrounded by the enemy's numbers or attacked in the flank or rear by flying units, a misfortune that often happens. Nor is your right to be negligent, though you might be less frequently in danger. There is only one remedy for this: to wheel back your wing and throw it into a circular position. By this evolution your soldiers meet the enemy on the quarter attacked and defend the rear of their comrades. Your best men should be posted on the angles of the flanks, since it is against them that the enemy makes their principal efforts.

There is a method of resisting the "wedge" when it is formed by the enemy. The wedge is an infantry formation widening gradually at the base and terminating in a point towards the front. It pierces the enemy's line by a multitude of darts directed to one particular place. The soldiers call it the swine's head. To oppose this disposition, they make use of another formation called the "pincers", resembling the letter V, composed of a body of men in close order. It receives the wedge, inclosing it on both sides, and thereby prevents it from penetrating the line.

The saw is another disposition formed of determined soldiers drawn up in a straight line advanced at the front against the enemy, to repair any disorder. The squad is a body of men separated from the line, that hovers on every side and attack the enemy wherever they find opportunity. Against this a stronger and more numerous squads should be detached.

Above all, a general must never attempt to alter his dispositions or break his order of battle during the time of action; such an alteration would immediately cause disorder and confusion which the enemy would not fail to press to their advantage.

VARIOUS FORMATIONS FOR BATTLE

An army may be drawn up for a general engagement in seven different formations. The first formation is an oblong square with a large frontage, of common use both in ancient and modern times, although not thought the best by various judges of the service, because an even and level plain of sufficient size to contain its front cannot always be found, and if there should be any irregularity or hollow in the line, it is often pierced in that part. Besides, an enemy superior in number may surround either your right or left wing, the consequence of which could be dangerous, unless you have a ready reserve to advance and sustain his attack. A general should make use of this disposition only when his forces are better and more numerous than the enemy's, it being in his power to attack both the flanks and surround them on every side.

The second and best disposition is the oblique. Although your army might consist of few troops, a thoughtful and advantageous posting will greatly contribute to you obtaining the victory, notwithstanding the numbers and bravery of the enemy. It is as follows: as the armies are marching up to the attack, your left wing must be kept back a distance from the enemy's right in order to be out of reach of their darts and arrows. Your right wing must advance obliquely upon the enemy's left, and begin the engagement. And you must endeavor with your best cavalry and infantry to surround the wing with which you are engaged, make it give way and fall upon the enemy in the rear. If they give ground at once and the attack is properly seconded, you will undoubtedly achieve victory, while your left wing, which continued at a safe distance, will remain untouched. An army drawn up in this manner bears some resemblance to the letter "A" or a mason's level. If the enemy should move in front of you in this evolution, action should be taken using the extra cavalry and foot posted as a reserve in the rear, as mentioned previously and they must be ordered to support your left wing. This will enable you to make a vigorous resistance against the designs of the enemy.

The third formation is like the second, but not as good, as it obliges you to begin the attack with your left wing on the enemy's right. The efforts of soldiers on the left are weak and imperfect from their exposed and weakened position in the line. I will explain this formation more clearly. Although your left wing should be much better than your right, yet it must be reinforced with some of the best horse and foot. They should be ordered to commence the action on the enemy's right in order to disorder and surround it as expeditiously as possible. The other part of your army, composed of the lesser troops, should remain at a distance from the enemy's left so as not to be disrupted by their darts or in danger of being attacked sword in hand. In this oblique formation care must be taken to prevent the line being penetrated by the wedges of the enemy, and should to be employed only when the enemy's right wing is weak and your greatest strength is on your left.

In the fourth formation your army is marching to the attack in order of battle and as you come within four or five hundred paces of the enemy, both your wings must be ordered unexpectedly to quicken their pace and advance with quickness upon the enemy. When they find themselves attacked on both wings at the same time, the sudden surprise may so disconcert them as to give you an easy victory. Through this method, if your troops are very resolute and experienced they may ruin the enemy quickly, yet it is also dangerous. The general who attempts it is obliged to abandon and expose his center and to divide his army into three parts. If the enemy is not routed at the first charge, they have a fair opportunity of attacking the wings which are separated from each other and the center which is destitute of assistance.

The fifth formation resembles the fourth but with this addition: the light infantry and the archers are placed in the center to cover it from the attempts of the enemy. With this precaution the general may safely follow the above mentioned method and attack the enemy's left wing with his right, and their right with his left. If he puts them to flight, he gains an immediate victory, and if he fails to succeed, his center is in no danger, being protected by the light infantry and archers.

The sixth formation is very good and almost like the second. It is used when the general cannot depend either on the number or courage of his troops. If the disposition is made with forethought, notwithstanding his inferiority, he often has a good chance for victory. As your line approaches the enemy, advance your right wing against their left and begin the attack with your best cavalry and infantry. At the same time keep the rest of the army at a great distance from the enemy's right, extended in a direct line like a javelin. Thus if you can surround their left and attack it in flank and rear, you must inevitably defeat them. It is impossible for the enemy to draw off reinforcements from their right or from their center to sustain their left in this emergency, since the remaining part of your army is extended and at a great distance from them in the form of the letter L. It is a formation often used in an action on a march.

The seventh formation owes its advantages to the nature of the ground and will enable you to oppose an enemy with an army inferior both in numbers and experience, provided that one of your flanks can be covered either with an encumbrance such as the sea, a river, a lake, a city, a morass or broken ground inaccessible to the enemy. The rest of the army must be formed, as usual, in a straight line and the unsecured flank must be protected by your light troops and all your cavalry. Sufficiently defended on one side by the nature of the ground and on the other by a double support of cavalry, you may then safely venture on action.

One excellent and general rule must be observed. If you intend to engage with your right wing only, it must be composed of your best troops. The same method must be taken with respect to the left or if you intend to penetrate the enemy's line, the wedges which you form for that purpose in your center, must consist of the best disciplined soldiers. Victory in general is gained by a small number of men. Therefore the wisdom of a general appears in nothing more than in such choice of disposition of his men as is most consonant with reason and service.

THE FLIGHT OF AN ENEMY SHOULD NOT BE PREVENTED, BUT FACILITATED

Generals unskilled in war think a victory is incomplete unless the enemy is stalemated or so entirely surrounded by numbers as to have no possibility of escape. In such a situation, where no hopes remain, fear itself will arm an enemy and despair inspires courage. When men find they must inevitably perish, they willingly resolve to die with their comrades and with their arms in their hands. The maxim of Scipio that, *"a golden bridge should be made for a flying enemy"*, has much been commended. When an enemy has free room to escape they think of nothing but how to save themselves by flight, and the confusion becoming general, great numbers are cut to pieces. The pursuers can be in no danger when the vanquished have thrown away their arms for greater haste. In this case the greater the number of the flying army, the greater the slaughter. Numbers are of no signification where troops once thrown into consternation are equally terrified at the sight of the enemy as at their weapons. But on the contrary, when men are surrounded, although weak and few in number, they become a match for the enemy from this very consideration, that they have no resource but in despair.
"The conquered safety is, to hope for none."

MANNER OF CONDUCTING A RETREAT

Having gone through the various particulars relative to general actions, it remains at present to explain the manner of retreating in presence of the enemy. This is an operation, which, in the judgment of men of greatest skill and experience, is attended with the utmost hazard. A general certainly discourages his own troops and animates his enemies by retiring from the field without fighting. Yet as this must sometimes happen, it is proper to consider how to perform it with safety.

In the first place your men must not imagine that you retire because you don't want to fight, but believe your retreat an artifice to draw the enemy into an ambush or more advantageous position where you may easier defeat them in case they follow you. Troops who believe their general despairs of success are prone to flight. You must be cautious lest the enemy should discover your retreat and immediately fall upon you. To avoid this danger the cavalry are generally posted in the front of the infantry to conceal their motions and retreat from the enemy. The lead divisions are drawn off first, the others following in their turns. The last maintain their ground till the rest have marched off, and then file off themselves and join them in a leisurely and regular succession. Some generals have judged it best to make their retreat in the night after reconnoitering their routes, and thus gain so much ground that the enemy, not discovering their departure till daybreak, were not able to come up with them. The light infantry are also sent forward to possess the eminences under which the army might instantly retire with safety; and the enemy, in case they pursued, be exposed to the light infantry, masters of the heights, seconded by the cavalry.

A rash and undisciplined pursuit exposes an army to the greatest danger possible that of falling into ambush and the hands of troops ready for their reception. As the temerity of an army is increased and their caution lessened by the pursuit of a flying enemy, this is the most favorable opportunity for such snares. It is said that the greater the security, the greater the danger. When troops are unprepared, at their meals, fatigued after a march, their horses are feeding, or in short, when they believe themselves most secure, they are generally most liable to a surprise. All risks of this sort should be carefully avoided and all opportunities taken of distressing the enemy by such methods; neither numbers nor courage avail misfortunes of this nature.

A general who has been defeated in a pitched battle may try to blame fortune on this outcome, although skill and conduct may have had a greater impact. If he has allowed himself to be surprised or drawn into the snares of his enemy, he has no excuse for his fault, because he might have avoided such a misfortune by taking proper precautions and employing spies on whose intelligence he could depend.

When the enemy pursues a retreating foe, the following snare is usually laid: a small body of cavalry is ordered to pursue them on the direct road. At the same time a strong detachment is secretly sent another way to conceal itself on their route. When the cavalry have overtaken the enemy, they may feint some attacks and retire. The enemy, imagining the danger past, and that they have escaped the snare, neglect their order and march without regularity. Then the detachment sent to intercept them, seizing the opportunity, falls upon them unexpectedly and destroys them with ease.

When obliged to retreat through woods, many generals send parties forward to seize the defiles and difficult passes, to avoid ambushes and block the roads with barricades of felled trees to secure themselves from being pursued and attacked in the rear. In short both sides have equal opportunities of surprising or laying ambushes on the march. The army which retreats should leave troops behind for that purpose posted in convenient valleys or mountains covered with woods, and if the enemy falls into the snare, it returns immediately to their assistance. The army that pursues detaches different parties of light troops to march ahead through side roads and intercepts the enemy, who are surrounded and attacked at once in front and rear. The fleeing army may return and fall on the enemy while asleep in the night. The pursuing army may, even though the distance is great, surprise the adversary by forced marches. The former attempts may be at the crossing of a river in order to destroy the part of the enemy's army that has already crossed. The pursuers hasten their march to fall upon those units of the enemy that have not yet crossed.

ARMED CHARIOTS AND ELEPHANTS

The armed chariots used in war by Antiochus and Mithridates at first terrified the Romans, but they afterwards made a jest of them. As a chariot of this sort does not always meet with plain and level ground, the least obstruction stops it. And if one of the horses be either killed or wounded, it falls into the enemy's hands. The Roman soldiers rendered them useless chiefly by the following contrivance: at the instant the engagement began, they strewed the field of battle with caltrops, and the horses that drew the chariots, running full speed on them, were infallibly destroyed. A caltrop is a machine composed of four spikes or points arranged so that in whatever manner it is thrown on the ground, it rests on three and presents the fourth upright.

By their vast size, Elephants, with their horrible noise and the novelty of their form are at first very terrible both to men and horses. Pyrrhus first used them against the Romans in Lucania. Afterwards Hannibal brought them into the field from Africa. Antiochus in the east and Jugurtha in Numidia had great numbers of them. Many expedients have been used against them. In Lucania a centurion cut off the trunk of one with his sword. Two soldiers armed from head to foot in a chariot drawn by two horses, also covered with armor, attacked these beasts with lances of great length. They were secured by their armor from the archers on the elephants and avoided the fury of the animals by the swiftness of their horses. Foot soldiers completely armored, with the addition of long iron spikes fixed on their arms, shoulders and helmets, to prevent the elephant from seizing them with his trunk, were also employed against them.

But among the ancients, the velites usually engaged them. They were young soldiers, lightly armed, active and very expert in throwing their missile weapons on horseback. These troops kept hovering round the elephants continually and killed them with large lances and javelins. Afterwards, the soldiers, as their apprehensions decreased, attacked them in a body and, throwing their javelins together, and destroyed them by the multitude of wounds. Slingers with round stones from the fustibalus killed both the men who guided the elephants and the soldiers who fought in the towers on their backs. This was found by experience to be the best and safest expedient. At other times on the approach of these beasts, the soldiers opened their ranks and let them pass through. When elephants got into the midst of the troops, they surrounded them on all sides and were captured with their guards unhurt.

Large balistae, drawn on carriages by two horses or mules, should be placed in the rear of the line, so that when the elephants come within reach they may be transfixed with the darts[531]. The balistae should be larger and the heads of the darts stronger and broader than usual, so that the darts may be thrown farther, with greater force and the wounds be proportioned to the bodies of the beasts. It was proper to describe these several methods and contrivances employed against elephants, so that the manner to oppose those prodigious animals may be known.

---

[531] By darts he means short javelins or spears.

RESOURCES IN CASE OF DEFEAT

While one part of your army is victorious the other could be defeated and you are by no means to despair, since even in this extremity the constancy and resolution of a general may arrive at a complete victory. There are innumerable instances where the party that did not give way to despair was esteemed the conqueror. Where losses and advantages seem nearly equal, he is reputed to have the superiority that bears up against his misfortunes with greatest resolution. The general is therefore to be first, if possible, to seize the spoils of the slain and to make rejoicings for the victory. Such marks of confidence dispirit the enemy and redouble your own courage.

Notwithstanding an entire defeat, all possible remedies must be attempted, since many generals have been fortunate enough to repair such a loss. A prudent officer will never risk a general action without taking such precautions as will secure him from any considerable loss in case of a defeat, for the uncertainty of war and the nature of things may render such a misfortune unavoidable. The neighborhood of a mountain, a fortified post in the rear or a resolute stand made by a good body of troops to cover the retreat, may be the means of saving the army.

After a defeat an army sometimes rallies, turns on the enemy, disperses him by pursuing in order and destroys him without difficulty. Nor can men be in a more dangerous situation than, when in the midst of joy after victory, their exultation is suddenly converted into terror. Whatever the event is, the remains of the army must be immediately assembled, reanimated by suitable exhortations and furnished with fresh supplies of arms. New levies should immediately be made and new reinforcements provided. It is of much greater consequence that proper opportunities should be taken to surprise the victorious enemies, to draw them into snares and ambushes and by this means to recover the drooping spirits of your men. It will not be difficult to meet with such opportunities, as the nature of the human mind is apt to be too elated and to act with too little caution in prosperity. If anyone should imagine no resource is left after the loss of a battle, let him reflect on what has happened in similar cases and he will find that they who were victorious in the end were often unsuccessful in the beginning.

GENERAL MAXIMS

It is the nature of war that what is beneficial to you is detrimental to the enemy and what is of service to him always hurts you. It is therefore a maxim never to do, or to omit doing, anything as a consequence of his actions, but to consult invariably your own interest only. You depart from this interest whenever you imitate such measures as he pursues for his benefit. For the same reason it would be wrong for him to follow such steps as you take for your advantage.

The more your troops have been accustomed to camp duties on frontier stations and the more carefully they have been disciplined, the less danger they will be exposed to in the field.

Men must be sufficiently tried before they are led against the enemy.

It is much better to overcome the enemy by famine, surprise or terror than by general actions, for in the latter instance fortune has often a greater share than valor. Those designs are best which the enemy is entirely ignorant of till the moment of execution. Opportunity in war is often more to be depended on than courage.

To demoralize the enemy's soldiers and encourage them in surrendering themselves is of special service, for an adversary is more hurt by desertion than by slaughter.

It is better to have several bodies of reserves than to extend your front too much.

A general is not easily overcome who can form a true judgment of his own and the enemy's forces.

Valor is superior to numbers.

The nature of the ground is often of more consequence than courage.

Few men are born brave; many become so through care and force of discipline.

An army is strengthened by labor and enervated by idleness.

Troops are not to be led to battle unless confident of success.

Novelty and surprise throw an enemy into consternation; but common incidents have no effect.

He who rashly pursues a flying enemy with troops in disorder, seems inclined to resign that victory which he had before obtained.

An army unsupplied with grain and other necessary provisions will be vanquished without striking a blow.

A general whose troops are superior both in number and bravery should engage in the oblong square, which is the first formation.

He who judges himself inferior should advance his right wing obliquely against the enemy's left. This is the second formation.

If your left wing is strongest, you must attack the enemy's right according to the third formation.

The general who can depend on the discipline of his men should begin the engagement by attacking both the enemy's wings at once, the fourth formation.

He whose light infantry is good should cover his center by forming them in its front and charge both the enemy's wings at once. This is the fifth formation.

He who cannot depend either on the number or courage of his troops, if obliged to engage, should begin the action with his right and endeavor to break the enemy's left, the rest of his army remaining formed in a line perpendicular to the front and extended to the rear like a javelin. This is the sixth formation.

If your forces are few and weak in comparison to the enemy, you must make use of the seventh formation and cover one of your flanks either with an obstruction, a city, the sea, a river or some protection of that kind.

A general who trusts to his cavalry should choose the proper ground for them and employ them principally in the action.

He who depends on his infantry should choose a situation most proper for them and make most use of their service.

When an enemy's spy lurks in the camp, order all your soldiers in the day time to their tents, and he will instantly be apprehended.

On finding the enemy has notice of your designs; you must immediately alter your plan of operations.

Consult with many on proper measures to be taken, but communicate the plans you intend to put in execution to few, and those only of the most assured fidelity; or rather trust no one but yourself.

Punishment and fear of it are necessary to keep soldiers in order in quarters; but in the field they are more influenced by hope and rewards.

Good officers never engage in general actions unless induced by opportunity or obliged by necessity.

To distress the enemy more by famine than the sword is a mark of consummate skill.

Many instructions might be given with regard to the cavalry. As this branch of the service has been brought to perfection since the ancient writers and considerable improvements have been made in their drills and maneuvers, their arms, and the quality and management of their horses, nothing can be collected from their works. Our present mode of discipline is sufficient.

Dispositions for action must be carefully concealed from the enemy, lest they should counteract them and defeat your plans by proper expedients.

This abridgment of the most eminent military writers, invincible Emperor, contains the maxims and instructions they have left us, approved by different ages and confirmed by repeated experience. The Persians admire your skill in archery; the Huns and Alans endeavor in vain to imitate your dexterity in horsemanship; the Saracens and Indians cannot equal your activity in the hunt; and even the masters at arms pique themselves on only part of that knowledge and expertness of which you give so many instances in their own profession. How glorious it is therefore for Your Majesty with all these qualifications to unite the science of war and the art of conquest, and to convince the world that by Your conduct and courage You are equally capable of performing the duties of the soldier and the general!

Romans at a Siege (Blinder Atlas)

Index of People Mentioned in the Text

A

Scipio Africanus (236–183 BCE), also known as Scipio the African, Scipio the Elder, and Scipio the Great, was a general in the Second Punic War and statesman of the Roman Republic. He was best known for defeating Hannibal at the final battle of the Second Punic War at Zama, a feat that earned him the name Africanus, the nickname "the Roman Hannibal", as well as recognition as one of the finest commanders in military history.

Agathocles (361 – 289 BCE), was a Greek tyrant of Syracuse (317–289 BCE) and king of Sicily (304–289 BCE).

Agesilaus (444–360 BCE) was a king of Sparta, ruling from approximately 400 to 360 BCE, during most of which time he was, in Plutarch's words, "as good as thought commander and king of all Greece," and was for the whole of it greatly identified with his country's deeds and fortunes.

Alcibiades (450 – 404 BCE), was a prominent Athenian statesman, orator, and general. His family fell from prominence after the Peloponnesian War. He played a major role in the second half of that conflict as a strategic advisor, military commander, and politician.

Alexander of Macedonia (b. 20/21 July 356 – 10/11 June 323 BCE), (reigned 336-323 BCE), was commonly known as Alexander the Great. He was a king of Macedon, a state in northern ancient Greece. He was born in Pella in 356 BCE, Alexander was tutored by Aristotle until the age of 16. By the age of thirty, he had created one of the largest empires of the ancient world, stretching from the Ionian Sea to the Himalayas. He was undefeated in battle and is considered one of history's most successful commanders.

Anaxibius was the Spartan admiral who worked against the Greek troops of Cyrus the Younger who figures prominently in Xenophon's work entitled, Anabasis.] In the year 389 BCE, Anaxibius was sent out from Sparta to supersede Dercyllidas in the command at Abydus, and to check the rising fortunes of Athens in the Hellespont. Here he met at first with some success, till Iphicrates ambush his forces on the march. Foreseeing the certainty of his own defeat, told his men to save themselves and flee. His own duty, he said, required him to die there; and, with a small body of comrades, he remained on the spot, fighting till he fell, in 388 BCE.[6]

Antigonus "Antigonus the One-eyed", (382–301 BC), son of Philip from Elimeia, was a Macedonian nobleman, general, and satrap under Alexander the Great. During his early life he served under Philip II, and he was a major figure in the Wars of the Diadochi after Alexander's death, declaring himself king in 306 BC and establishing the Antigonid dynasty.

Antiochus was a Macedonian that lived during the time of Philip II of Macedon, who ruled from 359-336 BCE. He originally came from Orestis, Macedonia. Antiochus served as a military general under Philip II, who gained distinction as one of Philip's officers. Antiochus was from an upper noble family. His son was Seleucus I Nicator, who would become a general of Alexander the Great and later founded and became the first king of the Seleucid Empire. When Seleucus became king, he founded and named sixteen cities in honor of his father, these include the Syrian city of Antioch (now situated in modern Turkey) and the Seleucid Military Outpost, Antioch, Pisidia. Through Seleucus, Antiochus would have thirteen Seleucid kings bearing his name and various monarchs bearing his name from the Kingdom of Commagene. Antiochus would have various descendants through his son from the 3rd century BC until the 5th century and possibly beyond.

Antonius is the family name of the gens Antonia, one of the most important families in ancient Rome, with both patrician and plebeian branches. Marcus Antonius claimed that the family was descended from Anton, a son of Heracles. Women of the family were called Antonia. The Antonii produced a number of important generals and politicians,

Mark Antony (January 14, 83 BCE – August 1, 30 BCE), is also known to us as Marcus Antonia. He was a Roman politician and general. As a military commander and administrator, he was an important supporter and loyal friend of his mother's cousin Julius Caesar. After Caesar's assassination, Antony formed an official political alliance with Octavian (the future Augustus) and Lepidus, known to historians today as the Second Triumvirate. The triumvirate broke up in 33 BC. Disagreement between Octavian and Antony erupted into civil war, the Final War of the Roman Republic, in 31 BC. Antony was defeated by Octavian at the naval Battle of Actium, and in a brief land battle at Alexandria. He committed suicide shortly thereafter.

Archelaus was a king of Macedon from 413 to 399 BC. He was a capable and beneficent ruler, known for the sweeping changes he made in state administration, the military, and commerce. By the time that he died, Archelaus had succeeded in converting Macedon into a significantly stronger power. Thucydides credited Archelaus with doing more for his kingdom than all of his predecessors together.

Archidamus was the name of several kings of Sparta who ruled from 600 to 227 BCE.

Aristonicus of Alexandria was a distinguished Greek grammarian who lived during the reigns of Augustus and Tiberius, contemporary with Strabo. He taught at Rome, and wrote commentaries and grammatical treatises.

Aristippus of Cyrene, (c. 435 – c. 356 BCE), was the founder of the Cyreniac School of Philosophy. He was a pupil of Socrates, but adopted a very different philosophical outlook, teaching that the goal of life was to seek pleasure by adapting circumstances to oneself and by maintaining proper control over both adversity and prosperity.

Artaxerxes was the name of five king of Persia who reigned from 424 – 329 BCE.

Atheas (ca. 429 BC–339 BC) was described in Greek and Roman sources as the most powerful King of Scythia, who lost his life and empire in the conflict with Philip II of Macedon 339 BC.

Autophradates (lived 4th century BC) was a Persian who distinguished himself as a general in the reign of Artaxerxes III and Darius Codomannus.

B

Barca is the family name of several famous generals of Carthage from the third to second centuries BCE. They include the most famous leaders of the Punic Wars with Rome – Hamilcar, Hannibal, Hasdrubal and Mago.

Bardylis (c. 448 – 358 BCE) was a king of the Dardanian Kingdom. Bardyllis created one of the most powerful Illyrian states, that of the Dardanians. His state reigned over Macedonia, Epirus and the lake lands. Bardylis was killed in battle against Phillip II of Macedon.

Brasidas (died 422 BC) was a Spartan officer during the first decade of the Peloponnesian War.

Decimus Brutus (April 27, either 85 or 81 BCE, died 43 BCE) was a Roman politician and general of the first century BCE and one of the leading instigators of Julius Caesar's assassination. Decimus Brutus is not to be confused with the more famous Brutus among the conspirators, Marcus Brutus.

C

Quintus Servilius Caepio the Elder was a Roman statesman and general, consul in 106 BCE, and proconsul of Cisalpine Gaul in 105 BCE. He was the father of Quintus Servilius Caepio the Younger and the grandfather of Servilia Caepionis. In the Battle of Arausio in 105 BCE, Caepio led one of the two forces against the Germanic tribes (the Teutones, the Cimbri, and Tigurini/Marcomanni/Cherusci) along with the consul Gnaeus Mallius Maximus. His refusal to cooperate with Maximus led to the total destruction of a Roman. Upon his return to Rome, Caepio was tried for "the loss of his army" by a tribune of the plebs, Gaius Norbanus. Caepio was convicted, and was given the harshest sentence allowable: he was stripped of his citizenship, forbidden fire and water within eight hundred miles of Rome.

Gaius Caesar (July 100 –15 March 44 BCE) was a Roman general, politician and notable author of Latin prose. He played a critical role in the events that led to the demise of the Roman Republic and the rise of the Roman Empire. In 60 BCE, Caesar, Crassus and Pompey formed a political alliance that was to dominate Roman politics for several years. Their attempts to amass power through populist tactics were opposed by the conservative elite within the Roman Senate, among them Cato the Younger with the frequent support of Cicero. Caesar's conquest of Gaul was completed by 51 BCE extending Rome's territory to the English Channel and the Rhine. Caesar became the first Roman general to cross both when he built a bridge across the Rhine and conducted the first invasion of Britain.

Atilius Calatinus (died by 216 BCE) was a politician and general in Ancient Rome. He was the first Roman dictator to lead an army outside Italy (then understood as the Italian mainland), when he led his army into Sicily.

Marcus Furius Camillus (ca. 446 – 365 BCE) was a Roman soldier and statesman of patrician descent. According to Livy and Plutarch, Camillus triumphed four times, was five times dictator, and was honored with the title of "Second Founder of Rome".

Cannicus (or Gannicus) was a Gallic gladiator, from the gladiatorial school of Lentulus Batiatus in Capua. Together with the Thracian Spartacus, and the fellow Gauls Crixus, Oenomaus and Castus, he became one of the leaders of rebellious slaves during the Third Servile War (73-71 BC). In the winter of 71 BC Cannicus along with Castus broke off from Spartacus taking a large number of Celts and Germans with them marking the second break off of the rebellion. Cannicus and Castus met their end in Lucania near Mount Soprano (Mount Camalatrum) where Marcus Licinius Crassus, Lucius Pomptinus and Quintus Marcius Rufus entrenched their forces in battle and defeated them.

Titus Quinctius Capitolinus Barbatus was a Roman statesman and general who served as Consul five times between 471 and 439 BCE. Titus Quinctius was a member of the family Quinctia, one of the oldest patrician families in Rome.

Castor was one of twins in Greek and Roman mythology, Castor and Pollux or Polydeuces were twin brothers, together known as the Dioscuri. In Latin the twins are also known as the Gemini or Castores. Their mother was Leda, but Castor was the mortal son of Tyndareus, the king of Sparta, and Pollux the divine son of Zeus, who seduced or raped Leda in the guise of a swan. When Castor was killed, Pollux asked Zeus to let him share his own immortality with his twin to keep them together, and they were transformed into the constellation Gemini. The pair was regarded as the patrons of sailors, to whom they appeared as St. Elmo's fire, and were also associated with horsemanship.

Castus was a Gallic gladiator, and escaped from the gladiatorial school of Lentulus Batiatus in Capua. Together with Spartacus, and the fellow Gauls Crixus, Oenomaus and Cannicus, he became one of the leaders of rebellious slaves during the Third Servile War (73-71 BCE). He was killed along with his co-commander Cannicus and their Gallic and Germanic followers by Roman forces under Marcus Licinius Crassus at the Battle of Cantenna in Lucania in 71 BCE.

Marcus Porcius Cato (73-42 BCE), son of Cato the Younger by his first marriage to Atilia, was a Roman soldier and in his earlier years spent some time in politics with his father. He was admired by close friends and relatives, serving his father loyally. Although he was pardoned by Caesar following the death of his father, he joined the "liberators" in the assignation of Caesar and eventually died in battle.

Chabrias was a celebrated Athenian general of the 4th century BC. In 388 BC he defeated the Spartans and Aeginetans under Gorgopas at Aegina and commanded the fleet sent to assist Evagoras, king of Cyprus, against the Persians. He won several battles against the Spartans, most notably at Thebes in 378 BCE, Naxos in 376 BCE and Corinth also in 376 BCE. In 366 BCE, he and Callistratus were accused of treachery in advising the surrender of Oropus to the Thebans. He was acquitted and later joined Chares in the command of the Athenian fleet. He lost his life in an attack on the island of Chios.

Chares was an Athenian general, who was a key commander of Athenian forces in the fourth century BCE.

Cimon (510 – 450 BCE), was an Athenian statesman, strategos (general), and major political figure in mid-5th century BC Greece, the son of Miltiades, victor of Marathon. Cimon played a key role in creating the powerful Athenian maritime empire following the failure of the Persian invasion of Greece by Xerxes I in 480-479 BCE. Cimon became a celebrated military hero and was elevated to the rank of admiral after fighting in the Battle of Salamis.

Quintius Cincinnatus (519 BC – 430 BC) was a Roman aristocrat and statesman whose service as consul in 460 BC and dictator in 458 BC and 439 BC made him a model of civic virtue. When his son was convicted and condemned to death, Cincinnatus was forced to live in humble circumstances, working on his own small farm, until an invasion caused him to be called to serve Rome as dictator, an office which he immediately resigned after completing his task of defeating the rival tribes of the Aequians, Sabines, and Volscians. His immediate resignation of his absolute authority with the end of the crisis has often been cited as an example of outstanding leadership, service to the greater good, civic virtue, lack of personal ambition and modesty.

Appius Claudius Pulcher (ca 70 BCE – 30 BCE) was a Roman politician. An early supporter of Augustus, he was elected consul in 38 BCE.

Claudius II, Gothicus (268 – 270 AD) who defeated the Goths at Naissus in 268/9 AD

Cleandridas was a Spartan general of the 5th century BCE, who advised the young king Pleistoanax during the early part of the latter's reign. According to Plutarch, both Cleandrides and Pleistoanax were banished from Sparta (most likely between the years 446 and 444 BCE), for allegedly accepting a bribe from the Athenian leader Pericles to call off their planned attack on the Athenian region Attica. Although Pleistoanax was later recalled to Sparta, Cleandrides had a death sentence imposed upon him in his absence.

Cleomenes (died c. 489 BC) was an Agiad, King of Sparta in the late 6th and early 5th centuries BCE. Starting around 520 BC, he pursued an aggressive foreign policy aimed at crushing Argos and extending Sparta's influence both inside and outside the Peloponnese. He was supposed to be a brilliant tactician and he successfully intervened twice in Athenian affairs but kept Sparta out of the Ionian Revolt.

Cleon (died 422 BCE) was an Athenian statesman and a strategos during the Peloponnesian War who opposed Pericles and eventually died in battle.

Cleonymus was a political ally of Cleon and an Athenian general. In 424 BCE, Cleonymus had dropped his shield in battle and fled which caused him to be branded a coward.

Clisthenes was a noble Athenian credited with reforming the constitution of ancient Athens and setting it on a democratic footing in 508/7 BCE. For these accomplishments, historians refer to him as "the father of Athenian democracy." Also, he was credited with increasing the power of the Athenian citizens' assembly and for reducing the power of the nobility over Athenian politics.

Horatio Cocles was an officer in the army of the ancient Roman Republic who famously defended the Pons Sublicius from the invading army of Lars Porsena, king of Clusium in the late 6th century BCE, during the war between Rome and Clusium. He is most famous for his defense of a bridge to protect the Roman Army against the Etruscans.

Commius, was appointed King of the Atrebatian by Caesar during his Gallic Campaigns in the 50's BCE and was supposedly loyal despite revolts of other Gallic tribes. Hirtius' book, however, he was supposedly accused of treachery and an attempt was made on his life, but he escaped never to be heard from again.

Domitius Corbulo (c. 7 - 67 AD) was a Roman general and a brother-in-law of the Emperor Caligula.

Cornelius Cossus was a Roman politician and general who lived in the 5th century BCE.

Marcus Licinius Crassus (ca. 115 – 53 BCE) was a Roman general and politician who played a key role in the transformation of the Roman Republic into the Roman Empire. Amassing an enormous fortune during his life, Crassus is considered the wealthiest man in Roman history, and among the richest men in all history. A political and financial patron of Julius Caesar, Crassus joined Caesar and Pompey in the unofficial political alliance known as the First Triumvirate. After his second Consulship, Crassus was appointed as the Governor of Roman Syria which he used as the launch pad for a military campaign against the Parthian Empire. Crassus' campaign was a disastrous failure, resulting in his defeat and death at the Battle of Carrhae and hastened the end of cooperation between Caesar and Pompey.

Craterus (ca. 370 – 321 BCE) was a Macedonian general under Alexander the Great and one of the Diadochi. Craterus commanded the phalanx and all infantry on the left wing in Battle of Issus (333 BCE). In 322 BCE Craterus aided Antipater in the Lamian War against Athens. He sailed with his Cilician navy to Greece and led troops at the Battle of Crannon in 322 BCE. When Antigonus rose in rebellion against Perdiccas and Eumenes, Craterus joined him, alongside Antipater and Ptolemy. He was killed in battle against Eumenes in Asia Minor when his charging horse fell over him, somewhere near the Hellespont, in 321 BCE.

Croesus (595 – 547 BCE) was the King of Lydia from 560 to 547 BCE until his defeat by the Persians.

Manius Curius (died 270 BCE), son of Manius, was a three-time consul and a plebian hero of the Roman Republic, noted for ending the Samnite War.

Papirius Cursor was a Roman general who was a Consul five times and dictator twice.

Cyrus II of Persia (600 or 576–530 BCE), commonly known as Cyrus the Great, also known as Cyrus the Elder, was the founder of the Achaemenid Empire. Under his rule, the empire embraced all the previous civilized states of the ancient Near East, expanded vastly and eventually conquered most of Southwest Asia and much of Central Asia and the Caucasus. He created the largest empire the world had seen at that time which stretched from the Mediterranean Sea and Hellespont in the west to the Indus River in the east.

D

Publius Decius Mus, son of Quintus, of plebeian origins, who was a Roman consul in 340 BC. He is noted particularly for sacrificing himself in battle through the ritual of devotio, as recorded by the Augustan historian Livy. After performing the religious ritual, the fully armored Decius Mus plunged his horse into the enemy with such supernatural vigor and violence that the awe-struck Latins soon refused to engage him, eventually bringing him down with darts. Even then, the Latins avoided his body, leaving a large space around it; and so the left wing of the Romans, once faltering, then attacked the weakened enemy lines. Manlius, conducting the right wing, held fast, allowing the Latins to use up their reserves, before crushing the enemy host between the renewed left and Samnite foederati at their flank, leaving only a quarter of the enemy to flee.

Diocletian (22 December 244 – 3 December 311 AD), He was a Roman Emperor from 284 to 305. Diocletian's reign stabilized the Empire and marks the end of the Crisis of the Third Century. He appointed fellow officer Maximian Augustus his senior co-emperor in 285.

Titus Didius was a general and politician of the Roman Republic. He is credited with the restoration of the Villa Publica, and is notorious for his proconsulship in Hispania Citerior (modern-day Spain).

Diodotus I Soter (285 – 239 BCE) was Seleucid satrap of Bactria, rebelled against Seleucid rule soon after the death of Antiochus II in c. 255 or 246 BCE, and wrested independence for his territory. He died in 239 BCE.

Domitian (Titus Flavius Caesar Domitianus Augustus) (24 October 51 – 18 September 96AD) was Roman Emperor from 81 to 96. Domitian was the third and last emperor of the Flavian dynasty who was assassinated by one of his officers. He fought major wars in his lifetime in Britain and against the Dacians. Stratagems was written during the reign of and dedicated to Domitian.

Gaius Duilius (lived 3rd century BCE) was a Roman politician and admiral involved in the First Punic War.
Little is known about his family background or early career, since he was a novus homo, meaning not belonging to a traditional family of Roman aristocrats. He managed, nevertheless, to be elected consul for the year of 260 BCE, at the outbreak of the First Punic war. As junior partner of the patrician Gnaeus Cornelius Scipio Asina, Duilius was given the command of the rear fleet, not expected to see much action. However, the naivety of Scipio Asina got him captured in the Battle of the Lipari Islands, leaving Duilius as senior commander. He won a victory over the Carthage at Mylae using the corvus.

E

Eumenes (ca. 362—316 BCE) was a Greek general and scholar. He participated in the wars of the Diadochi as a supporter of the Macedonian royal house.

Epaminondas (418 – 362 BCE), was a Theban general and statesman of the 4th century BCE who transformed the Ancient Greek city-state of Thebes, leading it out of Spartan subjugation into a preeminent position in Greek politics. In the process he broke Spartan military power with his victory at Leuctra and liberated the Messenian helots, a group of Peloponnesian Greeks who had been enslaved under Spartan rule for some 230 years, having been defeated in the Messenian War around 600 BC. He is largely remembered for a decade (371-362 BCE) of campaigning that sapped the strength of the great land powers of Greece and paved the way for the Macedonian conquest.

F

Marcus Fabius Ambustus (active 360–351 BCE) was a statesman and general of the Roman Republic. He was the son of Numerius Fabius Ambustus. His consulships occurred during a time in which Rome was reasserting itself following its defeat at the hands of the Gauls in the Battle of the Allia of 387 BCE. He defeated the Hernici in 356 BCE, and Tibur in 354 BCE, earning a triumph for the latter victory. He further succeeded against the Falisci, but was defeated by Tarquinia.

Quintus Fabius(ca. 280 – 203 BCE) was a Roman politician and general. His nickname *Cunctator* means "delayer" in Latin, and refers to his tactics in deploying the troops during the Second Punic War. He is widely regarded as the father of guerilla warfare due to his, at the time, novel strategy of targeting enemy supply lines in light of being largely outnumbered.

Marcus Calpurnius Flamma was a Roman military leader and hero in the First Punic War. Flamma was a military tribune who led 300 volunteers on a suicide mission to free a consular army from a defile in which they had been trapped by the Carthaginians. Flamma was found gravely wounded under a pile of bodies but survived

Gnaeus Fulvius Centumalus Maximus (d. 210 BCE) was a consul of the Roman Republic in 211 BCE. As consul, Fulvius defended Rome against Hannibal with his colleague Publius Sulpicius Galba Maximus during the Second Punic War.

Lucius Furius was a Roman commander who aided Publius Varinus and Lucius Cossinius against Spartacus in the Third Servile War.

G

Gaius Sulpicius Gallus was a general, statesman and orator of the Roman Republic. He commanded the 2nd legion in the campaign against Perseus, king of Macedonia, and gained great reputation for having predicted an eclipse of the moon on the night before the Battle of Pydna (168 BCE).

Gelo (died 478 BCE), a Greek who was the son of Deinomenes, was a 5th-century BC ruler of Gela and Syracuse.

Acilius Glabrio was a consul of the Roman Republic in 191 BCE. He came from an illustrious plebian family whose members held magistracies throughout the Republic and into the Imperial era.

Tiberius Sempronius Gracchus (died 212 BCE) was a Roman Republican consul in the Second Punic War. He was son of Tiberius Sempronius Gracchus who the first man from his family to become consul. Gracchus is first mentioned in 216 BC as curule aedile in which capacity he was inducted as Master of the Horse to the newly elected Dictator Marcus Junius Pera after the defeat at Cannae.

Gratian (18 April/23 May 359 – 25 August 383) was Roman Emperos from 375 to 383. The eldest son of Valentinian I, Gratian accompanied his father on several campaigns as a young man along the Rhine and Danube frontiers. Upon the death of Valentinian in 375, Gratian's brother Valentinian II was declared emperor by his father's soldiers. In 378, Gratian's generals won a decisive victory over the Lentienses, a branch of the Alamanni, at the Battle of Argentovaria. Gratian subsequently led a campaign across the Rhine, the last emperor to do so, and attacked the Lentienses, forcing the tribe to surrender. That same year, his uncle Valens was killed in the Battle of Adrianople against the Goths – making Gratian essentially ruler of the entire Roman Empire.

H

Hannibal (c. 300-290 – 258 BC) was a Carthaginian military commander in charge of both land armies and naval fleets during the First Punic War against Rome. His efforts proved ultimately unsuccessful and his eventual defeat in battle led to his downfall and execution.

Hanno the Great was a politician and military leader of the 4th century BCE. In 367 Hanno the Great commanded a fleet of 200 ships which won a decisive naval victory over the Greeks of Sicily. His victory effectively blocked the plans of Dionysius I of Syracuse to attack Lilybaeum, a city allied to Carthage in western Sicily.

Hasdrubal (245–207 BCE) was Hamilcar Barca's second son and a Carthaginian general in the Second Punic War. He was a younger brother of the much more famous Hannibal. He won several major battles for his brother, but was decisively defeated at the Battle of the Metaurus. Hasdrubal himself died bravely in the fight.

Hermocrates (died 407 BCE) was an ancient Syracusan general during the Athenians' Sicilian Expedition in the midst of the Peloponnesian War.

Himilco a Carthaginian navigator and explorer who lived during the height of Carthaginian power, the 5th century BCE. Himilco is the first known explorer from the Mediterranean Sea to reach the north-western shores of Europe. His lost account of his adventures is quoted by Roman writers.

Hirtuleius is the trusted lieutenant of the Populares Quintus Sertorius, who fought in the Sertorian War from 80 BCE until his death in 75 BCE.

Tullus Hostilius (ruled 673 – 642 BCE) was the legendary third of the Kings of Rome. He succeeded Numa Pompilius and was succeeded by Ancus Marcius . Unlike his predecessor, Tullus was known as a warlike king.

I

Iphicrates (418 - 353 BCE) was an Athenian general. He owes his fame as much to the improvements he made in the equipment of the peltasts or light-armed mercenaries (named for their small *pelte* shield) as to his military successes. Historians have debated about just what kind of "peltasts" were affected by his reforms; one of the most popular positions is that he improved the performance of the Greek skirmishers so that they would be able to engage in prolonged hand-to-hand fighting as part of the main battle line. Another possibility is that his reforms were limited to hoplites serving as marines on board ships of the Athenian navy.

I

Jugurtha (160 – 104 BCE) was a King of Numidia, born in Cirta (modern-day Constantine). He started out as an ally of Rome, but eventually engaged in a protracted war – The Jugurthine War (112-105 BCE). He was finally defeated by Sulla and paraded through the streets of Rome, where he was thrown into the Tullianum where he died of starvation in 104 BCE.

L

Titus Labienus (100 – March 17, 45 BCE) was a professional Roman soldier in the late Roman Republic. He served as Tribune of the Plebs in 63 BCE, and is remembered as one of Julius Caesar's lieutenants, mentioned frequently in the accounts of his military campaigns.

Gaius Laelius general and statesman, was a friend of Scipio Africanus, whom he accompanied on his Iberian campaign (210 - 206 BCE; the Roman Hispania, comprising modern Spain and Portugal). His command of the Roman fleet in the attack on New Carthage and command of the Roman & Italian cavalry at Zama contributed to Scipio's victories.

Publius Valerius Laevinus was commander of the Roman forces at the Battle of Heraclea in 280 BC, in which he was defeated by Pyrrhus of Epirus. In his Life of Pyrrhus, Plutarch wrote that Caius Fabricius said of this battle that it was not the Epirots who had beaten the Romans, but only Pyrrhus who had beaten Laevinus.

Leptines was an Athenian orator. He is known as the proposer of a law that no Athenian, whether citizen or resident alien (with the sole exception of the descendants of Harmodius and Aristogeiton), should be exempt from the public charges for the state festivals.

Publius Licinius Crassus (86/82 – 53 BCE) was one of two sons of the Marcus Licinius Crassus, the so-called "triumvir", and Tertulla. Publius Crassus served under Julius Caesar in Gaul 58–56 BC. Too young to receive a formal commission from the senate, Publius distinguished himself as a commanding officer in campaigns among the Armorican nations (Brittany) and in Aquitania. He was highly regarded by Caesar and also by Cicero, who praised his speaking ability and good character. Publius's promising career was cut short when he died along with his father in an ill-conceived war against the Parthian Empire.

Sempronius Longus (260 – 210 BCE) was a Roman consul during
the Second Punic War and a contemporary of Publius Cornelius Scipio. In
218 BC, Sempronius was sent to Africa with 160 quinqueremes to gather
forces and supplies, while Scipio was sent to Iberia to intercept Hannibal. It
was at this time, striking from Lilybaeum, on the island of Sicily, that
Sempronius Longus captured Malta from the Carthaginians.

Lysander the Spartan (died 395 BCE), was a Spartan admiral who
commanded the Spartan fleet in the Hellespont which defeated
the Athenians at Aegospotami in 405 BCE. The following year, he was able to
force the Athenians to capitulate, bringing the Peloponnesian War to an end;
he organized the dominion of Sparta over Greece in the last decade of his life.

Lysimachus (360 – 281 BCE) was a Macedonian officer and diadochus (i.e.
"successor") of Alexander the Great, who became a basileus ("King") in 306
BCE, ruling Thrace, Asia Minor and Macedon.

M

Mago (243 – 203 BCE), was a member of the Barcid family, and played an
important role in the Second Punic War, leading forces of Carthage against the
Roman Republic in Hispania, Gallia Cisalpina and Italy. Mago was the third
son of Hamilcar Barca, brother to Hannibal and Hasdrubal, and brother-in-law
to Hasdrubal the Fair.

Maharbal (2nd century BCE) was Hannibal's cavalry commander during
the Second Punic War. He was often critical to the success of the side
of Carthage over Rome. Throughout his Italian campaign Hannibal maintained
an advantage in mounted soldiers and thus relied upon them and Maharbal to
give himself a sizeable edge.

Gnaeus Manlius was a Roman Praetor who was involved in the Third Servile
War with Gnaeus Tremellius Scrofa.

Claudius Marcellus (268–208 BCE), five times elected as consul of
the Roman Republic, was an important Roman military leader during the
Gallic War of 225 BCE and the Second Punic War. Marcellus gained the most
prestigious award a Roman general could earn, the spolia opima, for killing the
Gallic military leader and king Viridomarus in hand-to-hand combat in 222
BCE at the battle of Clastidium.

Gaius Marius (157– January 13, 86 BCE) was a Roman general and statesman. He held the office of consul an unprecedented seven times during his career. He was also noted for his important reforms of Roman armies, authorizing recruitment of landless citizens, eliminating the manipular military formations, and reorganizing the structure of the legions into separate cohorts. Marius defeated the invading Germanic tribes (the Teutones, Ambrones, and the Cimbri), for which he was called "the third founder of Rome." His life and career were significant in Rome's transformation from Republic to Empire.

Masinissa, (240 or 238 BCE -148 BCE), was the first King of Numidia. During his younger years he fought in the Second Punic War (218-201 BC), first against the Romans as an ally of Carthage and later switching sides when he saw which way the conflict was going. With Roman help, he united the eastern and western Numidian tribes and founded the Kingdom of Numidia. He is most famous for his role as a Roman ally in the Battle of Zama and as husband of Sophonisba , a Carthaginian noblewoman whom he allowed to poison herself to avoid being paraded in a triumph in Rome.

Maximian (c. 250 – c. July 310), was Roman Emperor from 286 to 305. He shared the latter title with his co-emperor and superior, Diocletian, whose political brain complemented Maximian's military brawn. Maximian established his residence at Trier but spent most of his time on campaign.

Quintus Fabius Maximus (died December 31, 45 BC) was a general and politician of the late Roman Republic. He was a trusted lieutenant of Ceasar who commanded forces during the Civil War and helped Caesar win at the battle of Munda (17 March 45 BCE).

Memnon the Rhodian (380 – 333 BCE) was the commander of the Greek mercenaries in the service of the Persian king Darius III when Alexander the Great of Macedonia invaded Persia in 334 BCE. Memnon advocated a scorched earth policy against Alexander, aware of the Macedonian's lack of supplies and funds. He commanded the mercenaries at the Battle of Granicus River, where his troops were massacred by the victorious Macedonians.

Quintus Caecilius Metellus Pius (130 – 63 BCE) was a pro-Sullan politician and general. He was the principal Senatorial commander during the Sertorian War, fighting alongside Pompeius Magnus. He was given the agnomen (nickname) "Pius" because of his constant and unbending attempts to have his father officially recalled from exile

Miltiades (550 – 489 BCE) is known mostly for his role in the Battle of Marathon. He also convinced the generals of the necessity of not using the customary tactics, as hoplites usually marched in an evenly distributed phalanx of shields and spears, a standard with no other instance of deviation until Epaminondas. Miltiades feared the cavalry of the Persians attacking the flanks, and asked for the flanks to have more hoplites than the center. Miltiades had his men march to the end of the Persian archer range, called the "beaten zone", then break out in a run straight at the Persian horde. This was very successful in defeating the Persians, who then tried to sail around the Cape Sounion and attack Attica from the west. Miltiades got his men to quickly march to the western side of Attica overnight, causing Datis to flee at the sight of the soldiers who had just defeated him the previous evening.

Mindarus was a Spartan admiral who commanded the Peloponnesian fleet in 411 and 410 BCE, during the Peloponnesian War. Successful in shifting the theater of war into the Hellespont, he then experienced a string of defeats; in the third and final of these, he himself was killed and the entire Peloponnesian fleet was captured or destroyed.

Quintus Minucius was an officer serving under Q. Fulvius Flaccus when Roman forces took back Capua in 211 BCE after their defeat the previous year by Hannibal.

Mithridates VI or **Mithradates VI** 134–63 BCE, also known as Mithradates the Great and Eupator Dionysius, was king of Pontus and Armenia Minor in northern Anatolia (now Turkey) from about 120–63 BCE. Mithridates is remembered as one of the Roman Republic's most formidable and successful enemies, who engaged three of the prominent generals from the late Roman Republic in the Mithridatic Wars: Lucius Cornelius Sulla, Lucullus and Pompey. He was also the greatest ruler of the Kingdom of Pontus.

Myronides was an Athenian general of the First Peloponnesian War. In 458 BCE he defeated the Corinthians at Megara and then in 457 BCE he defeated the Boeotians at the Battle of Oenophyta. Myronides' victory at Oenophyta led to a decade of Athenian domination over Boeotia, Locris and Phocis sometimes called the Athenian 'Land Empire'.

N

Claudius Nero (15 December 37 – 9 June 68) was Roman Emperor from 54 to 68, and the last in the Julio-Claudian dynasty. Nero was adopted by his great uncle Claudius to become his heir and successor, and succeeded to the throne in 54 following Claudius' death. During his reign, Nero focused much of his attention on diplomacy, trade, and enhancing the cultural life of the Empire. He ordered theaters built and promoted athletic games. He also began the First Roman-Jewish War.

Fulvius Nobilior served with distinction in Spain, and as consul in 189 BCE he completely broke the power of the Aetolian League. On his return to Rome, Nobilior celebrated a triumph (of which full details are given by Livy) remarkable for the magnificence of the spoils exhibited. On his Aetolian campaign he was accompanied by the poet Ennius, who made the capture of Ambracia, at which he was present, the subject of one of his plays. For this Nobilior was strongly opposed by Cato the Censor, on the ground that he had compromised his dignity as a Roman general. In 179 BCE he was appointed censor together with Marcus Aemilius Lepidus.

O

Gnaeus Octavius (died 87 BC) was a Roman senator who was elected consul of the Roman Republic in 87 BCE alongside Lucius Cornelius Cinna. He died during the chaos that accompanied the capture of Rome by Cinna and Gaius Marius.

Orestes (died 28 August AD 476) was a Roman general and politician of Germanic ancestry, who was briefly in control of the Western Roman Empire in 475–6.

Osaces (d. 51 BCE), he was a Parthian general during the war between the Roman Republic and Parthia. He was subsequently killed in an ambush during the war.

P

Pacorus I of Parthia (died 38 BCE) was the son of king Orodes II and queen Laodice of the Parthian Empire. Following the defeat of the Roman general Marcus Licinius Crassus at the Battle of Carrhae in 53 BCE, Pacorus launched an invasion of Syria in 51 BC, briefly conquering the Roman territory before being driven out by Cassius. Pacorus invaded Syria again in 40 BC in alliance with the Roman rebel Quintus Labienus. In 39 BCE, a Roman counterattack under Publius Ventidius Bassus killed Labienus in a battle in the Taurus Mountains and recovered Anatolia. Pacorus returned to Syria in 38 BCE, but was killed in the Battle of Mount Gindarus.

Pammenes was a Theban general of considerable celebrity during the 4th century BCE.

Aemilius Paulus (229 – 160 BCE) was a two-time consul of the Roman Republic and a noted general who conquered Macedon putting an end to the Antigonid dynasty. He won the decisive battle of Pydna. Perseus of Macedonia was made prisoner and the Third Macedonian War ended.

Pelopidas (died 364 BC) was an important Theban statesman and general in Greece. He helped to liberate Thebes from Spartan control. About 375 he routed a much larger Spartan force at the battle of Tegyra. This victory he owed mainly to the valor of the Sacred Band, an elite corps of 300 seasoned soldiers. At the battle of Leuctra (371 BC) he contributed greatly to the success of Epaminondas' new tactics by the rapidity with which he made the Sacred Band close with the Spartans. Epaminondas, an intuitive and genius general used at Leuctra for the first time the oblique order in which a local superiority of numbers can be used to defeat a superior force. Then, by winning in detail, one can hope to win in the whole. After the battle at Leuctra Thebes became the strongest city of Greece and Sparta withdrew as a leading city.

Perdiccas (died 321/320 BCE) was one of Alexander the Great's generals. After Alexander's death in 323 BCE he became regent of all Alexander's empire.

Pericles (495 – 429 BCE) was the most prominent and influential Greek statesman, orator, and general of Athens during the Golden Age — specifically, the time between the Persian and Peloponnesian Wars. He was descended, through his mother, from the powerful and historically influential Alcmaeonid family. Pericles turned the Delian League into an Athenian empire and led his countrymen during the first two years of the Peloponnesian War.

Perseus, King of Macedonia (c. 212 – 166 BCE) was the last king of the Antigonid dynasty, who ruled the successor state in Macedon created upon the death of Alexander the Great. He also has the distinction of being the last of the line, after losing the Battle of Pydna on 22 June 168 BCE; subsequently Macedon came under Roman rule.

Phalaris of Agrigentum was the tyrant of Acragas in Sicily, from approximately 570 to 554 BCE.

Pharnabazus III (370 - after 320 BCE) was a Persian satrap who fought against Alexander the Great.

Pharasmanes I (died 58) was a King of Iberia (Kartli, modern eastern Georgia) who plays a prominent role in Tacitus' account of Rome's eastern policy and campaigns under Tiberius, Claudius and Nero. He reigned from 1 to 58.

Philip II of Macedonia (382–336 BCE), was king (basileus) of Macedon from 359 BCE until his assassination in 336 BCE. He was the father of Alexander the Great and Philip III.

Phormio the son of Asopius, was an Athenian general and admiral before and during the Peloponnesian War. A talented naval commander, Phormio commanded at several famous Athenian victories in 428 BEC, and was honored after his death with a statue on the acropolis and a state funeral. He is considered the first great admiral in history.

Lucius Piso was a Roman statesman of the 1st century. He was the grandson and son of men who had made huge fortunes from selling armaments which were used by the Roman legions.

Metellus Pius (130 – 63 BCE) was a pro-Sullan politician and general who was Roman consul in 80 BCE. He was the principal Senatorial commander during the Sertorian War, fighting alongside Pompeius Magnus.

Pompey also known as **Gnaeus Pompeius Magnus** (29 September 106 – 28 September 48 BCE), was a military and political leader of the late Roman Republic. He was part of the First Triumvirate with Marcus Licinius Crassus and Gaius Julius Caesar. Pompey would later contend with Julius Caesar for leadership of Rome leading to a civil war in Rome. His defeat would lead Rome towards its transformation from a Republic to a Principate and later Empire.

Porsenna was an Etruscan king known for his war against the city of Rome. He ruled over the city of Clusium.

Porus King of Paurava, an ancient state within the territory of modern day Punjab, located between the Jhelum river and the Chenab River (in Greek, the Hydaspes and the Acesines) rivers. Porus fought Alexander the Great in the Battle of the Hydaspes River in 326 BCE (at the site of modern day Mong) and was defeated. He then served Alexander as a client king.

Aulus Postumius Albinus was a general of the Roman Republic in the 1st century BCE. He attained the praetorian rank, and commanded the fleet in the Marsic War in 89 BC. He was subsequently killed by his own soldiers who claimed that he had been guilty of treason.

Tarquinius Priscus was the legendary fifth King of Rome from 616- 579 BCE.

Pyrrhus (319/318–272 BCE) was a Greek general and statesman of the Hellenistic era. He was king of the Greek tribe of Molossians , of the royal Aeacid house (from c. 297 BCE), and later he became King of Epirus (306–302, 297–272 BCE) and Macedon (288–284, 273–272 BCE). He was one of the strongest opponents of early Rome. Some of his battles, though successful, cost him heavy losses, from which the term "Pyrrhic Victory" was coined.

Q

Titus Quinctius (c. 229 BC – c. 174 BC) was a Roman politician and general instrumental in the Roman conquest of Greece.

R

Gaius Atilius Regulus (killed 225 BCE at Telamon in battle) was one of the two Roman consuls who fought a Celtic invasion of Italy in 225-224 BCE. He was killed in battle and beheaded.

Romulus was part of the twin brothers who were central characters of Rome's foundation myth. He kills his brother Remus over a quarrel about where the city should be founded. Romulus names the city "Rome" after himself and becomes the first king of Rome.

Marcus Minucius Rufus (died August 2, 216 BCE) was a Roman consul in 221 BCE. He was also Magister Equitum during dictatorship of Quintus Fabius Maximus. He was a political enemy of Fabius Maximus. He was against his delaying defensive strategy during the Second Punic War. Minucius finally accepted Fabius commands after Fabiussaved his life during Hannibal's attack at Gerontium. Marcus Minucius Rufus was killed in the Battle of Cannae.

S

Marcus Livius Drusus Salinator (254 – 204 BCE), was a Roman consul who fought in both the First and the Second Punic Wars most notably during the Battle of the Metaurus.

Sallust was a Roman historian, politician, and *novus homo* from a provincial plebian family. Sallust is the earliest known Roman historian with surviving works to his name, of which we have *Catiline's War* (about the conspiracy in 63 BCE of L. Sergius Catilina), *The Jugurthine War* (about Rome's war against the Numidians from 111 - 105 BCE), and the *Histories* (of which only fragments survive).

Marcus Scaurus (163 – 89 BCE) was a Roman consul in 115 BCE and considered one of the most talented and influential politicians of the Republic.

Publius Cornelius Scipio (died 211 BCE) was a general and statesman of the Roman Republic. He served as consul in 218 BCE, the first year of the Second Punic War.

Scorylo (27 BC – AD 14) was a Dacian King who unified Dacian tribes.

Semiramis was the legendary queen of King Ninus, succeeding him to the throne of Assyria.

Quintus Sertorious (126 – 73 BCE) was a Roman statesman and general, born in Nursia, in Sabine territory. His brilliance as a military commander was shown most clearly in his battles against Rome for control of Hispania.

Publius Servilius Rullus was a cavalry leader in 40 BCE of Octavian (the future Emperor Augustus).

Spartacus (109–71 BCE) was a Thracian gladiator, who along with the Gauls, Crixus and Oenomaus, Roman Castus and Celt Cannicus, was one of the slave leaders in the Third Servile War, a major slave uprising against the Roman Republic.

Lucius Sulla (138 - 78 BCE), was a Roman general and conservative statesman. He had the distinction of holding the office of consul twice, as well as reviving the dictatorship. Sulla was awarded a grass crown, the most prestigious and rarest Roman military honor, during the Social War.

Syphax was a king of the ancient Algerian tribe Masaesyli of western Numidia during the last quarter of the 3rd century BCE.

T

Tarquinius Superbus (535 – 496 BCE) was the legendary seventh and final King of Rome, reigning from 535 BCE until the popular uprising in 509 BCE that led to the establishment of the Roman Republic.

Thamyris son of Philammon and the nymph Argiope, was a Thracian singer who was so proud of his skill that he boasted he could best the Muses. He competed against them and lost. As punishment for his presumption they blinded him, and took away his ability to make poetry and to play the lyre.

Themistocles (524–459 BCE) was an Athenian politician and general. He was one of a new breed of non-aristocratic politicians who rose to prominence in the early years of the Athenian democracy. As a politician, Themistocles was a populist, having the support of lower class Athenians, and generally being at odds with the Athenian nobility. Elected archon in 493 BCE, he convinced the polis to increase the naval power of Athens, which would be a recurring theme in his political career.

Tigranes II more commonly known as Tigranes the Great (140–55 BCE) was emperor of Armenia under whom the country became, for a short time, the strongest state east of the Roman Republic. Under his reign, the Armenian kingdom expanded beyond its traditional boundaries, allowing Tigranes to claim the title Great King, and involving Armenia in many battles against opponents such as the Parthian and Seleucid empires, and the Roman Republic.

Timarchus was a usurper in the Seleucid Empire between 163-160 BCE.

Tisamenus or **Tissamenus,** in Greek mythology, was a son of Orestes and his cousin Hermione. He succeeded his father to the thrones of Argos, Mycenae and Sparta and was later killed in the final battle with the Heracleidae.

Tissaphernes (died 395 BC) was a Persian soldier and statesman. In 413 BC he was satrap of Lydia and Caria, and commander in chief of the Persian army in Asia Minor

Sempronius Tuditanus (3rd century BC) was a Roman Republican consul and censor, best known for leading about 600 men to safety at Cannae in August, 216 BCE.

Tydeus was an Aeolian hero of the generation before the Trojan War. He was one of the Seven Against Thebes, and the father of Diomedes.

V

Valentinian II (371 – 15 May 392), was Roman Emperor from AD 375 to 392.

Publius Varinius was a Roman praetor in 73 BCE, proconsul in 72 BCE, and an unsuccessful military commander during the Third Servile War.

Ventidus was a Roman general and one of Julius Caesar's protégés. He won impressive victories against the Parthians which resulted in the deaths of key leaders - victories which redeemed the losses of Crassus and paved the way for Antony's incursions.

Virgil (October 15, 70 – September 21, 19 BCE), was an ancient Roman poet of the Augustan period. He is known for three major works of Latin literature, the *Eclogues*, the *Georgics*, and the epic *Aeneid*. The Aeneid is especially important as it tells the story of the Trojan refugee Aeneas as he struggles to fulfil his destiny and arrive on the shores of Italy—in Roman mythology the founding act of Rome.

Viriathus (died 138 BCE) was the most important leader of the Lusitanian people that resisted Roman expansion into the regions of western Hispania or western Iberia, where the Roman province of Lusitania would be established. Viriathus led the Lusitanians to several victories over the Romans between 147 BCE and 139 BCE before he was betrayed to the Romans and killed.

X

Xanthippus was a wealthy Athenian politician and general during the early part of the 5th century BCE. He was the son of Ariphron and father of Pericles. In 479 BCE, Xanthippus succeeded Themistocles, an old rival, as commander of the Athenian fleet. Xanthippus' greatest military accomplishment was his command of the Athenian naval forces at the decisive Battle of Mycale against the Persians, which was fought off the coast of Lydia in Asia Minor under the command of Leotychidas of Sparta.

Xerxes I of Persia, also known as Xerxes the Great (519–465 BC), was the fourth King of Kings of Persia. He was famous for his invasion of Greece that involved the Battle of Thermopylae, the capture of Athens, the Battles of Salamis and Plataea.

Places Mentioned in the Text

A

Abydus was the name of a city in ancient Egypt as well as on the Hellespont in Asia Minor.

Aemilian Way was a trunk Roman road in the north Italian plain, running from Ariminum (Rimini), on the Adriatic coast, to Placentia (Piacenza) on the river Padus (Po). It was completed in 187 BC. The Via Aemilia connected at Rimini with the Via Flaminia to Rome, which had been completed 33 years earlier.

Aetolians is a mountainous region of Greece on the north coast of the Gulf of Corinth, forming the eastern part of the modern regional unit of Aetolia-Acarnania.

Amphipolis it was a city in the region once inhabited by the Edoni people in the present-day region of Central Macedonia.

Arbela is currently called the city of Erbil. The Persian emperor Cyrus the Great occupied Assyria in 547 BC, and established an Achaemenid satrapy there with Arbela as the capital.

Arpi was an ancient city of Apulia in south-western Italy near modern Foggia. The legend attributes its foundation to Diomedes, and the figure of a horse, which appears on its coins, shows the importance of horse-breeding since early times.

Asculum also known as **Ausculum**, was the ancient name of two Italian cities. The first is Ascoli Piceno, situated in the valley of the Truentus (modern. Tronto) river on the via Salaria. It was originally a Sabine city. In the triumviral period or under Augustus it became a colonia. The second is Ascoli Satriano, a small village of the Satriani people, on a branch of the Appian Way in Apulia, South East Italy.

Athens was the capital city of the state of the same name. Athens dominates the Attica region and is one of the world's oldest cities, with its recorded history spanning around 3,400 years.

B

Baleric Islands an archipelago of Spain in the western Mediterranean Sea, near the eastern coast of the Iberian Peninsula.

Boii were a Gallic tribe of the later Iron Age, attested at various times in Cisalpine Gaul (northern Italy), Pannonia (Hungary and its western neighbours), in and around Bohemia (after whom the region is named), and Transalpine Gaul. In addition the archaeological evidence indicates that in the 2nd century BCE Celts expanded from Bohemia through the Kłodzko valley into Silesia, now part of Poland.

Brundisium is a city in the Apulia region of Italy, the capital of the province of Brindisi, off the coast of the Adriatic Sea. Historically, the city has played an important role in commerce and culture, due to its position on the Italian Peninsula and its natural port on the Adriatic Sea. The city is a major port for trade with Greece and the Middle East.

C

Chalcidians were people from the chief town of Chalcis on the island of Euboea in Greece. It is situated on the strait of the Evripos at its narrowest point. The name is preserved from antiquity and is derived from the Greek word for cooper and bronze, though there is no trace of any mines in the area. In the late Middle Ages, it was known as Negropont a name that was applied to the entire island of Euboea as well.

The **Battle of Canusium** was a three-day engagement between the forces of Rome and Carthage. It took place in Apulia during the summer of 209 BC, the tenth year of the Second Punic War.

Cappadocia is a historical region in Central Anatolia that today is largely in Nevşehir Province, in Turkey. In the time of Herodotus, the Cappadocians were reported as occupying the whole region from Mount Taurus to the vicinity of the Euxine (Black Sea).

Carpetani were one of the Celtic pre-Roman peoples of the Iberian Peninsula (the Roman Hispania, modern Spain and Portugal), akin to the Celtiberians, dwelling in the central part of the meseta - the high central upland plain of the Iberian Peninsula.

Carthage is a suburb of Tunis, Tunisia, and was the centre of the Carthaginian Empire in antiquity. The city has existed for nearly 3,000 years, developing from a Phoenician colony of the 1st millennium BC into the capital of an ancient empire.

Casilinum was an ancient city of Campania, Italy, situated some 3 miles north-west of Capua. The position of Casilinum at the junction of the Via Appia and Via Latina, at their crossing of the river Volturnus by a still-existing three-arched bridge, gave the town considerable strategic importance during the Roman Republic.

Chaeronea is a village and a former municipality in Boeotia, Greece. It is located by the mountain Thourion and in the Kifisós river valley, NW of Thebes. Chaeronea was the site of several historical battles. Best known is that of 338 BCE, between Philip II of Macedon and a coalition of various South Greek states, mainly Thebes and Athens. During the battle, the elite unit of Theban soldiers known as the Sacred Band of Thebes was wiped out completely.

Chersonesus is an ancient Greek colony founded approximately 2,500 years ago in the south-western part of the Crimean Peninsula, known then as Taurica. The colony was established in the 6th century BC by settlers from Heraclea Pontica.

Cimbrians refers Germanic tribe who resided in north-eastern Italy/Switzerland.

Ciminian Forest was the unbroken primeval forest that separated Ancient Rome from Etruria. According to the Roman historian Livy it was, in the 4th century BCE, a feared, pathless wilderness in which few dared tread. The Ciminian Forest received its name from the Monti Cimini, which are still a densely wooded range of volcanic hills northwest of Rome. They form the part of the forerange of the Apennine main range that faces towards the Tyrrhenian Sea.

The **Battle of Caudine Forks**, 321 BC, was a decisive event of the Second Samnite War. Its designation as a battle is a mere historical formality: there was no fighting and there were no casualties. The Romans were trapped in a waterless place by the Samnites before they knew what was happening and nothing remained but to negotiate an unfavorable surrender. The action was entirely political, with the magistrates on both sides trying to obtain the best terms for their side without disrespecting common beliefs concerning the rules of war and the conduct of peace. In the end the Samnites decided it would better for future relations to let the Romans go, while the Romans were impeded in the prosecution of their campaign against the Samnites by considerations of religion and honor.

Clusium was an ancient city in Italy, one of several found at the site. The current municipality of Chiusi (Tuscany) partly overlaps this Roman walled city. The Roman city remodeled an earlier Etruscan city, found in the territory of a prehistoric culture, possibly also Etruscan or proto-Etruscan. The site is located in northern central Italy on the west side of the Apennines.

Cyrrhestica is a district of Greater Syria which owes its name to the Macedonian occupation of the country. It lies between the plain of Antioch, and was bounded on the east by the Euphrates and on the west by Amanus and Commagene; to the south, it extended as far as the desert. It was the scene of the campaign in which Ventidius defeated the Parthian Pacorus and avenged Crassus and the Roman army which had fallen at Carrhae. Constantine I united it with Commagene under the name of Provincia Euphratensis.

Cyzicenes or **Cyzicus** was an ancient town of Mysia in Anatolia in the current Balıkesir Province of Turkey. It was located on the shoreward side of the present Kapıdağ Peninsula a tombolo which is said to have originally been an island in the Sea of Marmara only to be connected to the mainland in historic times either by artificial means or an earthquake.

D

Dardani was a tribe that occupied the region of Dardania. Located between the Thracians-Illyrians, their identification as either an Illyrian or Thracian tribe is uncertain. Their territory itself was not considered part of Illyria by Strabo.

Decelea modern **Dekeleia** or **Dekelia**, **Deceleia** or **Decelia**, previous name **Tatoi**, was an ancient village in northern Attica serving as a trade route connecting Euboea with Athens, Greece. The historian Herodotus reports that its citizens enjoyed a special relationship with Sparta. The Spartans took control of Decelea around 413 BCE. With advice from Alcibiades in 415 BCE, the former Athenian general wanted on Athenian charges of religious crimes, the Spartans and their allies, under Agis the Spartan king, fortified Decelea as a major military post in the later stage of the Peloponnesian War, giving them control of rural Attica and cutting off the primary land route for food imports.

Dyrrhachium is the modern city of Durrës. It was founded in the 7th century BC by Greek colonists from Corinth and Corcyra under the name Epidamnos. It has been continuously inhabited for 2,700 years and is one of the oldest cities in Albania.

E

The **Enipeus** is a river in central Greece, tributary of the Pineios. Its source is in the northern part of Phthiotis, near Domokos. It flows generally northwest, through Thessaly. It flows through Farsala and Fyllo, and flows into the Pineios near Farkadona.

Epirotes is s a geographical and historical region in south-eastern Europe, shared between Greece and Albania. It lies between the Pindus Mountains and the Ionian Sea, stretching from the Bay of Vlorë in the north to the Ambracian Gulf in the south.

The **Erythraean Sea** is also known as "The Red Sea", is one of the names found in ancient cartography. This name may have derived from the seasonal blooms of the red-coloured Trichodesmium erythraeum near the water's surface, and it must be noted that such kind of algea was first found during 17th century on the research based so the botanical named after the sea. Etruria

Etruscan is the modern English name given to a civilization of ancient Italy in the area corresponding roughly to Tuscany, western Umbria, and northern Latium. The ancient Romans called its creators the Tusci or Etrusci. Their Roman name is the origin of the terms Tuscany, which refers to their heartland, and Etruria, which can refer to their wider region. Culture that is identifiably Etruscan developed in Italy after about 800 BC approximately over the range of the preceding Iron Age Villanovan culture. The latter gave way in the 7th century to a culture that was influenced by Greek traders and Greek neighbors in Magna Graecia, the Hellenic civilization of southern Italy. After 500 BC the political destiny of Italy passed out of Etruscan hands.

The **Euphrates** is the longest and one of the most historically important rivers of Western Asia. Together with the Tigris, it is one of the two defining rivers of Mesopotamia. The river originates in eastern Turkey and flows through Syria and Iraq to join the Tigris in the Shatt al-Arab, which empties into the Persian Gulf.

F

Fidenae or **Fidenes**, home of the **Fidenates**, was an ancient town of Latium, situated about 8 km north of Rome on the *Via Salaria*, which ran between Rome and the Tiber. As the Tiber was the border between Etruria and Latium, the left-bank settlement of Fidenae represented an extension of Etruscan presence into Latium. The site of the arx of the ancient town was probably on the hill on which lies the contemporary Villa Spada, though no traces of early buildings or defences are to be seen; pre-Roman tombs are in the cliffs to the north.

G

Gabii was an ancient city of Latium, located 18 km (11 mi) due east of Rome along the Via Praenestina, which in early times was known as the Via Gabina.

Gaul was a region of Western Europe during the Iron Age and Roman era, encompassing present day France, Luxembourg and Belgium, most of Switzerland, Northern Italy, as well as the parts of the Netherlands and Germany on the west bank of the Rhine. According to the testimony of Julius Caesar, Gaul was divided into three parts, inhabited by the Gauls, the Belgae and the Aquitani, and the Gauls of Gaul proper were speakers of the Gallic language distinct from the Aquitanian language and the Belgic language. .

H

The **Halys River**, now known as the **Kızılırmak** (Turkish for "Red River") is the longest river in Turkey among the rivers which originates and ends in Turkey.

Hydaspes is a river that flows in India and Pakistan that today is called the Jhelum River. Alexander the Great and his army crossed the Jhelum in BC 326 at the Battle of the Hydaspes River where it is believed that he defeated the Indian king, Porus. According to Arrian, he built a city "on the spot whence he started to cross the river Hydaspes", which he named Bukephala to honour his famous horse Bukephalus or Bucephalus which was buried in Jalalpur Sharif. It is thought that ancient Bukephala was near the site of modern Jhelum City.

I

Iapydes were an ancient people who dwelt north of and inland from the Liburnians, off the Adriatic coast and eastwards of the Istrian peninsula. They occupied the interior of the country between the Colapis (Kupa) and Oeneus (Una) rivers, and the Velebit mountain range (Mons Baebius) which separated them from the coastal Liburnians. Their territory covered the central inlands of modern Croatia and Una River Valley in today's Bosnia and Herzegovina. Archaeological documentation confirms their presence in these countries at least from 9th century BC, and they persisted in their area longer than a millennium.

Ilergetes were an ancient Iberian people who inhabited the area around present-day Lleida. They are believed to be of Iberian language.

L

Lacedaemonians is one of the regional units of Greece. It is part of the region of Peloponnese. It is situated in the south-eastern part of the Peloponnese peninsula. Its administrative capital is Sparti (Sparta). The word "laconic" is derived from the name of the region by way of analogy - to speak in a long and round-about way.

Liburnae were an ancient Illyrian tribe inhabiting the district called Liburnia, a coastal region of the north-eastern Adriatic between the rivers Arsia (Raša) and Titius (Krka) in what is now Croatia.

Ligurians were an ancient Indo-European people who gave their name to Liguria, a region of north-western Italy.

Lilybaeum is the ancient name for Marsala. It is located in the Province of Trapani in the westernmost part of Sicily.

Lucania was an ancient district of southern Italy, extending from the Tyrrhenian Sea to the Gulf of Taranto. It thus comprised almost all the modern region of the Basilicata, with the greater part of the province of Salerno (the so-calledCilento) and a portion of that of Cosenza.

Lydia was an Iron Age kingdom of western Asia Minor located generally east of ancient Ionia in the modern Turkish provinces of Uşak, Manisa and inland İzmir. Its population spoke an Anatolia language known as Lydian.

M

Molossians were an ancient Greek tribe that inhabited the region of
Epirus since the Mycenaean era. On their northeast frontier, they had
the Chaonians and on their southern frontier the kingdom of
the Thesprotians; to their north were the Illyrians. The Molossians were part
of the League of Epirus until they sided against Rome in the Third
Macedonian War (171–168 BC). The result was disastrous, and the vengeful
Romans enslaved 150,000 of its inhabitants and annexed the region into
the Roman Empire.

Mount Callidromus a mountain range in Macedonia.

Munychia is the ancient Greek name for a steep hill
in Piraeus, Athens, Greece known today as Kastella. In 403 BCE, Athenian
democrats defeated forces of the thirty tyrants at the Battle of Munychia.

N

Numantines is the name of an ancient Celtiberian tribe whose principal city
was called Numantia settlement, whose remains are located 7 km north of the
city of Soria, on a hill known as Cerro de la Muela in the municipality
of Garray. Numantia is famous for its role in the Celtiberian Wars. In the year
153 BC Numantia experienced its first serious conflict with Rome. After 20
years of hostilities, in the year 133 BC the Roman Senate gave Scipio
Aemilianus Africanus the task of destroying Numantia. He laid siege to the
city, erecting a nine kilometre fence supported by towers, moats, impaling
rods and so on. After 13 months of siege, the Numantians decided to burn
the city and die free rather than live and be slaves.

Numidian was an Ancient Libyan kingdom in modern-day Algeria and a
smaller part of western Tunisia in North Africa. Numidia was originally
divided between Massyliis in Eastern Numidia
with Massinissa and Masaesylis in Western Numidia led by Syphax. It
is Massinissa who historically won over Syphax and unified Numidia into one
kingdom. The kingdom began as a sovereign state and later alternated
between being a Roman province and being a Roman client state.

The Battle of **Numistro** was fought in 210 BC between Hannibal's army and one of the Roman consular armies led by Consul Marcus Claudius Marcellus. It was the fourth time both generals met in a battle. Previous encounters were all located around the walls of Nola (Campania) in 216, 215 and 214 B.C.E. and had been favourable for the roman side.

O

Old Pharsalus was a town in Thessaly near Pharsalus.

Orchomenos the setting for many early Greek myths, is a municipality and a rich archaeological site in Boeotia, Greece, that was inhabited from the Neolithic through the Hellenistic periods

P

Pannonia was an ancient province of the Roman Empire bounded north and east by the Danube, coterminous westward with Noricum and upper Italy, and southward with Dalmatia and upper Moesia. Pannonia was located over the territory of the present-day western Hungary, eastern Austria, northern Croatia, north-western Serbia, Slovenia, western Slovakia and northern Bosnia and Herzegovina.

The Battle of **Panormus** was fought in 251 BC between a Roman consular army led by Lucius Caecilius Metellus and Carthaginians led by Hasdrubal during the First Punic War. The resulting Roman victory allowed for Panormus to remain in Roman control for the remainder of the war.

Parthia is a region of north-eastern Iran, best known for having been the political and cultural base of the Arsacid dynasty, rulers of the Parthian Empire. The name "Parthia" is a continuation from Latin Parthia, from Old Persian Parthava, which was the Parthian language self-designator signifying "of the Parthians" who were an Iranian people.

Pharsalia is a Roman epic poem by the poet Lucan, telling of the civil war between Julius Caesar and the forces of the Roman Senate led by Pompey the Great. The poem's title is a reference to the Battle of Pharsalus, which occurred in 48 BC, near Pharsalus, Thessaly, in northern Greece. Caesar decisively defeated Pompey in this battle, which occupies the epic's entire seventh book. Though probably incomplete, the poem is widely considered the best epic poem of the Silver Age of Latin literature.

Phrygia was a kingdom in the west central part of Anatolia, in what is now modern-day Turkey, centered on the Sakarya River. The Phrygians are most famous for their legendary kings of the heroic age of Greek mythology: Gordias who's Gordian Knot would later be untied by Alexander the Great, Midas who turned whatever he touched to gold, and Mygdon who warred with the Amazons. According to Homer's Iliad, the Phrygians were close allies of the Trojans and participants in the Trojan War against the Achaeans. Phrygian power reached its peak in the late 8th century BC under another, historical King Midas, who dominated most of western and central Anatolia and rivaled Assyria and Urartu for power in eastern Anatolia. This later Midas was however also the last independent king of Phrygia before its capital Gordium was sacked by Cimmerians around 695 BC. Phrygia then became subject to Lydia, and then successively to Persia, Alexander and his Hellenistic successors, Pergamon, Rome and Byzantium.

Picentines or **Picentini** were an Italic tribe who lived in Picenum in the northern Adriatic coastal plain of ancient Italy.

Pisidia was a region of ancient Asia Minor located north of Lycia, and bordering Caria, Lydia, Phrygia and Pamphylia. It corresponds roughly to the modern-day province of Antalya in Turkey.

Pontus is a historical Greek designation for a region on the southern coast of the Black Sea, located in modern-day north-eastern Turkey. The name was applied to the coastal region in antiquity by the Greeks who colonized the area, and derived from the Greek name of the Black Sea, "Hospitable Sea", or simply "Pontos". The extent of the region varied through the ages, but generally it extended from the borders of Colchis (modern Georgia) until well into Paphlagonia in the west. Several states and provinces bearing the name of Pontus or variants thereof were established in the region in Hellenistic, Roman and Byzantine times. Pontus is known for the residence of the Amazons, with the name Amasia not only used for a city (Amasya) but for all of Pontus in Greek mythology.

The **Via Praenestina** (modern Italian: **Via Prenestina**) was an ancient Roman road of central Italy. It was initially called **Via Gabina**, from Gabii, the ancient city of Latium where it ended. It received the new name having been prolonged to Praeneste (modern Palestrina); after the latter city it continued towards the Apennines the towards the source of the Anio River until joining the Via Latina at Anagni.

R

Regium commonly known as **Reggio Calabria** or **Reggio**, is the biggest city and the most populated of Calabria, southern Italy, is the capital of the Province of Reggio Calabria and is the seat of the Regional Council of Calabria.

S

Sabines were an Italic tribe that lived in the central Apennines of ancient Italy, also inhabiting Latium north of the Anio before the founding of Rome.

Saepinum is the modern name for Altilia, near Sepino. It was a Samnite town located approximately 12 miles south of the modern Campobasso (in south central Italy. Saepinum was on the ancient road from Beneventum to Corfinium.

Samos a Greek island in the eastern Aegean Sea, south of Chios, north of Patmos and the Dodecanese, and off the coast of Asia Minor. **Segobrigenses** were a Celtic tribe of Gaul, whose fortress was located at Lugdunum (modern Lyons). The name "Segusiavi" may have been an alternative name of the "Segobriges" who were legendarily involved with Greeks in pre-Roman Gaul and the foundation myth of Massalia.

Scordiscans were a Gallic Iron Age tribe from present-day Serbia, along the Dravus (Drava) and Danube rivers. They emerged at the beginning of the third century BC until the first century AD. Their influence stretched over regions comprising parts of the present-day Serbia, Austria, Bosnia and Herzegovina, Croatia, Hungary, Slovakia and Slovenia. Their tribal name may be connected to the name of the Scordus Mountain

Sentinum was an ancient town currently located in the Marche region of Italy.

Sythians were diverse group of Iranian horsemen. These groups inhabited the western and central Eurasian steppes during the Iron Age, the area known to classical Greek sources as "Scythia". Their rise in importance coincided with the rise of equestrian semi-nomads from the Carpathian Mountains of Europe to Mongolia in the Far East during the 1st millennium BC.

T

Tarentines were from the town of Taranto, which is a coastal city in Puglia, Southern Italy. It is the capital of the Province of Taranto and is an important commercial port. Taranto was founded as a Gerek Colony in 706 BCE. The Greek colonists from Sparta called the city Taras, after the mythical hero Taras, while the Romans, who connected the city to Rome with an extension of the Appian Way, called it Tarentum.

Taurus Mountains are a mountain range in southern Turkey, dividing the Mediterranean coastal region of southern Turkey from the central Anatolian Plateau.

Teutons were a Germanic tribe mentioned by Greek and Roman authors, notably Strabo and Marcus Velleius Paterculus. According to a map by Ptolemy, they originally lived in Jutland.

Tigranocerta was a city that was possibly located near present-day Silvan, Turkey. It was founded by the Armenian Emperor Tigranes the Great in the 1st century BC. Tigranakert was founded as the new capital of the Armenian Empire in order to be in a more central position within the boundaries of the expanding empire. It was one of four cities in Armenia named Tigranakert.

Lake Trasimenus is the largest lake on the Italian Peninsula, part of the province of Perugia, in the Umbria region.

Triballi were an ancient tribe whose dominion was around the plains of modern southern Serbia and western Bulgaria and the Iskar River, roughly centered where Serbia and Bulgaria are joined.

Troezen is a small town and a former municipality in the north eastern Peloponnese, Greece.

U

Umbria is a region of central Italy. It is the only peninsular region that is landlocked; however, the region includes the Lake Trasimeno and is crossed by the River Tiber.

V

Veientines were people of the Etruscan city of Veii. Its site lies in Isola Farnese in the Province of Rome. Veii was the richest city of the Etruscan League, on the southern border of Etruria. It was alternately at war and in alliance with Rome for over 300 years. It eventually fell to the Roman general Camillus' army in 396 BC. Veii continued to be occupied after its capture by the Romans.

Vetulonia was an ancient town of Etruria, Italy.

Volscians were an italic tribe of the Volsci, who were well known in the history of the 1st century of the Roman Republic. At that time they inhabited the partly hilly, partly marshy district of the south of Latium, bounded by the Aurunci and Samnites on the south, the Hernici on the east, and stretching roughly from Norba and Cora in the north to Antium in the south.

Greece at the Time of the Persian Invasion

Terms Mentioned in the Text

A

Antesignani were troops posted in front of the standards in order to defend them from capture.
Armatura

Arcubalistae is a crossbow like device, but is probably identical with the scorpiones minores.

Augustales were an order of Roman priests created by Tiberius to maintain the cult of Augustus and the Iulii in 14 AD

B

Balistaria is an arrow slit or loophole used by archers to shoot at an enemy. In later times, this was a very narrow opening

Ballista is a missile weapon that launched a large projectile at a distant target. It was developed from earlier Greek weapons, it relied upon different mechanics, using two levers with torsion springs instead of a prod, the springs consisted of several loops of twisted skeins.

Bebrae describes the weapons on the barbarous nations.

Buccina was a curved brass horn played over the shoulder

Buccinatores were players of the *buccina*

C

Caltrops were anti-personnel devices consisting of four spikes, that when thrown on the ground, always have a pointed side up. They were used against men and horses to disable them.
Campignei

Centurions were professional officers of the Roman army after the Marian reforms of 107 BC. Most centurions commanded 60 to 80 men despite the commonly assumed 100, but senior centurions commanded cohorts, or took senior staff roles in their legion. Centurions were also found in the Roman navy. Centuries or Centuriae, derives its name from the term for tribe or company. Theoretically, this word traces its roots to centum which is Latin for one hundred. By the fourth century they were officers appointed to each century, now called Centenarii and Decani, who commanded ten men, now called heads of messes

Chevaux-de-frise is a portable frame or log covered with many projecting long iron or wooden spikes or spears. They were principally intended as an anti-cavalry obstacle, but could also be moved quickly to help block a breach in another barrier. They remained in occasional use until they were replaced by wire obstacles in the late 19th century.

Classicum is a particular sound of the buccina or horn, is appropriated to the commander-in-chief and is used in the presence of the general, or at the execution of a soldier, as a mark of its being done by his authority.

Cornicines, coronet players

D

Decanus, the head of the mess

Decumane Gate is directly opposite to the Praetorian in the rear of the camp. Soldiers on their way to punishment or execution passed through this gate.

Decurion is one of three officers commanding a troop or turma consisting of thirty men. In the early Republic on officer was in charge with the others being his deputy. They were often members of the Equestrian order. In the Empire there was just one Decurion in charge of a turma, they were often auxiliary troops and in many cases conscripted.

Draconarii is the name of the dragon pennant of the later Empire. Each cohort has also its own peculiar ensign, the Dragon, carried by the Draconarius

Draconarius known as a dragon bearer

F

Fascines are bundles of wood used in military defenses for shoring up trenches or ramparts, especially around artillery batteries, or filling in ditches from earliest military actions. Military fascine bridges were used on a regular basis by the Romans to cross obstacles. Subsequently, the use of fascines by military engineers continued almost wherever armies were deployed.

Foederatus or **foederati** the name changed over time between the early Roman Republic and the end of the Western Roman Empire. Early in the history of the Roman Republic, a foederatus identified one of the tribes bound by treaty who were neither Roman colonies nor Roman citizenship but were expected to provide a contingent of fighting men when trouble arose, thus were allies.

Ferentarii were light infantry and the troops armed with shields, loaded javelins, swords and common missile weapons.

Flaviales, were an order of priests from the Empire.

Fustibalus or staff sling. The fustibalus consists of a staff (a length of wood) with a short sling at one end. One cord of the sling is firmly attached to the stave and the other end has a loop that can slide off and release the projectile. Staff slings are extremely powerful because the stave can be made as long as two meters, creating a powerful lever. Ancient art shows slingers holding staff slings by one end, with the pocket behind them, and using both hands to throw the staves forward over their heads.

H

Hastati were a class of infantry in the armies of the early Roman Republic who originally fought as spearmen, and later as swordsmen. They were originally some of the poorest men in the legion, and could afford only modest equipment—light armour and a large shield, in their service as the lighter infantry of the legion. Later, the *hastati* contained the younger men rather than just the poorer, though most men of their age were relatively poor. Their usual position was the first battle line. They fought in a quincunx formation, supported by light troops. They were eventually done away with after the Marian reforms of 107 BC

I

Iusiurandum a voluntary oath taken before a tribune when the soldiers were assigned to separate divisions

L

Librarii, a soldier charged with keeping the legionary accounts

M

Manubalistae translates roughly to 'hand ballista', was a late Roman siege engine. It was originally thought to have been designed by Hero of Alexandria and primarily composed of metal (the spring mechanism and the skeins), it fired bolts that were smaller than those in other forms of ballistae and generally made of metal. It was the next major improvement after the scorpio. The name of the weapon implies that portable versions might also have existed, similar to crossbow.

Martiobarbuli exercise of the weighted javelins

Mensores, were surveyors that were part of the regular army structure used in constructing roads and forts.

Metatores was a senior officer in charge of laying out the castra, or legionary marching camp.

Millarian Cohorts the first cohort of a legion

Munifices, or working soldiers, from their being obliged to every kind of military work without exception

O

Onagri were smaller versions of the ballista, a small catapult like device used for hurdling missiles and projectiles. They derived their power from a twisted hair rope.

Ordinarii is the name of an officer of the legions. The ten centuries of the first cohort were commanded by five Ordinarii

P

Palisades is sometimes called a "stakewall". It is typically a wall or fence made from wooden stakes or tree trunks as a defensive barrier.

Pass under the Yoke was a custom of making prisoner bow under the wooden beam used by oxen as a sign of submission and embarrassment.

Postsignani were troops posted behind the standards in the field.

Praefect in the late Republic and early Empire was the formal title of many, fairly low to high-ranking, military or civil officials. In the late Empire (4th C) the Praefect was always a count of the first order. He took over command in the absence of the general.

Praetorian Gate is the main gate of a Roman camp that should either front the east or the enemy

Praetorium originally signified a general's tent within a Roman castra, castellum, or encampment

Principes were a type of soldier, in the armies of the early Roman Republic. They were men in the prime of their lives who were fairly wealthy, and could afford decent equipment. They were the heavier infantry of the legion who carried large shields and wore good quality armor. Their usual position was the second battle line. They fought in quincunx formation, supported by light troops. They were eventually done away with after the Marian reforms of 107 BC.

Q

Quingentarian Cohort (Cohors) was a cohort of auxiliary infantry from the second century AD onward.

Quincunx formation was a checkered formation of five units adopted by the consular legions when deployed for battle.

S

Sacramentum militare (also as *militum* or *militiae*) was the oath taken by soldiers in pledging their loyalty to the consul in the Republican era or later to the emperor

Semispathae – small swords

The Social War is a name given to several wars between the Roman Republic and Italian cities that were traditionally its allies. The one referenced in this book most likely applies to the war of 91-88 BCE which also goes by the name "The Italian War", "The War of the Allies" or "The Marsic War".

Spathae was a long Gallic slashing sword adopted by the Roman cavalry that was used for cutting and slashing. Its reach was useful for horseback, but cumbersome on foot for the Roman mode of battle.

Speculum is a later day name for a pilum

Spolia Opima are spoils taken by a victorious commander from the leader of the enemy.

T

Tesserarius was a watch commander in the Roman army. They organized and had command over the nightly guard assigned to keep watch over the fort when in garrison or on campaign and were responsible for getting the watchwords from the commander and seeing that it was kept safe. There was one tesserarius to each centuria. They held a position similar to that of a non-commissioned officer in modern armies and acted as seconds to the optiones.

Testudo or tortoise formation was commonly used by the Roman Legions during battles, particularly sieges. Testudo is the Latin word for "tortoise". The Greek term for this formation is "chelone" and during the Byzantine era, it seems to have evolved to what military manuals of the era call the "foulkon".

A body of soldiers, in forming a testudo, held their shields firmly together over their heads, and were protected from such missiles thrown from above, while those of the outer files held their shieldssloping in such a manner as to protect the flanks. They thus presented an appearance like the back of a tortoise, "testudo;" from which the name was derived. A testudo could also mean a moving penthouse on wheels, which the besiegers worked the battering-ram under cover. The name in this case was readily suggested by the resemblance which the ram presented to a tortoise thrusting its head forward from its shell and drawing it back again.

Torquati denominated from the gold collars given to soldiers in reward for their bravery, in addition to which they were allowed a higher rate of pay. Those who received double were called Torquati Duplares, and those who had only single were called, Simplares

Tragularii who annoyed the enemy with arrows from the manubalistae or arcubalistae

Triari were one of the military elements of the early Roman Republic used in the Manipular legions (509 BC – 107 BC). They were the oldest and among the wealthiest men in the army, and could afford good quality equipment. They wore heavy metal armor and carried large shields, their usual position being the third battle line. During the Camillan era, they fought in a shallow phalanx formation, supported by light troops. They were meant to be used as a decisive force in the battle, thus prompting an old Roman saying: 'Going to the triarii' which meant carrying on to the bitter end.

Tubicines trumpet players

V

Verriculum a small light-weight javelin

Verutum a later day name for the Verriculum

Vexillations was a detachment from a Roman legion formed as a temporary task force created by the Roman army of the Principate. It was named from the standard carried by legionary detachments, the vexillum, (which bore the emblem and name of the parent legion. Although commonly associated with legions, it is likely that vexillationes included auxiliaries. The term is found in the singular, referring to a single detachment, but is usually used in the plural to refer to an army made up of picked detachments. Vexillationes were assembled ad hoc to meet a crisis on Rome's extensive frontiers. They varied in size and composition, but usually consisted of about 1,000 infantry and/or 500 cavalry.

Bibliography and Further Reading

Siculus, Diodorus. *Library of History, Volume I, Books 1-2. 34.*
Leob Classical Libray: New York 1933

Smith, William. *Dictionary of Greek and Roman Biography and Mythology, Vol. I.* Oxford University: London 1844

Visit our website to find out about the selection of e-books, paperbacks and limited edition publications from Winged Hussar Publishing, LLC at:

http: // www.wingedhussarpublishing.com

or follow us on facebook at *WingedHussar Publishing LLC* and on twitter at *WingHusPubLLC* for information on upcoming publications.

Other books to look into from Winged Hussar Publishing concerning ancient history and military strategy include:

The Gallic Wars by Gaius Julius Caesar
978-0-6157232-8-0 Paperback
978-1-6201807-3-0 E-book
978-0-9889532-0-8 Ltd. Edition Hardcover

Frederick's Orders: Frederick the Great's Orders to His Generals and His Way of War by Frederick Hohenzollern
978-0-6157547-1-0 Paperback
978-1-6201809-5-2 E-book
978-0-9889532-2-2 Ltd. Edition Hardcover